Sir John Fortescue's
The Hard Learned Lesson

Sir John Fortescue's
The Hard Learned Lesson

The British Army & the Campaigns in Flanders &
the Netherlands against the French 1792-99

J. W. Fortescue

LEONAUR

Sir John Fortescue's The Hard Learned Lesson
The British Army & the Campaigns in Flanders & the Netherlands against the French
1792-99
by J. W. Fortescue

FIRST EDITION

Text taken from *A History of the British Army*

Leonaur is an imprint of Oakpast Ltd

Copyright in this form © 2016 Oakpast Ltd

ISBN: 978-1-78282-499-2 (hardcover)
ISBN: 978-1-78282-500-5 (softcover)

http://www.leonaur.com

Publisher's Notes

Contents

CHAPTER 1

The Armies of Revolution

In 1791 France plunged inexorably into the chaos of revolution until, at last, in January of the following year the Bourbon king, Louis XVI., was executed upon the guillotine. At the fall of the royal head on the 21st January, England was thrilled with horror, and Pitt seized the moment to order the ambassador, Chauvelin, to withdraw from England. His arrival in Paris brought matters to a climax, and on the 7th of February Pitt received the expected news that on the 1st the Convention had declared war against England and Holland.

Probably there never was a moment in the whole history of France when her military impotence was so abject, as on this declaration of war. The world's annals of military maladministration are rich and varied, but it is doubtful whether they afford any parallel to the unspeakable wickedness which characterised the three months of Pache's reign at the French War Office. It is sufficient to say that by the end of 1792 the French forces on the frontier had lost sixty thousand men by desertion alone, without counting those who had perished of cold, starvation, and sickness. The nominal establishment of the forces was eight hundred thousand men; and officers and staff for that number were actually on the pay-list.

Official accounts further proclaimed that France had ten armies on foot; but, of these, two had never existed except in name, while the remaining eight did not comprise above one hundred and fifty thousand effective men, including regulars and volunteers; and they were not only lacking in arms and ammunition, but absolutely destitute in respect of pay, clothing, and equipment. It is hardly necessary to add that the troops, having been forced to live by brigandage during great part of the winter, had lost such discipline as their officers had contrived to instil into them; while the soldiers of the Line, who still wore the white coats of the Monarchy, were by no means friendly to the volunteers.

The situation was so alarming that it was found necessary to displace Pache, though not with dishonour, and to make Beurnonville, an accomplished soldier, Minister in his stead. Further, on receiving the report as to the lack of recruits, the Convention passed a series of decrees for a levy of six hundred thousand men; each commune being called upon to furnish its contingent, and, if the number of voluntary recruits were insufficient, to make up the number as it thought best. Lastly, it was ordained that the Line and the volunteers should both alike enjoy the higher rate of pay and the privilege of electing officers, and should both wear the blue national uniform; a change which placed them upon an equal footing in every respect, except that the regulars were enlisted till the end of the war, and the volunteers for one year only. (Poisson, ii.; Rousset).

Further reforms were deferred till the close of the campaign; and it is easy to see that those above given could have little effect beyond putting an end to the volunteers by destroying their privileges. The levy itself necessarily required several weeks to collect, and, since personal service was not enforced, was not likely to be of any great value. Further, the execution of the king had alienated most of the older officers that remained, and among them Dumouriez himself. That general indeed had many causes of complaint against the ruling faction. His plan of campaign had been subordinated to Custine's; his cherished design of invading Holland had been checked; the operations of the entire army had been suspended; the whole of his honest and politic work in Belgium had been undone; the people had been driven into hostility by oppression, and the discipline of the army destroyed by starvation and want.

On the 27th of January he secretly sent an agent to open negotiations with Lord Auckland at the Hague, and to arrange a conference with him; but, before the two could meet, war was declared, and Dumouriez was ordered to invade Holland forthwith. The Convention, thirsting for the wealth of the Bank of Amsterdam, was anxious to make sure of it before the Allies could put their strength into the field.

Two months earlier, when his troops were heartened by the victory of Jemappe, no order could have been more welcome to Dumouriez than this; and even now, though he had few men upon whom he could depend, he resolved if possible to make good the defects of his army by swift and sudden action. The French troops on the north-

Battle of Jemappes

ern frontier were very widely scattered, their cantonments extending north and south on the lower Meuse from Roermond to Maastricht, and east and west from the upper Rhine through Aachen to Liege and Namur. His original plan had been to turn all the waterways and fortresses that bar the entrance into Holland from the south, and to invade it by way of Nimeguen; but time was so precious that he resolved to collect a small force of but seventeen thousand men at Antwerp, and to march from thence with all secrecy direct upon Amsterdam. At the same time he directed thirty thousand men from the east under General Miranda to take the Dutch fortresses of Maastricht and Venloo, and then to make for Nimeguen. Speed, in his view, was everything, for the Austrians had already forty thousand men cantoned to the east of the Rhine, and were shortly to be reinforced.

Meanwhile the Allies were still making up their plans for the next campaign. Brunswick and Prince Frederick Josias of Coburg-Saalfeld, who had been appointed Commander-in-Chief of the Austrian Army, met at Frankfurt and, after many conferences between the 6th and the 14th of February, decided upon a scheme of operations, which by their own showing required forty thousand more men than they had any expectation of collecting. They saved themselves, however, by laying it down as a cardinal principle that, until Mainz was recovered from the French, the Allied forces must not attempt to pass from the east to the west bank of the Meuse. Belgium (so argued the Austrians) had been eaten up, and so long as the navigation of the Rhine was blocked at Mainz, the subsistence of the Imperial troops on the west of the Meuse must be difficult; moreover, if the French should retire before an Austrian advance, and mass all their forces on the Rhine, then they might beat Brunswick, who, unless his retreat were assured by the possession of Mainz, would be in danger of utter destruction.

The reader should take note of this decision, for not only is it the key to much that appears puzzling in the coming campaign, but it is an excellent example of the principle on which Coburg and Brunswick conducted war, namely, to look at risks first and at objects afterwards. The immediate problem of the defence of the Dutch provinces was left without so much as an attempt at solution. Both Grenville in England and Auckland at the Hague had long foreseen the certainty of a French attack upon them, and had strained every nerve to stir the authorities to action. But the *stadtholder* was a man of almost inhuman dullness, apathy and stupidity; and all popular energy was paralysed by the spirit of faction, which, never inactive in Holland, had under the

BATTLE OF JEMAPPES

influence of French agents become almost a spirit of revolution.

The Dutch Army was so defective in training, equipment and discipline that it had ceased to exist as an efficient force; and its few foreign corps, which alone deserved the name of regiments, had been driven to mutiny by a reduction of their pay below the rate fixed by their contract. Even in January and February, Auckland wrote that the *stadtholder* looked for British ships and British troops to save him, and that the French party was derisively insinuating that England, nominally the faithful ally of the Dutch Republic, was content to desert her in the hour of danger. (*Dropmore Papers,* Auckland to Grenviile, 21st and 25th January; 14th and 15th February. *F.O. Holland*, 16th February 1793. And see *Auckland Correspondence* and *Dropmore Papers* generally, November 1792 to February 1793).

Finally, on the 15th of February he begged that the Duke of York might be sent over with a few officers of experience, even if without troops, to take command of the Dutch, he wrote:

> Men, commanders, ships and money, we could not ask for more if this country were a part of Yorkshire, but I incline to think that it should be considered so for the present; and if it is brought to a question whether we are to conquer it and keep it, or whether Dumouriez is to do it, I have no doubt as to the decision.

Still the British Government hesitated, for, thanks to its neglect of the army, it possessed but a handful of troops, and was unwilling to move them to the Continent. Then suddenly, on the 16th of February, 1793, Dumouriez dashed out from Antwerp with his tiny force in four columns. One small body instantly pushed northward towards Moerdyk, to collect boats for the passage of the arm of the sea called the Hollandsdiep; another marched upon Klundert and Willemstadt, a third north-eastward to attack Breda, and a fourth to the north-west to blockade Bergen-op-Zoom and Steenbergen. Everywhere his coming was welcomed by the Dutch. Breda, with large stores of munitions of war, was disgracefully surrendered on the 26th of February; Klundert and Gertruydenberg fell in quick succession; Willemstadt was then besieged with the captured cannon, and by the 9th of March Dumouriez was prepared to essay the passage of the Hollandsdiep. But here his course was stayed, for his activity had stirred his enemies on every side.

On the 20th of February the seven battalions of British Guards were suddenly paraded before the Horse Guards; and the Duke of York, announcing that the first battalions of the three regiments were ordered to proceed on active service, called for volunteers from the others to bring them up to strength. The whole brigade thereupon stepped forward as one man; and five days latter the three battalions, numbering under two thousand men of all ranks and denominations, marched to Greenwich amid the cheers, and something more than the cheers, of an enormous and enthusiastic crowd.

★★★★★★

The head of the column was able to keep sober; the rear, under the endearments of the populace, subsided dead drunk on the road and was brought on in carts. *Narrative of an Officer of the Guards.*

★★★★★★

By nightfall the whole were embarked upon transports too small to carry more than two-thirds of their number in safety, without medicines or medical appliances, without the slightest reserve of ammunition, and of course without transport of any description. Their commander was Colonel Gerard Lake of the First Guards, and his orders were on no account to move his men above twenty-four hours' distance from Helvoetsluis, so as to be able to return on the shortest notice. By the mercy of Heaven these troops safely reached that port, March 1, narrowly escaping a gale which would probably have condemned them either to drowning or asphyxiation; and four days later they proceeded to Dort to oppose Dumouriez's passage of the Hollandsdiep. About the same time a flotilla of Dutch gunboats arrived in the Meuse, many of them manned by British sailors and flying British colours. Auckland, by threatening to take command of Holland himself, had at last compelled the miserable *stadtholder* to issue orders for the defence of his country. (Lake to Dundas, 2nd March 1793. Lake's Instructions, 23rd February. Grenville to Auckland, 20th February 1793. *F.O. Holland*, Auckland to Grenville, 4th March 1793).

But the obstacles which were multiplying in Dumouriez's front were as nothing to the storm that suddenly broke upon his flank, Feb. 20th. Miranda had duly moved up to the siege of Maastricht with a force inadequate to the task and, moreover, dangerously dispersed; but the Austrians, declaring themselves too weak to move, still remained torpid in their cantonments, perhaps the more stubbornly because the Prussian Agent at the Austrian headquarters was perpetually urging them to action. At last, however, Coburg on the 26th began to

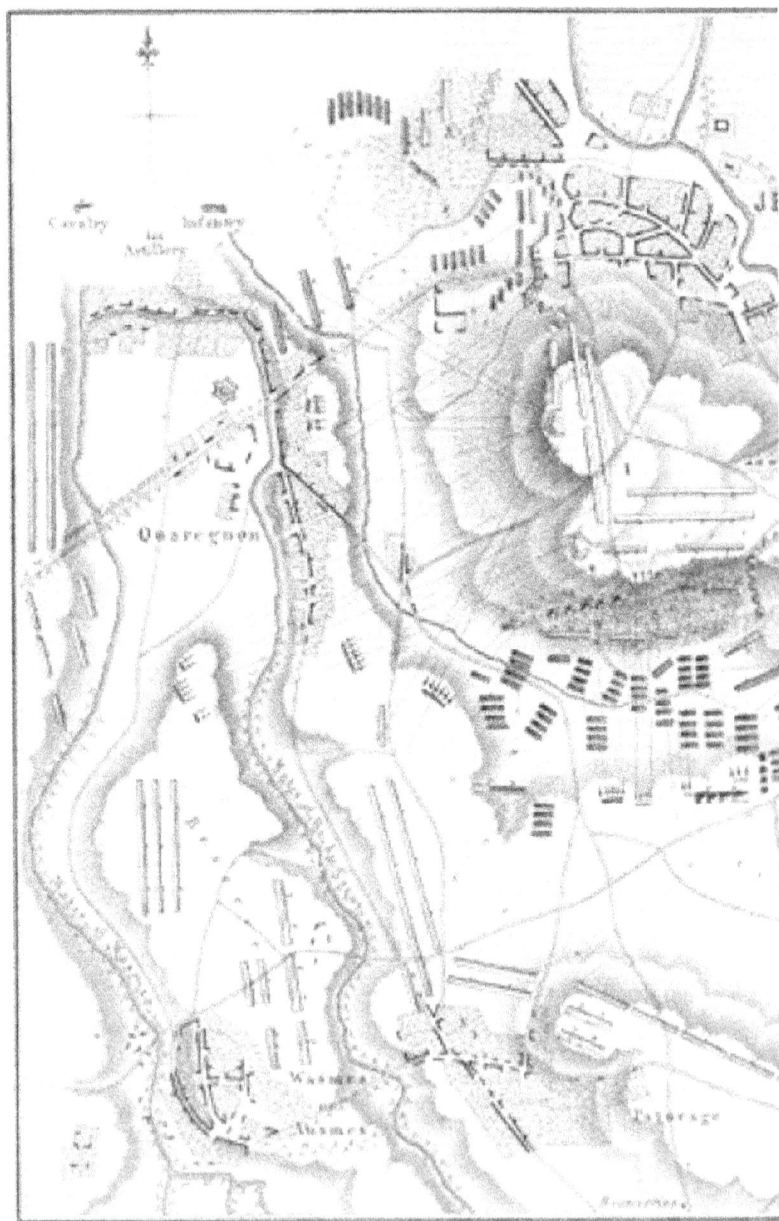

BATTLE

OF

JEMAPPES

6 November 1792.

French   Austrians

Position on the 5th Nov.   Position at the 5th Nov.
... during the battle   ... during the battle

SCALES
Military Steps 2½ feet each

1 English Mile

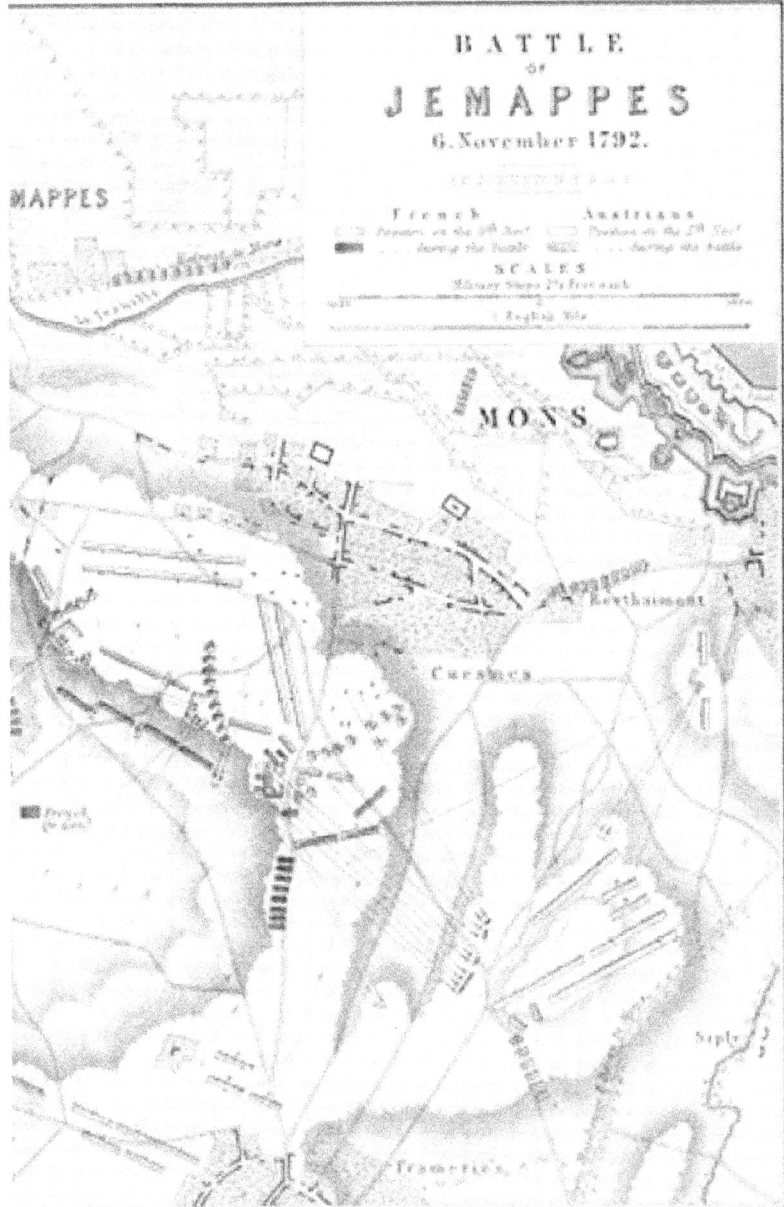

MAPPES

MONS

Battle of Jemappes

concentrate his forty thousand men and to pass them in five columns across the river; and on the 1st of March, to the great surprise of the French, he burst upon their cantonments on the Meuse, and for four days drove them in utter rout before him.

Coburg himself and the left wing halted before Liege, but on the right the Archduke Charles, with the impetuosity of twenty-one and the instinct of a born soldier, followed up the disorderly rabble from Maastricht southward upon Tongres, boldly attacking wherever he met the enemy. Such of the French as had been in action fled in all directions, abandoning everything; ten thousand deserters hurried across the frontier into France; and a small remnant took refuge behind the canal at Louvain, where it was joined by such French divisions as had not been engaged.

Had Coburg pursued his advantage and advanced instantly with all his forces, he could have ended the campaign at once, for the people, furious at the exactions of the Jacobins, and, above all, at the theft of the plate from their churches, had turned savagely upon the retreating French. Instead of this he halted on the 5th, and wasted ten whole days in cantonments between Maastricht and Tongres. The Convention now ordered Dumouriez at once to proceed to Louvain and assume command, which he did with a very bad grace, March 9th, leaving General Flers to take his place in Holland. His presence did much to restore confidence in the French Army, and he was not a little helped by Coburg's inaction.

Nevertheless the news that reached him was singularly disquieting. Fresh regiments were embarking from England for Helvoetsluis; two reinforcing columns of Austrians were advancing from the Rhine upon Namur; and eight thousand Prussians, under the Duke of Brunswick-Oels, had arrived at Bois-le-Duc on the 11th, and were moving with five thousand British and Dutch upon Breda, to cut off the troops on the Hollandsdiep from France and himself from Antwerp. In so desperate a situation there was no choice but to take the offensive.

On the 15th Coburg at last resumed his advance with forty-two thousand men; and on the 16th Dumouriez marched with forty-eight thousand to meet him. On the 18th the decisive action was fought at Neerwinden, when the French were totally defeated, with a loss of five thousand men and three guns. The volunteers and the National Guards were the troops that failed in the battle; after which the men broke up and fled by whole battalions. Ten thousand deserted in the ten days following the action, and Dumouriez was fain to form a

BATTLE OF NEERWINDEN

rearguard out of his artillery and his few battalions of the Line, and to fall back on Louvain.

Coburg, who had lost about three thousand men, made little attempt at pursuit, keeping his main body halted at Tirlemont until the 22nd, but exhorting the Duke of Brunswick-Oels to hasten from Bois-le-Duc to Malines to cut off Dumouriez's retreat to Antwerp. The Duke, who had already permitted Flers to withdraw with impunity the bulk of his forces to Antwerp, was evidently not disposed to further Austrian operations with Prussian troops, for he refused to move. However, the advance of the Austrians compelled Dumouriez to evacuate Louvain and Brussels in succession; and on the 25th, finding himself obliged to abandon Namur also, he opened negotiations with Coburg.

He had quarrelled beyond hope of reconciliation with the Convention over the iniquity of its rule in Belgium, and he now proposed that the French should retreat from the whole country, and that he should march to Paris to re-establish the monarchy, the Allies meanwhile halting on the frontier and receiving the fortress of Condé as a guarantee. An agreement to this effect was duly made with the Chief of the Austrian Staff on the 27th, and a circular was issued from the Austrian headquarters, suggesting a conference of the representatives of the powers to decide as to the measures to be next taken.

There is no need to tell at length the story of Dumouriez's adventures during the following days. It must suffice that he was driven from the midst of his army, and on the 5th of April was fain to take refuge with the Austrians. Fragments of several corps and one complete regiment of Hussars followed him, unwilling to part with their beloved general; but several thousand French troops in Belgium and Holland, which might have been cut off to a man, were allowed to retire in peace to the frontier. None the less the fact remained that even a slow commander at the head of a force of discordant Allies had sufficed to drive the armies of the Revolution in shameful disorder from the Austrian Netherlands.

Neer Landen

Hacken

Kermael

Elixem

Laar

Racour

NEERWINDEN

Oberwinden

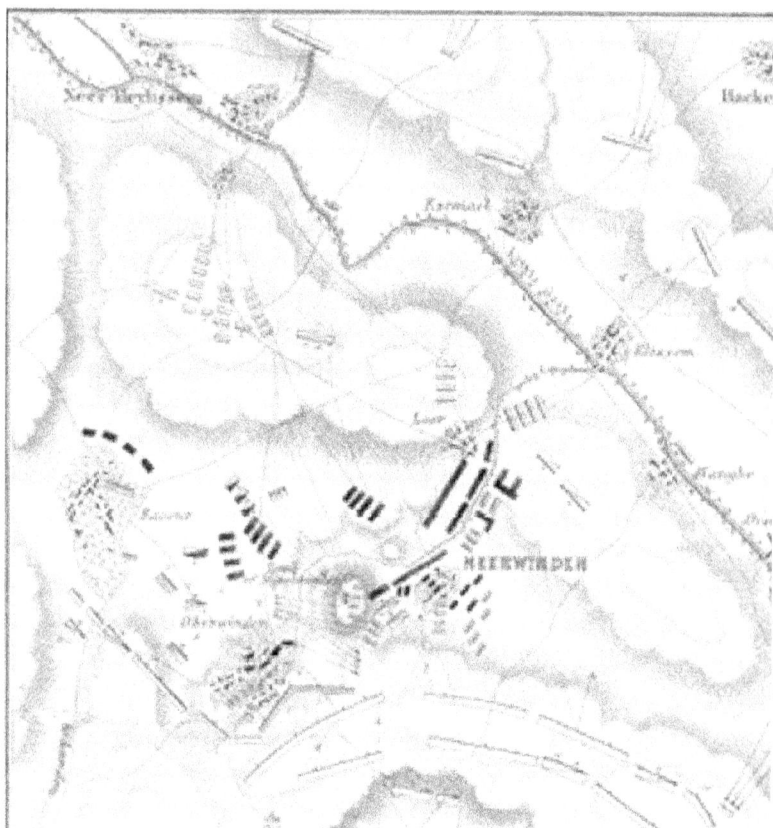

BATTLE
OF
NEERWINDEN
18. March 1793.

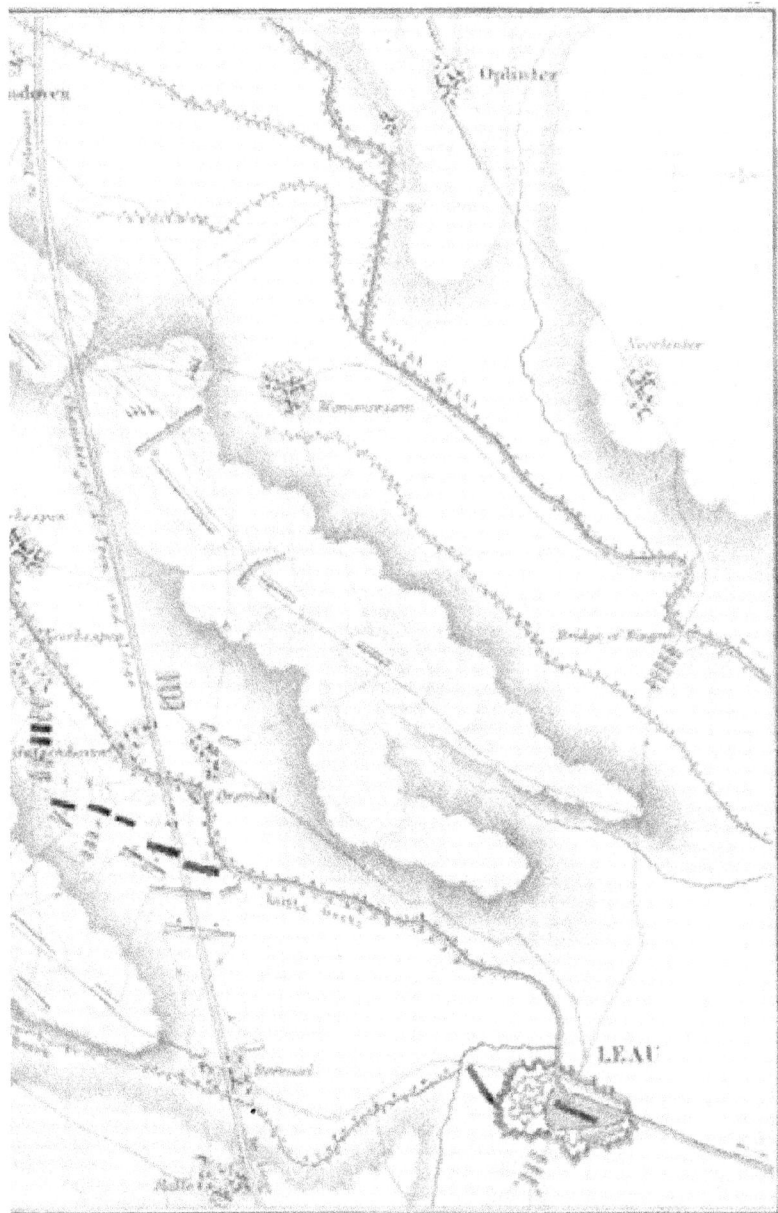

CHAPTER 2

From Bad Beginnings

England's Government at this period lay in the hands of three principal men, William Pitt, Henry Dundas, and William Grenville. Few readers need information as to the great talents of Pitt, his capacity in administration, his skill in finance, his eloquence in debate, his integrity, his courage, and his patriotism; but there were two important matters of which Pitt had no knowledge, namely, of war and of the world. The man whom he chose, or rather who thrust himself upon him, to supplement these defects was Henry Dundas.

The son of a Lord Advocate of Scotland, Dundas was born seventeen years before Pitt, and had been called to the Scottish Bar while Pitt was still in the nursery. Sprung from a well known legal family, and possessing not only ability of his own but a half-brother who was President of the Court of Session, he soon obtained a large practice, was made Solicitor-General for Scotland at twenty-four, and in 1774 was elected member of Parliament for Midlothian. Having some talent for speaking he soon made his mark in Parliament as one of the bitterest opponents of America, and, being made Lord Advocate in 1775, was one of Lord North's strongest supporters until that statesman's influence began to wane.

By great adroitness he kept his place under the Rockingham Ministry of 1781, and in 1782 received from Lord Shelburne the Keepership of the Scottish Signet for life, with the patronage of all places in his own country, where for thirty years he reigned practically with autocratic power, returning such peers and such commoners to Parliament as he chose to nominate.

In the year 1792 he was chairman of the Secret Committee appointed to report on the government of India, and gained much insight into the affairs of that country. It is characteristic of the man that he was foremost to accuse Warren Hastings in 1782, that he defended him at first in 1786 against Burke, and finally for no reason turned against him again. His principles in fact were plastic; and he had a singularly keen eye for the form in which it would be most profitable to mould them. Having early perceived the promise of Pitt, he attached himself to him, and became Treasurer of the Navy in his first administration. Finally, in 1791 he received the seals of the Home Office, which gave him charge of the Colonies, and also, as shall be seen, of the conduct of the war.

By that time Dundas had become Pitt's closest friend and most trusted colleague. Dundas wrote:

> Mr. Pitt, among the multitude of things which press upon him is at all times ready to accommodate himself to my call.

Pitt wrote in 1794:

> You know the difficulty (of the War Department) with other Departments, even with the advantages of Dundas's turn for facilitating business and of every act being as much mine as his.—*Dropmore Papers*, ii.

The alliance between two such men was strange. Pitt, though the wittiest and most delightful of persons when he consented to unbend, was naturally shy, haughty, reserved, and fastidious. Dundas was not only highly convivial over the bottle, as was the rule in those days, but genial to everyone, never forgetting, to his credit, those who had known him before he rose to high office; yet his mind was coarse and his ideals low. Pitt was an upright man, and in public affairs at large a patriotic and far-seeing statesman.

Dundas was honest in so far as he never sought to enrich himself with the public money; but in political matters he was little more than an unscrupulous though very successful intriguer. Votes were the end and aim of all his actions, and the horizon of his policy was bounded by the next general election. Such a man may be a faithful servant to a successful master; but he can never be a loyal master to an unsuccessful servant. Nor, despite his undoubted industry and "turn for facilitating business," can I find that the man had really any great talent for administration.

His State-papers are intolerably diffuse, verbose, and evasive of the point, while his orders, as shall be seen, are open to still harsher criticism. Probably, like Pitt, he was at his best in the House of Commons, where his speeches are said to have been eloquent, and were certainly disingenuous, but where his cheerful address and broad Scottish accent doubtless reconciled many to the chilling superiority of his young leader. Such was the man who from his knowledge of the world had gained Pitt's utmost confidence, and, as I believe, far greater ascendency over him than is generally supposed. To him, accordingly, was committed the direction of the war, with a sanguine trustfulness, to which he responded with as sanguine self-confidence. Yet so profoundly ignorant was Dundas of war that he was not even conscious of his ignorance.

A man of very different character was William Grenville, who after holding the seals of the Home Office for two years had made them over to Dundas in 1791, and taken over those of the Foreign Office in their stead. A younger son of the George Grenville who had passed the Stamp Act, he, like his father, had been Speaker of the House of Commons, and possessed a mind of the same academic cast. Indefatigable industry joined to great natural gifts had made him one of the best informed men in England. As a classical scholar he was deeper and sounder than Pitt or Fox; he was as familiar with Italian literature as with Greek; he spoke French with a purity of accent which had deceived even Frenchmen as to his nationality, and he wrote it with a facility and correctness that were the envy of the diplomatic service.

Withal he was deeply versed in history, and followed political, social, and religious movements all over Europe so closely, that few pamphlets of note or notoriety in any country failed to find their way to his library. He had, moreover, devoted as close attention to Indian and Colonial history as to European; and, above all his contemporaries he made a particular study of geography, sparing no pains to obtain the best maps, and amassing a collection of them which would not have been despised by any General Staff in Europe. And if his idea of an English statesman's intellectual equipment was high, his conception of his duty to his country as a patriot and to himself as a gentleman was no whit lower.

Intense pride and austerity of conduct forbade him even to recognise that there was more than one path for an upright and honourable man. Yet with all his great qualities he was diffident of his own powers, and painfully conscious that the gift of governing men had been denied to him. He could win their confidence and respect, but he could not command their sympathy; and, too honest to charge others with a failing which he knew to be his own, he confessed it with genuine self-abasement and humbleness of heart. Through his willingness to efface himself his name has been little remembered in history, yet he brought to the council-board not only knowledge, insight and sagacity, but a resolute will, dauntless courage, and inflexible constancy of purpose.

Pitt, as we have seen, had done his utmost to avoid war; but, since war had been forced upon him, it behoved him, or Dundas for him, to frame a military policy. On the continent of Europe there were two principal objects which seemed vital to England, namely, the integrity of the Dutch Netherlands, and the maintenance of an effective barrier between them and France. Holland, as Lord Auckland said, (Auckland to Grenville, 14th February 1793), was practically a great military magazine and military chest; and Antwerp was a base for naval operations which, in the hands of France, would be a standing menace to England's safety.

The Belgic barrier and the exclusive right of the Dutch to the navigation of the Scheldt were, in fact, not only matters of traditional foreign policy but an essential part of England's scheme of national defence; and Pitt imagined that he had secured both by the active diplomacy of Harris in 1787. Moreover, from the beginning of the Revolution he had watched the growing financial distress of France with the keen eye of a Chancellor of the Exchequer, and had made up his mind, not altogether unreasonably, that no country in such a state of disorganisation and bankruptcy as France could long support a war. He thought that he could fix a term at which her hand must drop the sword from sheer powerlessness, and he entered upon the contest in the assurance that the contest could not be a long one.

To hasten the process of financial exhaustion by destroying French trade over sea would, as he thought, be the surest and cheapest way of bringing the struggle to a close, as well as the means best suited to England's military resources; for, though she had practically no army, she possessed at any rate a navy and superiority at sea.

This policy once fixed, it was not difficult to decide where the naval force should be employed. Ever since the declaration of the Rights of Man by the National Assembly, Aug. 20th 1789, there had been unrest in the French West Indies generally, and especially in St. Domingo, the most important of them; the white planters everywhere taking alarm at the doctrine that the blacks were free and equal to themselves. On the contrary, the *mulattos* or coloured people, who were subject to degrading hardships and disabilities, claimed their privileges under this declaration, and were encouraged by a philanthropic society, known as the Negro's Friends, in Paris.

The grant of a constitutional government to the island naturally kindled between the two parties dissensions, which were artfully inflamed by the partisans of royalty and of the old order. The quarrel was carried to Paris, where the violent language of Brissot and others of the Negro's Friends encouraged the hot-headed *mulattos* to organise an insurrection. This was put down, March 1791, without great difficulty, and the ringleaders, were broken on the wheel; out this seventy gave the Negro's Friends an opportunity to pass a decree asserting, at whatever cost, the equality of the coloured man with the white.

"Perish the Colonies rather than one tittle of our principles," cried one of them; and therewith the full rights of citizenship were conceded to the coloured people at one stroke, May 15th. The whites thereupon trampled the National Tricolour under foot, and even threatened to hoist British colours; but before they could organise themselves for defence the negro slaves in two districts, stirred by incendiary addresses from Paris, rose up in general insurrection against them, August, devastating and slaughtering with hideous barbarity.

Alarmed at the ruin of their once rich and thriving colonies, the Constituent Assembly in Paris rescinded its mischievous decree, Sept. 24; but it was too late. The *mulattos* joined the blacks; and the whites, aided by the garrison of regular troops, turned upon both with the fury of despair. The combatants vied with each other in a savage emulation of cruelty. Civil commissioners arrived from Paris, Christmas, and endeavoured to restore peace, but in vain; a war of colour, once kindled, is not easily quenched; and they returned to France after three months, having accomplished nothing.

The Legislative Assembly then put the finishing stroke to the mischief by decreeing equality of rights with white men to all free *mulattos* and negroes, April 4th 1792, and by sending out violent Jacobins as commissioners to execute the decree in all the French islands. Those appointed to St. Domingo, namely, Santhonax and Polverel, arrived there in September, and at once allied themselves to the blacks, in order to enrich themselves with the plunder of the whites.

Having deposed two governors who presumed to dispute their authority, they, at the beginning of 1793, became practically masters of the island.

Meanwhile, as the month of January advanced and the prospect of war grew more certain, further orders were issued for augmenting the forces; and on the 25th Lord Amherst was appointed General on the Staff, as during the American War, with the duties though not with the title of Commander-in-Chief at the Horse Guards. Finally on the 11th of February a vote was submitted to Parliament for the increase of the army by twenty-five thousand men, a great number of which were raised by forming one hundred independent companies of one hundred men apiece, and drafting them into existing battalions.

Just at this time, as we have seen, the apathy of the *stadtholder* towards the entreaties of Lord Auckland compelled the Ministry to hasten three battalions of Guards, in a dangerous state of unreadiness, to Holland, but with express and repeated orders that they should be used for the protection of that country only, (Dundas to York, 19th March 1793).

It is perfectly plain that the Government had at first no intention of keeping these troops on the Continent; but their arrival, and still more that of the Duke of York, did so much to hearten the Dutch to activity, that on the 5th of March it was resolved to send the Fourteenth, Thirty-Seventh, and Fifty-Third Foot, completed by drafts from the new independent companies, to join the duke as a brigade under Major-General Ralph Abercromby. These regiments, however, were subject to the same instructions as the Guards, namely, to remain within immediate reach of their transports in case their services should be required elsewhere. Their quality was such that the adjutant-general felt constrained to apologise for them both to Abercromby and to the Duke of York. He wrote to the duke:

> I am afraid that you will not reap the advantage that you might have expected from the brigade of the Line just sent over to you, as so considerable a part of it is composed of nothing but undisciplined and raw recruits; and how they are to be disposed of until they can be taught their business I am at a loss to imagine. . . . I was not consulted upon the subject until it was too late to remedy the evil, but I hope that my remonstrances will be of some use in the modelling of troops for the Continent in future.

It need hardly be added that, on their arrival in Holland, April 1st, two out of the three battalions were found utterly unfit for service, the new recruits being old men and weakly boys, worse than the worst that had been accepted even at the period of greatest exhaustion during the American War. To send them on active service was, therefore,

27

simply waste of money. (*Dropmore Papers*, Auckland to Grenville, 5th and 13th March, 1793. *S.C.L.B.* 5th March; Abercromby's instructions, 9th March; Dundas to York, 15th March 1793; *C.C.L.B.* 2nd March; Adj.Gen. to York, 27th March, 12th April 1793. Calvert).

But this was only one of the evils which ensued, because an extremely ignorant civilian was too conceited to consult his military advisers before giving military orders. Any soldier at the War Office could have told him that the method of raising independent companies to recruit existing regiments had been found wasteful and unsatisfactory in the past; and, indeed, at this very time the Chief Secretary Cooke wrote to him from Ireland a strong protest against the whole system. It was expensive, because it meant the provision of half-pay for their officers as soon as the men had been drafted out; it was unfair to old subalterns, because they were passed over by boys who by good fortune had raised recruits cheaply.

It produced a bad class of recruit, because these young officers were poor judges of men; and finally it encouraged desertion, for the crimps, so long as they poured a certain number of recruits into the depots by a certain time, cared not the least whether they deserted afterwards. Nor was Cooke content only to criticise, for he produced an alternative plan for allowing each of the fourteen battalions in Ireland to raise two additional companies of one hundred men apiece, and for granting to the commanding officers the privilege of recommending officers for them. The scheme was approved and was found to be most successful; but it was not introduced into England, where, on the contrary, the number of independent companies was still further increased. (*S. P. Ireland*, Cooke to Hobart, 23rd April; Westmoreland to Hobart, 27th April; Dundas to Westmoreland, 16th May, 31st July 1793; *S.C.L.B.* 18th May 1793).

Again, the adjutant-general, if consulted, could have warned Dundas to be chary of his battalions, since some of them would certainly be required for the Fleet. The King's Navy was labouring under the grievances which in four years were to drive the seamen to mutiny; and as a natural consequence men were hardly to be obtained by any means. On the very day when the declaration of war was received, Feb. 7th, the Fleet swallowed up two battalions; and by the end of March it had absorbed so many men that only three regiments of the Line were to be found south of the Tweed.

In fact the Horse Guards did not know where to turn for another battalion. This, however, did not prevent Dundas from presently sending another emissary to Jamaica, to commit England still more deeply to operations in the most leeward sphere of the West Indies. Yet he had no reserve of any description to rely upon, except fourteen thousand Hanoverians and eight thousand Hessians, which, pursuant to the time-honoured practice, were taken into British pay; and of these the latter only, being mercenaries pure and simple, could be counted upon for service beyond sea. (*S.C.L.B.* 7th February. *C.C.L.B.* Adj.-Gen. to Duke of York, 2nd and 12th April 1793. Dundas to Williamson, 4th April).

Since the kingdom was thus stripped of regular troops, it was necessary to raise other forces for its security; but this also was done as foolishly as possible. Early in February 1793, it was rightly and wisely decided to call out nineteen thousand additional Militia; but in the execution precisely the same mistake was made as in France. Personal service was not insisted upon; there arose a great demand for substitutes; and the Militia, instead of gaining a substantial increase, simply cut off from the army the sources of its supply of recruits. In Scotland, which as yet had no Militia, recourse was made to the raising of Fencible regiments, that is to say, of regular troops enlisted for home-service and for the duration of the war only. This system had so far been applied only on a small scale, the regiments of Fencibles during the Seven Years' War and the American War of Independence having been but few; but it now received great and sudden expansion. (Duke of Argyll's and Earl of Sutherland's, 1759; Lord Fred. Campbell's, 1778; Earl of Sutherland's, Fauconberg's/Yorkshire, North's/Cinque Ports, 1779).

On the 2nd of March authority was issued for the raising of seven regiments of Fencible Infantry in Scotland at a stroke; besides one already authorised for the Isle of Man, Feb. 20th, and another, added in April, for the Orkney Islands. (Athol's or the Manx, Sir J. Grant's, Gower's/or Wemyss's, Eglinton's/or Montgomery's, Breadalbane's, Argyll's, Duke of Gordon's, Hopetoun's, Balfour's/Orkney. Their strength was 650 of all ranks, except the Manx, which were 323 strong).

With the leading magnates of Scotland at their head, these new corps were speedily completed; but there was one Scottish nobleman who went further than his peers, and raised a regiment in the Highlands for general service. This was Thomas Humberstone Mackenzie, afterwards the last Earl of Seaforth; and his regiment remains with us, still known by his name, but yet more famous under its number of the Seventy-Eighth. The reader should take note of the Fencible regiments, for in the years before us we shall see them increased and multiplied in all three kingdoms.

Meanwhile, he should remark that within a month of the declaration of war there were already three distinct forces, the Army, the Fencibles, and the Militia, all bidding against each other for the recruits which only the Regular Army could turn to efficient account.

It is not difficult to perceive the lurking possibilities of disaster in Dundas's military policy; but until April it showed at any rate a certain consistency. The despatch of troops to the Continent was treated as a temporary measure, designed for the protection of Holland only; and, though the Prince of Coburg had called upon the Duke of York to co-operate in his great sweeping movement from north-east to southwest, the duke had complied only so far as his instructions and, it may be added, his lack of transport permitted. (Murray to Dundas, 26th March 1793).

But much, besides the expulsion of the French from Holland and Belgium, had occurred in March, all tending to embarrass England in the principal object of her Continental policy, the securing of a strong barrier between France and Holland. The fatal question of indemnity, first brought forward by the King of Prussia, had aroused the cupidity of his brother potentate in Austria, who valued the recovery of Belgium chiefly in order that he might exchange it for Bavaria. Pitt had for a moment been willing, as we have seen, to consent to the Bavarian exchange, for the sake of peace; but upon the outbreak of war he reverted to absolute rejection of it; and, in an evil hour, March 2nd, the British Ambassador at Vienna, Sir Morton Eden, put forward a suggestion that Austria should be bribed to retain Belgium by the promise of an extension of her frontiers on the side of France.

Realising that Austria refused to act disinterestedly, 3rd April, Grenville reluctantly accepted the proposal; and at the same time the British Government seems to have taken it for granted that it must give the emperor some assistance towards the conquest of the new barrier, (Sybel, ii.; Grenville to Auckland, 3rd April 1793).

Accordingly, since no more infantry was to be spared from England, eleven regiments of cavalry were ordered to prepare for service on the Continent, though their numbers were so weak that they could not between them muster more than twenty-three squadrons, or about two thousand five hundred of all ranks, fit for service. But, at the same time, the British Ministers shrank from supplying British troops for the advantage of other nations without gaining some equivalent to satisfy the electors of England; wherefore they decided, apparently at the instance of Grenville's elder brother, Lord Buckingham, to claim Dunkirk as Great Britain's indemnity for the war. The choice, viewed from the standpoint of the party-politician, was a good one.

Dunkirk, having been taken by Cromwell, sold by Charles the Second, and dismantled under the conditions imposed by the sword of Marlborough, possessed sentimental attractions to the public at large and to the Whigs in particular; while, as a nest of privateers, its extirpation could not but be welcome not only to every merchant in England, but especially to the Chancellor of the Exchequer. No scheme of operations had yet been concerted with Austria, for, indeed, Coburg had advanced from the Roer before nearly all his forces had been collected; but Pitt seems to have thought that, while the Austrian reinforcements were on their way to the front, the mixed force of British, Hanoverians, Hessians and Dutch might very well master Dunkirk in the course of April, afterwards leaving the Austrians in sufficient strength to pursue their operations in Flanders alone, while the British struck at some other part of France.

Thus Pitt was not true even to his own plan of ruining his enemy by the destruction of her colonial trade; while what he meant by some other part of France is not very clear. The old Marquis of Bouillé, knowing that the heart of the Revolution could be pierced at Paris, had suggested a descent upon Havre with thirty thousand men; and, as shall be seen, there was by this time another vulnerable point in the west of France. But why it should have been necessary to seek out a new point of attack, when troops were already massed or massing on the French frontier within twelve days march of the capital, and with only a demoralised enemy before them, was a question which seems never to have occurred either to Pitt or to Dundas.

There can be no doubt that they fell into a common pitfall of the British politician. They gave so much thought to the treaty which they should lay before Parliament at the close of the war, that they omitted to consider the means of bringing the war itself to a close. (*S.C.L.B.* 2 1st March, 2nd April; *C.C.L.B.* 25th March 1793. *Dropmore Papers*, ii. Buckingham to Grenville, 20th January; the King to Grenville, 29th March; Pitt to Grenville, 1st April 1793. Auckland to Grenville, 31st May 1793).

Meanwhile the omnivorous rapacity of the Emperor Francis, of the Holy Roman Empire, was already reducing the coalition against France to hopeless weakness. The first trouble arose out of the project of the Bavarian exchange, which was so bitterly resented by the Wittelsbachs, the reigning house of Bavaria, that they not only raised difficulties about the passage of the Imperial troops through their territory to the Rhine, but refused to make over Mannheim to them as a place of arms. Much incensed, the emperor detained his reserves from the front with the idea of seizing Bavaria by force, to which the Bavarians replied by detaining their troops likewise to watch them; and thus both were lost for service in active operations. This was a bad beginning; but still more fatal in its results was the communication to Vienna of the treaty between Russia and Prussia for the partition of Poland, March 23rd.

The emperor, furious at having been outdone by Frederick William in the gain of territory, dismissed his ministers and took to himself a new adviser in Baron Thugut, an absolutely unprincipled politician, who cared for nothing but power and believed in nothing but success. To humour the greed of his master, he sent an emissary to England, March 27th, to press once again not only for her consent to the Bavarian exchange, but for the acquisition by Austria of certain places in Alsace also; agreeing in return that the emperor should do his best to increase the territory of Belgium by the conquest of French fortresses, but adding that, unless England consented to the exchange of the Belgic Provinces thus augmented, Austria would be obliged to take a portion of Poland.

Simultaneously, April 4th, he informed Russia and. Prussia, who had agreed to guarantee the Bavarian exchange to Austria if she would subscribe to the treaty of partition, that the Emperor renounced the exchange and looked for indemnity both in France and Poland. Finally, after hearing of the recapture of Belgium, he again approached Sir Morton Eden and offered, if England would conclude a close alliance with Austria, to abandon the Bavarian exchange. Thugut appears to have considered it a cardinal principle of statesmanship to involve himself in a tangle of lies; but this purposeless duplicity of course produced no good effect. Eden announced that England was immovable upon the Bavarian question, but would agree to concede indemnities of French territory. Frederick William simply replied that, if Austria thwarted his designs on Poland, he would withdraw all his troops from France except the twenty thousand men that formed his contingent, as a member of the Empire, to the Imperial army.

This placed the emperor in a dilemma. He would gladly have broken with Prussia, and drawn closer to England, but that Prussia could provide him with the troops that he needed, while England could not. It then remained for him to choose whether he would make peace with France and give all his attention to Poland, or renounce Poland and turn all his strength against France; but in his insane greed of territory he insisted upon trying to gain everything. The result of this double dealing speedily told upon the military operations. Brunswick, pursuant to agreement, had moved upon the 25th of March against Custine before Mainz; and in the course of ten days he drove the French in utter confusion south of the Lauter. But beyond that point he did not press them; and Frederick William, though he blockaded Mainz, resolved to make any further offensive movements conditional upon Austria's good behaviour.

It was in such inauspicious circumstances that the representatives of the various powers met in conference at Antwerp. Coburg, who loathed the war and had hoped to end it by an agreement with Dumouriez had issued a proclamation, April 5th, declaring himself to be the ally of all friends of order, and abjuring all projects of conquest in the emperor's name. Instantly Austrians, Prussians, and English with one voice required him to withdraw it, and to publish a new declaration that he would prosecute the war vigorously. He did so, but with great reluctance; indeed, so bitter was his opposition to the new policy that he tried to open further negotiations with the Convention, and even furnished it with information which he ought to have kept to himself. (Sybel, ii.)

Meanwhile Lord Auckland announced that England, as well as the other powers, would expect an indemnity for her share in the war; whereupon the Dutch representative announced that, as everyone else was taking compensation, he hoped that Holland's claims would not be forgotten.

★★★★★★

The insisting upon an indemnity must have been the work of Pitt, probably under the influence of Dundas. Grenville trembled at the word indemnity. *Dropmore Papers*, ii..

★★★★★★

The sharing of the lion's skin having thus been determined, the next thing was to decide upon a plan of operations for slaying the lion. A vague project was drawn out for the attack of the frontier-fortresses, in which Coburg reckoned upon the co-operation of over twenty thousand men, that is to say, of thirteen thousand Hanoverians and seven thousand five hundred British, in British pay, besides fifteen thousand Dutch. Dundas was staggered; for he had not yet the slightest idea what were the ultimate designs of either of the German powers, who, as he justly complained, were very backward to give an explicit account of their views either as to the conduct of the war or the termination of it, he wrote:

> We cannot advise the king to give a blind co-operation to measures not distinctly explained.

But he hinted that if the Austrians would spare a detachment to help the British to capture Dunkirk at once, England might make fewer difficulties about lending her troops for subsequent operations. The English, he explained, were prejudiced against Continental enterprises; wherefore it was important to convince the nation early that its troops in Holland were employed for an object intimately connected with the interests of Great Britain and the security of her commerce, he added:

> The early capture of Dunkirk by a prince of the blood would give much *éclat* to the commencement of the war.

In other words, Dundas was ready to employ British troops in the Low Countries only for a political campaign, and not for the military purposes of the war to use them, in fact, primarily to win votes rather than battles. The attitude is but too characteristic of British Ministers for War. (Protocol of conference of 7th April. Dundas to Auckland and to Murray, 16th April; Auckland to Grenville, 19th April 1793).

Meanwhile the Allies on the frontiers of France remained inactive; the Austrians, indeed, blockading Condé, where the French kept them engaged with incessant affairs of outposts, but the British contingent still awaiting the orders which Dundas hesitated to give. In the third week of April the chief of the British staff reported that a considerable force of French was entrenched about Dunkirk, too strong to be attacked by the Duke of York's troops, and that there was no operation on which the latter could be employed except in support of the Austrians, (Murray to Dundas, 22nd April 1793).

We shall presently recognise the unseen hand which had been working at Dunkirk. Ten days more of uncertainty passed away, and at last, on the 1st of May, Coburg produced a plan of operations. By the middle of May he hoped to have about ninety-two thousand men, (see list following), to which by the beginning of June would be added thirteen thousand more. He proposed, therefore, to hasten the fall of

Condé by a bombardment, and then to advance with fifty-two thousand men to the siege of Valenciennes, leaving a cordon of some forty thousand to cover every imaginable point along a front of some fifty miles from Maubeuge on the Sambre to Ostend on the sea.

Prussians, 8000, of which 1800 cavalry; Austrians, 55,000, of which 10,000 cavalry; Dutch, 15,000, of which 2500 cavalry; Hanoverians, 12,000, of which 3000 cavalry; Hessians, 8000, of which 1500 cavalry; British, 7200, of which 3000 cavalry. Total, 105,200, of which 27,200 in the pay of England. About 5000 of the Austrians and the 8000 Hessians were not expected till June. Witzleben, ii. Coburg to York, 1st and 3rd May; Murray to Dundas, 5th May; Dundas to Murray, 10th May 1793.

Valenciennes might be expected to fall at the end of July, and then ten thousand men could be left to mask Lille, while fifty thousand marched to the siege of Dunkirk. If this plan were accepted, Coburg pledged himself to the Duke of York to lend his best goodwill to the attack on Dunkirk. On this assurance the duke recommended the plan to which at last Dundas gave his consent, on the understanding that the other powers in general and Austria in particular should give an immediate explanation of their ulterior views. England, he repeated, could not allow so large a force in her pay to be employed on operations whose object was undefined; and he emphasised the statement by an inquiry as to the security of Ostend, which so far had been the British port of disembarkation, evidently as a hint that England reserved her right to withdraw her troops at any moment.

This is a good instance of the manner in which British Ministers evade their responsibility. The British general had, nearly three weeks before, laid before Dundas the following issue:

> There is no use for British troops in the Netherlands except to act in support of the Austrians. Their commander has submitted a plan based on the active co-operation of all our troops, present and expected. We think the plan a good one. Are we to act with him, or are we not?

Upon this it was for the Ministry to say at once to Austria:

> Our generals favour your plan of campaign, but until we know your ultimate intentions we cannot take part in it. Unless you come to a definite understanding with us by a certain day, we shall order our troops on the spot to re-embark, and meanwhile we have suspended the march of our reinforcements.

DUNKIRK AND ENVIRONS
showing
THE POSITION OF THE ALLIES
from 24 Aug to 6 Sept. 1793.

Allies ......
French ....
Advance of French ....

English Miles
0 1 2 3 4 5

Ost Dunkirk

The Dunes

Adinkerke

FRENCH GUNBOATS

Rosendael

Ghyvelde

DUNKERQUE

Dunkirk

Great Moor

Teteghem

Coudekerque

Warhem

White House

Bergues

Hondschoote

FREYTAG'S POSITION
7 SEPT.

Killem

Steene

F   R   Quaedypre

E   Rexpoede

Y   Ost Cappel   R. Yser

T   Rousbrugge

Wylder
er

Bambecque   A

R. Yser

G   Proven

Esquelbeck

Wormhoudt

Herzeele   Houtkerque

Watou

Poperinghe

Ypres

Cassel

Steenvoorde

Oxelaere

Eecke   Berthen

Sylvestre Cappel

Instead of this they said in effect:

> We approve the plan of campaign, and thereby commit our troops to it; but we reserve to ourselves the right to withdraw them, or, in other words, to wreck the operations, whenever we think proper.

If, therefore, the enemy should in the meantime take the offensive and press the Austrians hard, which, as shall be seen, was what actually happened, the responsibility for granting or withholding British assistance was thrown entirely upon the general.

It remains to say a word of the plan itself, and of the troops and commanders who were appointed to carry it out. The enormous front along which Coburg proposed to disperse his force is an example of the system known as the cordon system, which was in particular favour with the Austrians at this time. It consisted in covering every possible access to a theatre of war with some small body of troops, and had been formulated by Marshal Lacy upon the experience of the war of the Bavarian Succession in 1778, when he had held a front of fifty miles in the labyrinthine country of the Upper Elbe, and reduced the campaign to a mere scuffle of foraging parties.

Well calculated to exclude the plague or contraband goods from a country, it was, of course, ridiculous against the invasion of an enemy; for it meant weakness at all points and strength at none, and in fact simply invited the destruction of the army in detail by a force of inferior strength. Nevertheless it was in high favour with all armies of Europe, excepting the British, at that time; and it was a matter of rule that, wherever the enemy stationed a battalion or a company, a countervailing battalion or company must be posted over against it.

The Austrians had suffered much from this system in their recent war with the Turks; but their commanders, of whom Coburg had been one, had learned little from this experience. Apart from his adherence to this new and utterly false fashion, which precluded the concentration of troops for a vigorous offensive, Coburg was a sound, slow, cautious commander of the old Austrian type, more intent upon preserving his own army than destroying the enemy's, and, perhaps, happiest when firmly set down to conduct a siege in form according to the most scientific principles.

Withal he was a sensible and honourable gentleman, and extremely popular with his troops. The chief of his staff was the unfortunate Mack, then a colonel forty years of age, who enjoyed the reputation of being the most scientific officer in Europe. The theory of war, as then understood in many quarters, assigned as the first object not the annihilation of the enemy's force in the field, but the possession of certain geographical points, which were called Strategic Objects. At this game of maps and coloured labels Mack excelled; and, when called upon to fight an action, he so elaborated his plans for the overwhelming of his enemies by the simultaneous onslaught of a number of converging columns that, if everything went right and every column reached exactly the appointed place at exactly the appointed time, he assured to himself not only victory but conquest. But, since he made no allowance for the possible failure of any one of his combinations through unforeseen contingencies or accidents of any description, Mack's actions were rarely successful and always unduly hazardous.

He seems to have been an honest man, of real though misdirected ability; while his character gained for him a confidence and respect which the British in the field accorded to no other foreign officer. But though, as shall be seen, his methods by no means commended themselves to all British commanders, they nevertheless made a fatally favourable impression upon the British Ministry.

To judge with the wisdom that comes after the event, it may be said that the Allied Army was tactically deficient in two principal respects, namely, in the numerical weakness of its light infantry, and in the faulty organisation of its artillery. Light infantry and light cavalry at this time were still treated mainly as accessories, useful for the "little war" (to use the French expression) of outposts and reconnaissance, but as something apart from the "great war," which was reserved for the more solid squadrons and battalions that enjoyed the dignity of a place in the formal Order of Battle.

In fact, the work of outposts was supposed to fall wholly upon the light corps, while the regular troops husbanded their strength in security behind them. Hostilities with any nation which is driven back on primitive methods of self-defence, and which neither knows nor respects the contemporary usage of civilised warfare, invariably upset any such arrangement; and the British, after the experience of America, should have been awake to this truth. Indeed, in justice to the officers, many of them were alive to it; but Pitt, since 1783, had been more solicitous for the reduction than the training of the Army. In the matter of artillery the practice of all the nations was the same. Each battalion possessed its two guns, three-pounders or six-pounders, and the remainder of the ordnance was massed into a park, with or without an inner distribution into brigades or batteries. The handling of the artillery by the Count of Bückeburg at Minden had not yet found sufficient appreciation to be made the foundation of a system. (Ditfurth, i.; Witzleben, ii.; Calvert; Sybel, ii.).

The Austrian troops, in spite of the exhaustion of the long Turkish war, were for the most part worthy of their high reputation, and aroused at first the greatest admiration among British officers. They included, however, a certain number of irregular corps, both horse and foot, chiefly Slavs, which were simply savage banditti of the most dangerous type. They would murder or plunder any one, friend or foe, even to the vedettes of their own army; and no Austrian general would trust himself among them without an escort. The quality of the higher officers was, however, unworthy that of the men, many of them being old, supine, and narrow-minded; and the corps of officers at large was sharply divided between two factions, which espoused the two opposite schools of Loudon and Lacy.

The organisation also was imperfect, for, though the army was indeed distributed into brigades and divisions, these were not kept together, but all detachments were formed of squadrons and battalions arbitrarily collected and entrusted to a general as arbitrarily chosen, who knew no more of the men than they knew of him. In the matter of tactics the Austrians had made no progress since the Seven Years' War. Cavalry and infantry alike were still formed in three ranks, and the art of handling large bodies of cavalry had been nearly, though not wholly, forgotten.

The Prussians still enjoyed the fame which they had won under Frederick the Great, but they had not been improved by the false training observed by Cornwallis at their manoeuvres, while their commander, von Knobelsdorf, though full of zeal, was also full of years, having passed his seventieth birthday. Superior to them were the Hessians, the majority of whom had served in America, where they had learned to manoeuvre rapidly and to fight in dispersed order, though the lesson had never been practised since their return to their own land, (Ditfurth, i.). The Hessian Jäger were particularly good light troops, and were armed with rifles. The whole corps, moreover, was the more effective since it was equipped with regimental transport upon a lavish scale, and was therefore mobile and self-dependent.

★★★★★★

231 horses, draught and pack, and 116 drivers, etc., per battalion of 1100 men, of which 82 horses and 34 men were for the

officers. Each company had one four -horse waggon, and each battalion one pair-horse hospital-waggon.

★★★★★★

On the whole, the Hessians seem to have been the most valuable fighting men in the army, though they were not exempt from the love of plunder, a failing which mercenary veterans are apt to judge more leniently, at certain times, than other troops. The Hanoverians were then, as always, fine soldiers, but without the advantage of the Hessians in experience and training. The Dutch, being hastily raised, were ill organised, disciplined, trained, and equipped.

The British, with the exception of the Guards, were, in the opinion of foreign critics, very deficient in training and discipline, for precisely the same reason as the Dutch, namely, persistent neglect. The cavalry was of better material than the infantry, and was very well mounted; but both officers and men were so ignorant of their work that, at first, they could not even throw out vedettes and outposts without instruction from foreigners. The field-guns were inferior to those of the rest of the Allies; the ammunition-waggons were heavy and unwieldy; and the horses were harnessed one before the other instead of abreast, which made them difficult to drive, and took up much room on the road. The models of both harness and waggons were, in fact, of Marlborough's time; while the medical arrangements, or what passed for such, were those of a still remoter age.

Discipline for the most part was bad, especially among the officers, for reasons which have been explained in a former chapter; and, though there were still among their infantry good men who had learned their business in America, far too many were absolutely ignorant as well as neglectful of their duty. Hard drinking in all ranks accounted for much both of the indiscipline and the neglect.

To the men, of course, drunkenness brought a flogging at the halberts, but to the officers, unfortunately, it did not necessarily mean punishment; nor was it possible that it should, when respectful consideration was shown to both Prime Minister and Secretary of State for War if they appeared incapably drunk at the House of Commons, because the leaders of the Opposition drank even harder than they. This vice of drunkenness was the most formidable with which good officers had to contend throughout the twenty years of the war, simply because it was a fashion set in high places. (Ditfurth, i.; Witzleben, ii. York to Dundas, 25th January 1794).

It was no easy task to command such a force as the British, Hanoverians and Hessians, under the orders of such a man as Dundas, and the immediate direction of such generals as Coburg and Mack. Frederick, Duke of York, second son of King George the Third, was in 1793 twenty-eight years old. At the age of sixteen he had been sent to Berlin to study the profession of arms under the eye of Frederick the Great himself, and had returned with a practical knowledge which made him later an admirable commander-in-chief at the Horse Guards, but also with an undue preference for the weaker points of the stiff and formal Prussian system.

In 1791 he had become Colonel of the Coldstream Guards, in which post he had at first shown himself enough of a martinet to excite discontent, (*Dropmore Papers*, ii.); and, though he had wisely changed his ways after a year's experience, he was not at this time popular with his men, while his officers, who had been taught to look for preferment from politicians, resented his authority whether for good or ill.

In this respect he was hampered by the same disadvantages as had beset Lord Stair in 1743; and, unfortunately, he did not possess the qualifications to gain the confidence of his troops in the field. He had the cool personal bravery which belongs to his race, but not the higher moral courage which gives constancy and patience in difficulty or misfortune; and hence he was at once sanguine and easily discouraged. He had learned his work, so far as it could be acquired by the industry of a mediocre intellect, but he was slow of apprehension, without sagacity, penetration or width of view, and with so little imagination or resource that an unforeseen emergency confounded him.

On the other hand, his dutiful loyalty and submission, in most trying circumstances, towards Coburg on the one hand, and the Cabinet on the other, were beyond all praise. The Ministry had some just doubts as to his fitness to command, but the king had set his heart upon the appointment; and indeed, where so many Serene Highnesses were gathered together, the superior rank of the duke was a decided advantage. It was hoped, therefore, to make good his deficiencies by joining to him Sir James Murray, better known by the name which he afterwards assumed as Sir James Pulteney, nominally as adjutant-general, but really as Chief of the Staff and something more; for it was to his correspondence that the government looked for information and advice.

Murray was a singular character. He had served in the Seven Years' War; he had distinguished himself in the West Indies during the American War of Independence; and he had trained an intellect, which was of no common order, not only by shrewd observation of the world but by solid and extensive study. His knowledge was great, his grasp and outlook wide, his judgment cool and accurate, his indifference to danger and hardship absolute; but he was shy, awkward and diffident, with a dreamy indolence which led him too readily to surrender his own correct opinion, and to amuse himself with speculation upon the incorrect opinions of others, (Bunbury, *Great War with France*). When roused he could sum up a situation with an insight, terseness and vigour which showed how close was his hold upon facts; but he was not the helpmate who could make good the defects of the Duke of York.

The situation, indeed, demanded a Marlborough, with the insight to see the one thing that was needed, and the tact and ascendency to bring cautious commanders, intriguing Ministers, narrow-minded potentates and irresolute Cabinets into line, for the one true object,—an immediate march on Paris. Such a march could undoubtedly not have been made without risk, owing to the dearth of food in France; yet the opportunity was favourable, and the hazard was slight compared with the certain danger of delay. Already in February the Republic had wantonly made a fresh enemy by declaring war upon Spain, (19th); and the course of the campaign in Belgium had produced results for which the most sanguine of her enemies could hardly have hoped.

On the first news of the Austrian successes, (March 8th), the Convention instantly formed a special tribunal for the trial of traitors and conspirators against France, and summoned two of the defeated generals to appear before it. This done, it proceeded to take measures for hastening the levy of the three hundred thousand men, decreed a fortnight before. The scenes of ridiculous enthusiasm, which had become usual in Paris, followed as a matter of course; but the multitude of men who, for various reasons, claimed exemption, was astonishing, and the rascality of many who were enrolled was flagrant.

A great many of these rogues made a trade of fraudulent enlistment, receiving a bounty from several corps and selling the arms and clothing received from each of them; while the number of women, who claimed allowances for the removal of their husbands to the army, sufficed to warrant the belief that every recruit was a polygamist. In the provinces, both north and south, there was violent resistance to the levy; and on the 10th of March, at Saint Florent le Vieil on the Loire, the peasants turned upon the troops which had been brought up to enforce the ballot, and, though armed only with cudgels, dispersed them and drove them from the town.

That evening the alarm-bell rang in every church of the surrounding parishes; and five days later bands of peasants drove the National Guards from Chollet, some twenty miles south of Saint Florent, and took that town also. This was the first manifestation of a great counter-revolutionary movement, famous in history as the revolt of La Vendée.

The Convention, however, did not at first realise the importance of this outbreak, in the critical state of things in the north. At attempt to reinforce Dumouriez at Louvain, by calling out ten thousand of the National Guards of the northern provinces, provided only a few worn-out men and boys, (Poisson, ii.), whom the general contemptuously dismissed to their homes. Then came the defection of Dumouriez himself, which was well-nigh fatal to all military improvement. The general had disparaged the election of officers by their men; he had urged that the volunteers should be incorporated in the Line; he had tried to enforce discipline upon all; and, finally, he had turned traitor and taken some of his regular troops with him. It was therefore plain that discipline was an abomination, that all his recommendations were vicious, that the regular troops were not to be trusted, and that volunteers only were to be accounted faithful.

Never was the regular army of France so near to total dissolution at the hands of its countrymen as at this moment of supreme military peril. Beurnonville, having tried to abolish abuses, was driven from the War Office; a good Jacobin, Bouchotte, with a still better Jacobin, Vincent, at his elbow, was installed April 6th in his place, and the whole of Pache's vile following returned with them to office, (Rousset). A camp was ordered to be formed at Peronne, and in it were assembled, not with disgrace but with honour, all the soldiers who had been imprisoned by Dumouriez for misconduct, all the deserters, the cowards and the skulkers, who had fled from the army of Belgium.

Further, it was resolved that representatives of the people, with absolute powers, should be sent to rally and reorganise the northern forces, and to set the fortresses in order. If ever a nation seemed bent upon compassing its own destruction by piling madness upon madness, it was the French at this moment.

Yet, amid all the confusion, there appeared the first sign of the powers which by terrible means were to reduce France and, through France, the whole Continent of Europe to discipline and order. On the 6th of April the Convention chose nine of its members, renewable by monthly election, to wield the Dictatorship of France, with the title of the Committee of Public Safety. On the 10th of April a rough Alsatian officer, Kellerman by name, whose gallantry had raised him from the ranks to a commission during the Seven Years' War, came forward with a scheme which preserved the famous regiments of the French Line.

Finally, among the six representatives despatched to save the wreck of Dumouriez's army was Captain Lazare Carnot of the Engineers; by birth a younger son in a respectable family of Burgundy, by repute well known in Europe as an original thinker upon military matters in general, and upon the defence of fortresses in particular. Though now forty years of age and of twenty years' standing in the army, he was still a captain, for his military opinions had given offence in high quarters under the Monarchy; and it was as a simple captain that he was to appoint generals, and to organise victory under the Republic. Deeply read in theology and history, a passionate devotee of mathematics and of science, he had framed for himself high ideals, which, as he thought, the Revolution was appointed to fulfil; and he upheld its principles through good report and evil report, not with the Gallic effervescence that is bred of self-consciousness, but with the austere enthusiasm of a Scot who takes his stand upon the Covenant.

He believed; and in his faith he had buried all thought of self. Rank, wealth, fame alike were indifferent to this spare, stern, ascetic soldier. To give all that lay in him for the cause, to render faithful account of every trust reposed in him for the cause, to forward all that would further it, to combat all that could impede it—such were the principles that governed his conduct. With these motives to inspire him, with great natural gifts, and with every faculty of mind and body trained to the highest point, it is not surprising that his intellectual grasp was wide, his insight clear, his energy infectious, his industry indefatigable. Such was the man who in the early days of April hurried to the north, his brain teeming with thoughts, long since conceived, as to the training best suited to the French soldier, with his natural aptitude for attack.

Five years before, while advocating a scheme of short service, he had written that it is war and not a lifetime in the barrack-yard that makes the old soldier, (*Vie de Carnot*, i.). To General Dampierre, who had been appointed on his recommendation to succeed Dumouriez, Carnot left it to apply this precept, while he himself, with ominous directness, hurried northward to repair the half-ruined fortress of Dunkirk.

CHAPTER 3

The French Take the Initiative

The effect of Carnot's arrival at Dunkirk in overthrowing Pitt's original plan has already been told. There can be no doubt that the French had full information of the minister's designs, for it became a proverb that the most secret projects of the British War Office were always well known to the enemy and to everybody in England.

★★★★★★

"The squadron of men of war and transports was collected, the commodore's flag hoisted, and the expedition sailed with *most secret* orders, which as usual were as well known to the enemy and everybody in England as to those by whom they were given." (Marryat, *The King's Own*, ch. vii. *ad init.*). Marryat attributes this failing to the multitude of counsellors that compose a Cabinet. He may be right, but those who are acquainted with the scandalous carelessness with which ministers treat confidential military documents, find no difficulty in accounting for if otherwise. This evil still continues, and will continue until Cabinet Ministers are subjected to the same penalties for abuse of trust as other servants of the king.

★★★★★★

Nevertheless, if the British Cabinet had thereupon frankly abandoned any attempt upon Dunkirk, Carnot's labours might have been turned to naught. The French army was only slowly assembled during April, and even at the end of the month was of inferior force and scattered over a wide front; for the French were not free from the vices of the cordon-system, nor were likely to be, so long as civilians interfered with their military dispositions. Apart from the garrisons of Quesnoy, Valenciennes, Condé, Lille and Dunkirk, Dampierre kept ten thousand men on his right, under General Harville, between Maubeuge and Philippeville: ten thousand more, under General Lamarlière, lay on his left, in an entrenched camp thrown up by Carnot at Cassel and at other points between Lille and Dunkirk; and five thousand at Nomain, Orchies, and Hasnon, covered the interval between Lille and the main army. This last, consisting of thirty thousand men under Dampierre's immediate command, lay in an entrenched camp at Famars, a little to the south of Valenciennes, with a detachment in another entrenched position at Anzin, to the north-west of that town. In all, therefore, he had about fifty thousand men at hand for service in the field.

Meanwhile the Allies, who were still below their full strength, occupied the following positions, April 23rd. On their right, that is to say, to westward, six thousand Dutch and about three thousand Imperial troops, under the Hereditary Prince of Orange, lay at Furnes, Ypres and Menin; next to them two thousand five hundred British and about the same number of Austrians and Prussians, under the Duke of York, occupied Tournai; next to the Duke of York, Knobelsdorf, with about eight thousand Prussians, held the line of Maulde, Lecelles and Saint Amand on the Scarpe; next to Knobelsdorf, Clerfaye, with about twelve thousand men at Vicoigne and Raismes, and at Bruay and Fresnes, on the Scheldt, encompassed Condé on the south, while the Prince of Würtemberg with about five thousand men blockaded it on the north.

At Onnaing, due south of Condé, lay the principal army, about fifteen thousand strong, with the advance guard at Saint Saulve; and to the east of the main army General Latour with about six thousand men occupied Bettignies, in observation of Maubeuge, with a detachment at Bavai to preserve communication between Bettignies and Onnaing. The total force of the Allies may thus be taken, roughly, at over sixty thousand men, not including thirty thousand Imperial troops under the Prince of Hohenlohe-Kirschberg, which were uselessly detained at Namur, Treves and Luxemburg. The English cavalry, the Hanoverians and the Hessians, had not yet arrived, though the first detachments of the two former were drawing near to the front; but none the less the Allies were actually superior to the French in numbers, and very far superior in quality.

The whole of their multitudinous posts were strongly entrenched; but it will be observed that, besides the essential defect of the enormous extension of their front, their line was cut in two by the river Scheldt, which gave the greater opportunity for a successful attack upon one or other of their wings. The general distribution of the Allies corresponded in the main with their lines of retreat, that of the British lying west to the sea, that of the Dutch north-east upon Antwerp, that of the Austrians east upon Namur; so that a successful attack upon the British would probably lay bare the Austrian right, and a decided defeat of the Austrians must certainly uncover the British left. With their usual jealousy for supreme control, the Austrians mixed a contingent of their own troops with the Allies in every section of the army, an arrangement which gave rise to infinite confusion, since it made even small detachments dependent on two or three different sources of supply. For each nation made provision for its own troops in its own way, and, owing to diversities of system and of differences in calibre of muskets and cannon, it was impossible to make any effort towards uniformity.

Still, the inactivity of Coburg during April was marvellous. It never occurred to him to overwhelm any one of Dampierre's isolated divisions of untrained men by concentrating a superior force upon it. He never reflected that, even if both sides adhered to the cordon-system, the French could bring up the whole manhood of their country to make their cordon stronger than his own at every point. He allowed Dampierre to school his troops with impunity by perpetual affairs of outposts, without remembering that the French could more easily replace two men than he could replace one.

Finally (but this may be pardoned to him) he did not guess that, while he was wasting a campaign over formal sieges, the French would evolve from the experience of many skirmishes a new system of tactics—that they would abandon the old formal training, and, turning to account the indiscipline which springs from the principle of equality, would grant independence of action to the born fighting men, and trust to the national impetuosity to carry the rest forward in dense masses to the attack.

It is a shameful reproach to the Allies that, overmatched though he was in every respect, the French general took the initiative and made the first move of the campaign. On the 1st of May he assailed the whole line of the Allies from Saint Saulve to St. Amand; but, the attacks being unintelligent and incoherent, he was beaten back at every point with a loss of two thousand men and several guns.

Urged by the Convention to save Condé, he on the 8th essayed a second attempt, and on this occasion confined himself to demonstrations only upon the flanks of the Allies, concentrating a larger proportion of his force against Clerfaye's position in the centre. These sounder principles brought him within an ace of success. He himself directed a frontal attack from Anzin against Raismes and Vicoigne, and after four successive repulses carried the position of Raismes, excepting the village. Lamarlière meanwhile with little difficulty made his way towards St. Amand, while one of his divisions, crossing the Scarpe, pressed on unseen through the forest of Vicoigne, nearly to the road which leads from St. Amand to Valenciennes.

There this division began to throw up a redoubt and batteries to cannonade Clerfaye's defences of Vicoigne, so as to cut off communication between him and Knobelsdorf, and to ensure a junction with the garrison of Valenciennes. The situation was critical, for, if the French succeeded in holding possession of the road, the post at Vicoigne was lost, and the whole line of the Allies was broken. Fortunately the Duke of York had moved three battalions of Guards to Nivelle, a little to the north of St. Amand, having promised Knobelsdorf to help him in case of need; and at five o'clock in the evening the brigade came upon the scene, just as the French were gaining the upper hand of the Prussians. The country to north and west of Valenciennes is a level plain, broken only by the three forests, which bear the names of Marchiennes, Vicoigne, and Raismes, so that the duke could see little or nothing of what was going forward until his troops were actually on the scene of action.

Then the Coldstream, being first for duty, by Knobelsdorf's order entered the wood, and quickly driving the French back, followed them up to their entrenchments. There, however, they were met by musketry in front and a fierce fire of grape from a masked battery in flank; when, finding themselves unsupported by the Prussians, they fell back in good order with a loss of over seventy killed and wounded. Seeing, however, by the red coats, that Knobelsdorf had been reinforced, Lamarlière's division made no further effort to advance; and Dampierre, while leading a last desperate assault upon Vicoigne from the front, was mortally wounded by a cannon-shot.

This decided the fate of the day: his successor stopped the attack, and on the following morning retreated. On the next day Clerfaye and Knobelsdorf stormed the enemy's newly-built batteries and captured their garrison of six hundred men, but not the guns, which, according to the French custom of the time, had been withdrawn and kept limbered up for the night, in readiness for escape, (Calvert).

The loss of Clerfaye's and Knobelsdorf's corps in the two days was little short of eight hundred officers and men; that of the French was far heavier, and was aggravated by the death of Dampierre. It speaks highly for the man that with troops so raw he should have made so fine a fight against some of the best soldiers in Europe.

The losses suffered by the Coldstream Guards on the 8th were made the subject of much complaint both against Knobelsdorf and the Duke of York, and did not promote good feeling among the Allies in the field. The battalion was, in fact, lucky to escape annihilation. Murray blamed Lieutenant-Colonel Pennington, who was in command; but it seems that Knobelsdorf simply told him to enter the wood, which was full of dense undergrowth, without saying a word of the batteries or entrenchments hidden within it, though both an Austrian and a Prussian battalion had already suffered severely in an attempt to carry them. The Duke of York had never contemplated so foolhardy an attack, but wisely thought it best to make no complaint.

The battalion itself, to judge by a letter from one of the officers to Lord Buckingham, was very indignant with the duke; and there is every probability that its complaints reached the ear of Pitt. I mention this because, though the matter is in itself a small one, it gives conclusive evidence of the incessant friction which arose from the indiscipline of the British officers and from the mistrust which the Allies felt for each other. It is safe to conjecture that this uninformed criticism of generals by their subordinate officers continued throughout the campaign; and the preservation of the letter above-mentioned among Lord Grenville's papers is proof that such criticism was not disregarded by their powerful patrons at home. Unfortunately there is too much reason to fear that this evil even now is not unknown in our army.

★★★★★★

Dropmore MSS. Lieut.-Colonel Freemantle to Buckingham, 13th May 1793. Calvert, *Narrative by an Officer of the Guards,* i. Murray to Dundas, 10th May (private) 1793. There are some significant omissions from his public letter of the same date as published in the Gazette. *Auckland Correspondence,* iii.

★★★★★★

During the following days the Allies were considerably strengthened by the arrival of successive detachments of Hanoverians and of one brigade of British cavalry under General Ralph Dundas; (7th, 11th, 15th, 16th Light Dragoons), but already Murray, with his American experience, had awoke to his weakness in light troops, and was recommending the acceptance of two offers to raise corps of foreign riflemen and Polish Uhlans. (Murray to Dundas, 15th and 17th May 1793).

The primitive tactics of the French were beginning to tell. The raw levies understood war to signify the killing of the enemy—even of one man rather than none at all—and the saving of themselves. When therefore a mass of them was set in motion, the bravest men advanced, taking advantage of every shelter afforded by the ground, and did their utmost to shoot their opponents down; while the rest ran away or remained at a safe distance, to return in a fierce tumultous swarm if the enemy showed signs of wavering, but not otherwise.

However, on the 21st, Coburg, much rejoiced by the reinforcement of British and Hanoverians, judged himself strong enough to pursue his plan of campaign, and decided to drive the French from their camp at Famars preliminarily to the investment of Valenciennes. Meanwhile, to the general regret, Mack resigned his post on Coburg's staff, owing partly to ill-health, partly to his sense of Thugut's antagonism to him, (Witzleben, ii.); and the Prince of Hohenlohe, a veteran of seventy-one, was called from Luxemburg to take his place. It was, however, enough at that time that the attack should be designed by an Austrian general to ensure that it should be repugnant to all good sense.

The entrenched camp of Famars embraced two broad parallel plateaux, divided by the little River Rhonelle, which lie immediately to the south of Valenciennes. The western plateau, that of Famars, has a length of about four miles, and abuts on the village of Artres; the eastern, which is broader and less clearly defined than the other, has a length of about three and a half miles, and terminates at the village of Préseau. Both are practically flat upon the summit, unenclosed, and covered with crops. The ascent to them is steepest from the west and south, and the valley dug between them by the Rhonelle, though not deep, plunges down so abruptly as to present sides of sharp though short declivity.

The ridge of Famars was protected by a series of detached fleches and redoubts placed on every commanding point on the northern, western, and southern sides. The passages over the Rhonelle at Artres, and at Maresches, a mile and a half above it, were defended by strong entrenchments and batteries, and all the fords on this narrow but deep and sluggish stream, had been destroyed. The eastern ridge was fortified by a continuous entrenchment with three redoubts, which was carried for nearly a mile along the length of the summit. The force at hand for its defence was about twenty-five thousand men, besides which five thousand men held the fortified position of Anzin; while a small detachment due west of it at Aubry maintained communication with the post of Hasnon, still further to north and west.

The attack of the main position was assigned to two principal columns, of which the left or southern was placed under command of the Duke of York, with orders to assemble his force on the heights between Préseau and Maresches, and to assail the right flank of the position. This column was made up of sixteen battalions, eighteen squadrons, and thirty-eight reserve-guns, (*i.e.* guns not allotted to the infantry as battalion-guns), of which the brigade of Guards (reckoned at four battalions, the flank companies being massed into a fourth battalion), and the eight squadrons of Dundas's brigade were British.

The second principal column consisted of twelve battalions, of which three were the English of Abercromby's brigade, (see note following), twelve squadrons and twenty-three reserve-guns, with five pontoons, under the Austrian General Ferraris. His orders were to assemble between Saultain and Curgies, a little to the north-east of Préseau, to drive the enemy from their positions east of the Rhonelle, and to cross the river itself, or at least feint to do so.

Note:—The Fourteenth and Fifty-Third, with the flank companies of these two regiments and of the Thirty-Seventh, massed into a third battalion. Witzleben (ii.) gives a larger number of British troops, calling all squadrons and battalions in British pay by the name English.

Besides these, a third column under Count Colloredo was to observe Valenciennes from between Estreux and Onnaing, and to protect Ferraris's right flank; a fourth, further to the right, under Clerfaye, was to attack the entrenched camp of Anzin; a fifth still further to the right under Knobelsdorf was to march from St. Amand against Hasnon; and a sixth and seventh under the Crown Prince and Prince Frederick of Orange were to move respectively from Tournai upon Orchies, and from Menin upon Turcoing.

Finally, on the extreme left or eastern flank, there were an eighth column, under General Otto, to protect the Duke of York's left by an advance by Villerspol upon Quesnoy, and a ninth to disquiet the French on the Sambre from Bavai. The scheme was typically Austrian; that is to say, too full of science to leave room for sense.

The morning of May 23rd broke in dense fog, so that the main attack did not begin until near seven o'clock, when the Duke of York's column, after marching most of the night, made its way with little re-

Attack of the Allies
on the
CAMP OF FAMARS
23 May, 1793.

English Miles

Allies ▬▬ French ▬▬

Forest of

Raismes

Vieux Condé

Condé

Vicoigne

Forest
of
Vicoigne

CLERFAYE

St
Sauve

Onnaing

Aubry

Anzin

COLLOREDO

VALENCIENNES

Estreux

Demain

Saultain

Curgies

R. Scheldt

FERRARIS

Préseau

Famars

DUKE OF
YORK

Artres

Maresches

Quérénaing

DUKE OF YORK

Sepmeries

Villers-Pol

Sommaing-sur-Ecaillon

Verchain

Vendegies

Ruesnes

Haspres

Bermerain

sistance to Artres. There failing to force the passage of the river, which was defended by five batteries, the duke left his heavy guns with about a third of his force to engage the French artillery, and proceeded with the rest higher up the stream to Maresches, where a ford was found, and the passage was with some trouble and delay accomplished.

Meanwhile Ferraris attacked the long entrenchment on the eastern ridge, opening fire from three batteries, while Abercromby on the right and four Austrian battalions on the left advanced to the assault, and carried the works with little difficulty, capturing seven guns and over one hundred prisoners. Two French regiments of cavalry, which tried to turn the scale against the assaulting columns, were most gallantly charged by the Austrian Hussars and the Hanoverian Life Guards, and actually defeated, notwithstanding that the victorious troops had all the disadvantage of a steep ascent against them. Coburg then halted Ferraris's column, until further news should come of the Duke of York's advance.

But the duke, after making a wide turning movement by Querenaing and driving the French from their outlying defences, found himself at sunset at the foot of the most formidable ascent in the whole position, crowned at different points by four redoubts which flanked each other. Thereupon, since his men had been on foot for eighteen hours, he decided to defer the attack till next morning. Elsewhere, the success of the various columns was indifferent.

Knobelsdorf could win no more than the outworks of Hasnon; Clerfaye failed to take the camp of Anzin; and, though the Prince of Orange drove the French from Orchies, his brother, Prince Frederick of Orange, was foiled before Turcoing. Coburg gave orders for renewal of the attack on the entrenchments of Famars and Anzin at daybreak of the 24th; but it was found that the French, after reinforcing the garrison of Valenciennes, had evacuated all their positions and retired to Bouchain.

The trophies of the Allies were seventeen guns, captured at various points, and three hundred prisoners; and the further loss of the French was set down, doubtless with exaggeration, at three thousand killed and wounded. Still the results of the day were unsatisfactory. The Austrians, of course, blamed the Duke of York; and Murray, without specifying who was in fault, wrote privately that a great deal more might have been done, (Murray to Dundas, 24th May 1793). But, in truth, no one except an Austrian of that day could have looked for great results from so feeble and faulty a plan of attack.

However, the ground was now clear for the siege of Valenciennes; and Coburg, as a compliment to the Duke of York, offered him the command of the besieging force, including fourteen thousand Austrians. There was much division in the British Cabinet over this piece of politeness, for Ministers were still in the dark as to Austria's general intentions; and some of them feared that the troops under the Duke of York might be so crippled by the siege of Valenciennes as to be unfit for the subsequent siege of Dunkirk.

However, notwithstanding their suspicions of some sinister design on Austria's part, the duke received permission to accept the command; though Coburg was careful to attach General Ferraris to his staff with secret orders to take the entire direction of the operations upon himself.

★★★★★★

Witzleben, ii. This author states that the Duke of York asked for the command of the siege, which I believe to be absolutely incorrect, and indeed incredible. See Murray to Dundas, 26th and 29th May; Dundas to Murray, 30th and 31st May 1793.

★★★★★★

The chief of the English Engineers, Colonel Moncrieff, was urgent for storming the town without further ado, and was confident that, if his plans were followed, the place could be taken within twelve days; but though Murray was wholly of Moncrieff's opinion, Ferraris would not hear of it. A fortnight was therefore spent in collecting heavy artillery, after which ground was duly broken on the 13th of June, before a greater and a lesser horn-work on the east side of the town. About twenty-five thousand men were actually employed on the siege, while the remainder, about thirty thousand men, formed the covering army; and, practically speaking, active operations upon both sides ceased except round the walls of the beleaguered fortress.

Yet, far away to westward, there had been a movement disquieting to the British. On the 29th of May forty transports, convoying the second brigade of British cavalry, (Blues, Royals, Greys, Inniskillings), came into Ostend; whereupon Captain Carnot, knowing the slackness of the Dutch garrisons at Furnes and Nieuport, which covered that place, determined to surprise them from Dunkirk, and then by a swift march forward to seize and burn the British shipping. Moving out accordingly on the night of the 30th, he reached Furnes at daybreak, drove the Dutch headlong from the town, and was hoping to follow them up to Nieuport, when the whole of his troops with one accord fell to the plunder of the town, heedless of their officers, and in a short time were reeling or lying in all directions, hopelessly drunk. Far from seizing Ostend, he was thankful that the Dutch did not return and cut his helpless battalions to pieces, (*Vie de Carnot*, i.).

Nevertheless, the movement fulfilled the useful purpose of frightening the British Cabinet. Dundas was possessed by a kind of superstition respecting Ostend, having apparently some idea that it might be held as the gate of the Austrian Netherlands from the sea, even if the rest of the country were evacuated. Though the place itself was part of the Austrian dominions, the guardianship of the whole of the coast, and indeed of the right flank of the Allied army, was entrusted to the Dutch; and in spite of all protests the Dutch declined to do anything for its defence. Ostend was in fact indefensible, being divided by an unbridged estuary which cut it in two at every flood tide, and was safe from a French attack only for so long as Menin, Ypres, and Nieuport were held by the Allies.

The Duke of York and Murray therefore regarded it as of no military value, though of some temporary convenience, looking upon Antwerp and the Scheldt as their true base and channel of communication with England. Nothing, however, would convince Dundas of Ostend's insignificance. He took the place under his own control, sent heavy ordnance to be mounted for its defence, appointed a special officer, General Ainslie, to take command of it, and plagued Murray so incessantly to fortify it that the Duke of York, for the sake of peace, consented to raise a few entrenchments on a small scale. The duke had hardly done so, however, before he received a rebuke from Dundas for spending too much money; whereupon he, of course, suspended the work, being, as Murray said, at a loss to know how to proceed. This was the beginning of a more minute and persistent interference of Dundas with the conduct of the operations, with its inevitable consequence of strained relations between him and the general in the field. (Dundas to Murray, 29th May, 14th June, 12th July; Murray to Dundas, 18th June and 16th July 1793).

Meanwhile the siege of Valenciennes went forward slowly and methodically, much more so, indeed, than seemed necessary either to Murray or to Moncrieff, though bad weather was accountable in some measure for the delay. At length, on the 10th of July, Condé surrendered after a severe bombardment, and was occupied in the name of the Emperor Francis. Twelve days later Mainz opened its gates to the Prussians, though the garrison was twenty thousand strong, and had still bread and wine to last for some days. Finally, on the 26th, an assault was delivered in three columns upon the two horn-works of Valenciennes, one column being led by a storming party of the Guards, and supported by part of Abercromby's brigade. The attacks of all three succeeded with little loss, and Murray, after a strong altercation with the Austrian engineer, insisted, in defiance of Ferraris's orders, upon making a lodgement in the greater horn-work, (Murray to Dundas, 25th July).

Thereupon, on the 28th of July, the French General, Ferrand, capitulated. The place was taken over, like Condé, in the emperor's name, amid the loud applause not only of the citizens but of the garrison, who trampled the tricolour under foot and hailed the Duke of York as King of France. All three of the captured garrisons were permitted to return to their own place, on condition that they should not fight against the Allies during the remainder of the war.

The French Government, however, found important employment for these troops at home; for during the months of May, June, and July matters in France had gone from bad to worse. The arbitrary interference of the Jacobin Commune of Paris, May 5th, with property and commerce had irritated the better class of citizens all over the country; and Marseilles, Lyons, and all Brittany burst into revolt. The news of the reverse at Famars, and of a disaster which had occurred two days later in La Vendée, only made the Commune more desperate.

The Committee of Public Safety, supported by the Girondists, sought to conciliate both revolted towns and foreign enemies; but the Jacobins, by stirring the mob of Paris into insurrection, overawed the Convention into the total overthrow of the Girondists, June 2nd. The supremacy of the party of violence meant as usual the destruction of all obedience among the troops. At the end of April and during May, the Committee of Public Safety had passed sundry decrees, (Poisson, ii.), for reinforcing the army and for the improvement of its discipline, by the establishment of a military code and military courts, and by driving away the swarms of women who, whether as wives, mistresses, or actual soldiers, attached themselves to all ranks, from the general to the private.

The base and contemptible Minister of War, Bouchotte, took good care that these salutary orders should not be executed. Custine, on succeeding to the command of the army in Flanders after the death of Dampierre, May 25th, had by exhortation and a few terrible examples restored subordination in some measure, and gained the respect and confidence of his men. Bouchotte, insanely jealous of him, not only gave him no support but rather flooded his camp with low ruffians and with foul literature, for the deliberate encouragement of indiscipline. (Poisson, ii.; Rousset).

The same influences were employed in La Vendée, where the volunteers deserted in whole battalions, and the basest pretexts were put forward for the evasion of service.

★★★★★★

Poisson, ii. The Vendéens let their prisoners go on parole, shaving their heads for greater certainty of identification. Thereupon great numbers of the French soldiers voluntarily shaved their heads in order to evade further service, pleading that their parole could not be violated.

★★★★★★

Nothing indeed but failure upon failure in the field could result from the policy of the Jacobins. Kellerman complained that his army of the Alps was hopelessly overmatched; and on the 12th of June the army of Italy was utterly routed at Saorgio. Even the forces of corrupt and demoralised Spain successfully invaded Roussillon, captured Bellegarde, and threatened Ollioure and Perpignan. Yet Robespierre still held his shield over Bouchotte; and the Jacobins sought to escape from the consequences of their own folly by the execution of Custine, Biron, and other generals, and by the imprisonment, often followed by decapitation, of all officers who had met with defeat in the field.

Thus did the countrymen of Voltaire emulate and outdo the countrymen of Admiral Byng. Further decrees, ordaining the death of all grown men and the destruction of all property in Vendée, July 26th, and stigmatising Pitt as the enemy of the human race, showed sufficiently that the ruling faction in Paris was animated by the fearful desperation which springs from the consciousness of guilt.

Thus, at the beginning of August, the position of France seemed to be, and in the presence of active and intelligent enemies would actually have been, hopeless. Not only in the north and east was danger threatening; it was still more urgent in the south, where Lyons, Marseilles, and above all Toulon, the great naval arsenal of the Mediterranean, were in arms against the Convention. Great Britain had concluded alliances. with Sardinia, April 25th, with Spain, May 25th, and with the Court of Naples, July 12th, in order to unite all the forces of the Mediterranean against France; and Lord Hood's fleet of fifteen ships, though disgracefully belated, and indeed only manned by the help of three British regiments, had anchored at Gibraltar on the 19th of June. (The regiments were the 11th, 30th, and 69th. Hood hoisted his flag at Spithead on the 6th of May, and sailed the 24th of May).

Moreover, Corsica also had risen against the Convention, under the leadership of the old patriot Paoli, the hero of many a London drawing-room during the days of his exile in England. Such a series of events could not but attract Dundas's eye more strongly to the Mediterranean; and in July he sent Colonel, Lord Mulgrave, a very capable officer, to Turin, to stir up both Sardinia and the Austrians in Italy to an advance upon Lyons. Meanwhile the Convention summoned Kellerman with the army of the Alps to overawe the rebellious city, which, however, girded herself for a siege rather than yield, Aug. 8th; and before Kellerman could take measures to coerce her, he was recalled to his former station by a successful movement of the Piedmontese against his advanced posts, Aug. 19th.

Mulgrave, however, sent no very encouraging report from Turin. The King of Sardinia was eager for action in co-operation with the British fleet, but jealous of Austria. The Austrian General De Vins was also ready to march upon Lyons or Marseilles in command of an united force of Austrian, British, Sardinians, and Neapolitans, but only on condition that the various contingents were raised to a sufficient strength, and the arrangements for subsistence placed absolutely under his control.

Altogether Dundas came to the conclusion that nothing could be done in the Mediterranean during 1793, though Mulgrave gave a promising account of Corsica's readiness to place herself under British protection. The minister therefore contented himself with sketching an elaborate and characteristic plan for a future campaign in that sea during 1794, counting that by that time the troops in Flanders, as well as those under orders for the West Indies, would have finished their work and would be wholly at his disposal. None the less he continually warned the Duke of York that he should shortly withdraw eight thousand Hessians from his force on the frontier of France; although, in the distracted state of that country, the one thing needful was to prosecute the campaign in that quarter with energy.

★★★★★★

Dundas to Mulgrave, 8th July; Mulgrave to Dundas, 19th August; Memorandum dated Wimbledon, 27th August 1793. This last document is unsigned, and not in Dundas's handwriting, nor in his style. Possibly it was prepared by Pitt when staying with Dundas at Wimbledon; but I take the mention of Dundas's residence to be plain evidence that it represents his opinion.

★★★★★★

Unfortunately, after the fall of Valenciennes the Allies in Flanders, far from pressing their advantage, fell to debating what they should do next. It had been already agreed that the Austrians should give up ten thousand men to the Duke of York for the siege of Dunkirk; but Coburg, seeing the danger of the plan, made a last effort to avert it by submitting a new scheme for taking the offensive in concert with Prussia; he himself to move south-east upon Maubeuge from Valenciennes, while the Prussians advanced southwest from Mainz upon Sarrelouis.

King Frederick William gladly assented, but the Duke of York protested, as under his instructions he was bound to do; and he was upheld by a messenger who arrived from Vienna at Coburg's headquarters on the 6th of August. Thugut had been at work on one of his usual subtilties. He had soothed Pitt by renouncing the exchange of Belgium for Bavaria, but had begged that Prussia might not be informed of the renunciation; for he was still secretly bent on obtaining Bavaria by some means, and had resolved to purchase it by the cession of Alsace. Hence it was his wish that the King of Prussia, and particularly the Austrian troops under General Wurmser who were serving with him, should move south into Alsace, and that Coburg should pursue the plan, already agreed upon, of besieging Quesnoy, while the Duke of York invested Dunkirk. Coburg thereupon gave way, though with no very good grace; and it was resolved that, before his army was separated from the Duke's, a general action should be fought, as an essential preliminary to the subsequent operations, (Sybel, ii.).

The position of the French under General Kilmain was known as that of Caesar's Camp, which lies on the left bank of the Scheldt about two miles above Bouchain; but in reality it formed an irregular quadrilateral, of which a part of Villars's famous lines of La Bassée formed the northern side. Facing due east, Kilmain's front was covered by the Scheldt from Bouchain to Cambrai, his rear by the River Agache, which runs into the Sensée a little to the south of Arleux, his right by the Sensée, and his left by the wood and heights of Bourlon from Cambrai to Marquion.

All passages over the Scheldt were closed by entrenchments, and the valley itself was flooded; all passages over the Sensée were equally defended, while the right from Cambrai to Agache was strengthened by fieldworks and abatis. Such a position, held by sixty thousand men, was formidable, and Coburg accordingly resolved to turn it by the south. The turning column, consisting of fourteen thousand men under the Duke of York, was to assemble about Villers-en-Cauchies and Saint Aubert, and to cross the Scheldt at Masnières and Crevecoeur, about five miles south of Cambrai. A second column of about nine thousand men under the Austrian General Colleredo, and a third of about twelve thousand under General Clerfaye, were to force the passage of the Scheldt in the front of the position. The remainder of the army, little less than half of it, was uselessly frittered away in posts of observation.

Murray, foreseeing that the French would retire as soon as they perceived the turning movement, begged persistently that more cavalry should be given to the Duke of York, in order to inflict some punishment on them. His request was refused, and the result was exactly that which he had expected. The duke, after a march of eleven hours on a day of extraordinary heat, Aug. 7th, found his troops too much exhausted to pass the river at Masnières; and Kilmain, withdrawing quietly in the night, made good his retreat upon Arras with little loss, though the British cavalry made a few prisoners.

The Austrians, of course, blamed the Duke of York, though Coburg had sent Hohenlohe to him for the express purpose of superintending his operations; but the arrangements of the day opened Murray's eyes to the essential vices of the Austrian tactics, he wrote:

> We were not in force to attack the enemy, the duke's column was a long way from support, and between ourselves we were not sorry to see them go off.

It was only after long schooling by disaster that the Austrians at last abandoned a system of which the rottenness was clear to the much despised Briton. (Ditfurth, i. Witzleben, ii. Murray to Dundas (private), 9th August 1793).

After the engagement, Coburg pressed the Duke of York to remain with him for yet another fortnight, in order to renew the attack on the French army or to take Cambrai, the last fortress that blocked the way into France. But the duke could only obey his instructions as to Dunkirk, which had lately been reiterated by Dundas, (Witzleben, ii. Dundas to Murray, 1st August 1793), and the two armies accordingly parted. Coburg, weakened by the withdrawal of nine thousand Prussian troops, and not yet compensated by the restoration of fourteen thousand Austrians from the Rhine, resolved to besiege Quesnoy, and meanwhile spread his force in several detachments from Denain to Bettignies.

The duke assembled his whole force of about thirty-seven thousand men, (see list following), at Marchiennes on the Scarpe on the 13th of August, and on the 15th marched in two columns north-west by Baisieux and Turcoing upon Menin.

Ditfurth, i. 47½ battalions, 58 squadrons. British, 5200 infantry, 1300 cavalry; Austrians, 10,000 infantry, 1000 cavalry; Hanoverians, 9000 infantry, 1600 cavalry; Hessians, 5500 infantry, 1500 cavalry. Total, 29,700 infantry, 5400 cavalry, 1900 artillery.

From Baisieux the route lay across the front of the great fortress of Lille, and of the French fortified posts extending from that city to Dunkirk; and on the morning of the 18th, soon after the advanced guard of the southern column had moved from Turcoing, heavy firing was heard in the direction of Linselles, about two miles to the west of that place. The Prince of Orange, for reasons best known to himself, had seized the opportunity to sally out from Menin, and surprise the French posts of Blaton and Linselles, which being accomplished, he left two weak battalions to hold them, and retired.

About mid-day the French returned with five thousand men and drove out the Dutch; and an hour or two later an *aide-de-camp* came galloping into Menin to ask for help. The Duke of York at once ordered out the brigade of Guards, which had just arrived at Menin after a severe march, with a few guns, under General Lake. The three battalions, without their flank companies, and therefore little over eleven hundred strong, at once turned out, and traversed the six miles to Linselles in little more than an hour, but, on reaching it, found not a Dutchman there. They were, however, saluted by a heavy fire of grape from batteries which they had supposed to be in possession of the Dutch; and thereupon Lake determined to attack at once.

The hill, on which the village of Linselles stands, is fairly steep on its northern face, and was further strengthened by two redoubts before the village itself and by a barrier of palisades on the road, while its flanks were secured by woods and ditches. Lake at once deployed into line under a heavy fire of grape, and, after firing three or four volleys, charged with the bayonet and drove the French from the redoubts and village. He then halted and re-formed on the southern side of the hill, not without apprehensions lest the enemy should rally and make a counter attack while he was still unsupported.

Fortunately, however, the French were not equal to the attempt, being still of the inferior quality which was inevitable under the foolish administration of the Jacobins, and so puny in stature that the Guards cuffed and jostled them like a London mob, without condescending to kill them. (Hamilton, *History of the Grenadier Guards*, ii.).

Lake was therefore left unmolested on his ground, until at nightfall six battalions of Hessians arrived, in reply to his urgent messages for reinforcement, to relieve him. His trophies were twelve guns, seventy prisoners, and a colour, but his losses amounted to one hundred and eighty-seven officers and men killed and wounded; and no real object whatever was gained. The action was undoubtedly most brilliant, and the conduct of the men beyond all praise; while Lake's swift decision to escape from a most dangerous situation by an immediate attack stamps him as a ready commander. But it is a grave reflection upon the Duke of York that he should so thoughtlessly have exposed some of his best troops to needless danger, leaving them isolated and unsupported for several hours.

It is still less to his credit that, when he finally relieved them by a detachment of Hessians, he actually left these also isolated and unsupported within striking distance of a superior enemy during the whole night, for no better purpose than to raze some paltry French earthworks which a few hours would suffice to throw up again. Because the Prince of Orange was guilty of one act of signal foolishness, there was no occasion to outdo him by another.

At Menin the army was parted into two divisions. The first, consisting of the Hanoverians, ten British squadrons and foreign troops, or about fourteen thousand five hundred men, under the Hanoverian Marshal Freytag, was to form the covering army; the other, of nearly twenty-two thousand men, including the rest of the British troops, under the duke in person, was appointed to besiege Dunkirk. On the 19th, Freytag marched from Menin by Ypres upon Poperinghe, which he occupied with his main body on the 20th, at the same time pushing his advanced guard further northwest to Rousbrugge on the Yser.

On the following day a detachment of Hessians, with great skill and at small cost to themselves, drove the French from Oost Capel and Rexpoede into the fortress of Bergues, with the loss of eleven guns and some four hundred men; and Freytag then took up his line of posts to cover the besieging army. His left was stationed at Poperinghe, covered by the fortress of Ypres; and from thence the chain ran north-west to Proven on the Yser, and westward up that stream by Bambecque to Wylder, where it turned north, and passing midway between Bergues and Rexpoede rested its right on a point called the White House, hard by the canal that runs from Bergues to Furnes.

On the 23rd and 24th Freytag drove the French from Wormhoudt and Esquelbecque with the loss of nineteen guns, and surrounded Bergues by detachments at Warhem to east, Coudekerque to north, Sainte Quaedypre to south, and Steene to west. From this last an outer chain of posts was extended southward to Esquelbecque, and thence east by Wormhoudt and Herzeele to the Upper Yser at Houtkerque. The whole circuit thus embraced was about twenty-one miles; from which it will be concluded that Freytag was a believer in the cordon-system.

Meanwhile the Duke of York marched on the 20th to Furnes; and on the 22nd, moving thence parallel with the strand, he drove in the enemy's advanced posts upon the entrenched camp of Ghyvelde, which the French abandoned in the night. On the 24th, after several hours of sharp fighting, which cost the Allies nearly four hundred men, (British were flank cos. of the Guards and Line, and R.A., casualties 78 killed and wounded), the French were forced back from the suburb of Rosendahl into the town; after which the Duke entrenched himself in his chosen position, with his right resting on the sea and his left at Tetteghem, facing full upon the eastern side of the town and about two miles distant from the walls.

The field of operations for the duke's army may be described roughly as a quadrilateral, of which the sea forms the northern side, the canal from Dunkirk to Bergues the west, the canal from Bergues to Furnes the south, and a line drawn from Furnes to the sea the east. From east to west the ground thus enclosed was divided roughly into two parallel strips; the northern half consisting of the sandhills known as the Dunes, together with a narrow plain of level sandy ground within them; and the southern half of a huge morass called the Great Moor, which consisted partly of standing water, partly of swamp, but was all open to inundation by admitting the tidal water from the sluices of Dunkirk.

Tetteghem, which formed the left of the duke's position, rested upon this swamp, and commanded the only road that led across it to the White House, and so to Freytag's army. The position itself was in many respects disadvantageous. It was much broken up by innumerable little ditches, hedges, and patches of brushwood, all of which the troops had to clear away with their side-arms for want of better tools; it was wholly destitute of drinking water, that in the canals being brackish, and that found in the wells unpalatable; and, finally, it lay open to the minutest inspection from the tower of Dunkirk Cathedral.

But this was not the worst. The duke had looked for a fleet to cover his right flank, which had suffered from the enemy's gunboats during the march upon Ghyvelde, and for transports bringing heavy artillery and other materials for the siege; and so far there was not a sign of them. Murray had written to Dundas in July:

> The principal object is to have what is wanted and to have it in time.

Dundas had replied that he was preparing artillery for Dunkirk, but was in great want of gunners. (Murray to Dundas, 16th July; Dundas to Murray, 19th July).

At last, on the 27th, the transports came with gunners, but without guns; on the 29th a frigate, the *Brilliant*, and a few armed cutters appeared off the coast; and on the 30th Admiral Macbride arrived to concert operations, but without his fleet.

By an arrangement, which was repeated at least once more during the war, Macbride's squadron, being intended to act with the army, had been removed from the control of the Admiralty and placed under the orders of Dundas, so that he alone was responsible for this miscarriage. (*Dropmore Papers,* ii. Dundas to Grenville, 12th October).

He wrote angrily to Murray on the 29th:

> Why did you not earlier suggest to me naval co-operation at Dunkirk? I had always a conceit in my own mind as to its usefulness, but I had no authority to quote for it.

This is an instructive example of Dundas's methods as a War Minister. The project of besieging Dunkirk emanated from himself and his colleagues in the Cabinet, and from them alone. No military man approved it, though the Duke of York, out of loyalty to his masters, dutifully upheld it; and Dundas never quoted any authority but his own for undertaking it, nor for his constant interference with the conduct of the operations that preceded it. He had indeed a good many conceits in his own mind, the most fatal of which was that he understood how to conduct a campaign; and he had privately made vague inquiries of Murray, as to the need for naval co-operation, as far back as in April. (Dundas to Murray, 16th April 1793).

But the point was not one to be decided off-hand by a general, for the question was not whether a fleet would be useful, but whether it would be able to act in all weathers; and this purely naval matter appears never to have been considered at all. On the 15th of August, when the army was not yet committed to the siege, General Ainslie, the commandant at Ostend, warned Dundas that he had not realised the difficulties which might be raised by adverse weather at Dunkirk; and, as a matter of fact, the *Brilliant* and her little flotilla had not been on the coast three days before they were blown away from their station.

It was doubtless owing to the uncertainty of naval assistance that Murray gave the apparently astounding opinion, that he regarded a squadron as useful though not very material to the siege. But, apart from this, Dundas had so often pressed the Duke of York to spare his eight thousand Hessians, which formed almost one-third of the force under his command, for another service, that it was impossible for the duke to divine whether ministers really intended to pursue their design against Dunkirk or not.

If they did, he had a right to look to them for a siege-train and for the necessary naval assistance, neither of which were forthcoming, partly because Dundas did not know his own mind, partly because he had committed himself to a multiplicity of operations beyond the power of either Army and Navy to execute, after ten years of steady neglect. (Calvert, vi.; Murray to Dundas, 3rd September).

However, as a substitute for the much-needed ships and guns, he sent to Murray a plan for the siege of Dunkirk, drawn up by no less skilled a hand than that of Lord Chancellor Loughborough, possibly with some hope that the deficiencies of Downing Street might be made good by the wisdom of the woolsack. There are times when the conceit of British politicians becomes touchingly ridiculous.

Very different was the change that had come over military administration in France during the same month of August. Upon the re-election of the Committee of Public Safety, which took place on the 10th, Barrère, who was a member, approached Prieur of the Cote d'Or with the words, "We none of us understand military matters. You are an officer of Engineers; will you join us?"

"There is only one man in the Convention for the place," answered Prieur, "and that is Carnot; and I will be his second."

Accordingly, on the 14th of August two new members were added to the Committee, namely, Carnot, who assumed control of the formation, training, and movements of the armies, and Prieur, who took charge of arms, ammunition, and hospitals. These, together with Robert Lindet, formed the most remarkable group in one of the most remarkable administrative bodies which has ever existed. Three of the members, Barrère, Billaud Varennes, and Collot d'Herbois, were known as the Revolutionaries, their business being to guide and inspire political emotions; three more, Robespierre, Couthon, and Saint Just, were concerned with legislative proposals, police, and the revolutionary tribunal, and bore the ominous name of the High Hands; but the last three, Carnot, Prieur, and Lindet, were known simply as the Workers, a title which no men have ever more worthily earned.

Carnot's advent showed itself in prompt and energetic action. On the 16th of August a decree was passed for a levy *en masse*, which, it was estimated, would add four hundred and fifty thousand men to the army; and, since all exemptions and substitutes were disallowed, the flower of the nation began for the first time to flow into the ranks. Moreover, on the 29th of August, the old white coats of the Monarchy were abolished and the blue coat of the National Guard made uniform for the entire host, a significant hint that henceforth there were to be no further distinctions between regular troops and volunteers, but a single National Army. Prieur, on his side, set up manufactories of arms and gunpowder in Paris, and stimulated the search for saltpetre in all directions.

The result of these measures lay hid in the future; but immediate and important movements were made on the northern frontier. Carnot, with true insight, had divined that England was in reality the most dangerous member of the Coalition, and that to foil her before Dunkirk would, from its political results, be the most telling of all military operations, (*Vie de Carnot,* i.).

Withdrawing therefore several thousand troops from Coburg's front and from the army of the Moselle, he massed them to westward, until, on the 24th of August, there were, apart from the eight thousand men in Dunkirk itself, some twenty-three thousand in the entrenched camp at Cassel, four thousand about Lille, and twelve to fifteen thousand more from the Moselle within a few days' march. Kilmain had been recalled after the retreat from Caesar's camp, and replaced by General Houchard in supreme command. Among Houchard's subordinate generals was Jourdan: Dunkirk itself had for commandant General Souham, an energetic officer whose fame was soon to spread wide; and one of Souham's battalions was commanded by Lazare

Hoche.

Thus new men and a new principle of war, which were to crush the cordon-system out of existence, hung like an angry cloud to the south of Dunkirk; but the Generals of the Allies took no heed. Murray, indeed, had heard with anxiety of the increase of the French force in his front, and had begged Coburg for reinforcements, which, however, could not be spared.(Murray to Dundas, 28th and 31st August 1793).

On the east Coburg was busy besieging Quesnoy, with corps of observation thrown out to east and west. He had called up eight thousand men under General Beaulieu from Namur to strengthen his weak cordon about Bouvines and Orchies; but to west of Beaulieu the space from Lannoy to Menin was guarded by some thirteen thousand Dutch—spiritless, disaffected troops, whose leader, the Prince of Orange, was half inclined to give up the contest because he could obtain no assurance as to his indemnity. West of the Dutch was the gossamer line of Freytag, and behind it lay the Duke of York, conscious, first, that Souham had opened the sluices, and that the steady rise of the inundation would shortly sever his communication with Freytag; secondly, that his right flank was under perpetual menace from the French gunboats; and thirdly, that his rear was insecure, since there was nothing to hinder the French from moving troops by sea.

In this situation he was trying to take a fortress, which he was not strong enough to invest, and which the enemy could consequently reinforce at any moment, by attacking it upon one side only without heavy artillery. He endeavoured to protect his flanks by throwing up entrenchments in the Dunes, but found that they filled with water at the depth of two feet; and he was fain to disarm a frigate at Nieuport and bring up her heavy guns to the front, in order to arm batteries, not only against the town, but towards the sea, to drive away the French gunboats. Thus at the beginning of September he was able to open fire; but meanwhile Houchard had not been idle, for on the 27th he fell in force upon the posts of Beaulieu and the Prince of Orange at Cysoing and Turcoing.

He was beaten back by Beaulieu with the loss of four guns; but the Dutch abandoned Turcoing with suspicious alacrity, and would have retired to Tournai and Courtrai had not Murray sent a detachment to support them. Murray wrote, (Murray to Dundas, 31st August 1793); and indeed the fact is hardly surprising:

There is ill-will and disinclination to favour our present operations.

The marvel is that he and the Duke of York should have remained in so dangerous a position, when a successful attack on the Dutch and a bold push forward would have carried the French to Furnes, and cut off the whole of the army about Dunkirk beyond rescue. Indeed, though they knew it not, this operation had actually been projected at the French headquarters. (Sybel, ii.).

With the arrival of his last reinforcements from the Moselle, Houchard resolved to attack the scattered posts of Freytag, the nearest of which lay little more than five miles from Cassel. Assembling thirty thousand men, he led them forward early in the morning of the 6th of September in five columns, under Generals Vandamme, Hédouville, Colland, Jourdan, and himself, the three first against Poperinghe, Proven, and Rousbrugge, the two last against Wormhoudt, Herzeele, and Houtkerke. Though outnumbered by ten to one, the Hanoverians and Hessians fought most obstinately, and the troops opposed to Houchard and Jourdan would have held their own behind the Yser at Bambecque, had not the French already penetrated to Rexpoede in their rear.

The fighting lasted all day, the garrison of Dunkirk at the same time keeping the besieging army employed by a sortie; and at night Freytag retired upon Hondschoote, ordering General Walmoden, who commanded the posts about Bergues, to withdraw all his troops to the same place. Taking the road by Rexpoede, in ignorance that it was actually occupied by the French, Freytag blundered into the midst of a French picquet, and was, with the young Prince Adolphus (afterwards Duke of Cambridge), wounded and taken.

The prince was rescued, but the field-marshal was secured, and would have remained a prisoner, had not General Walmoden, guessing that his chief might have fallen into a trap, marched at once upon Rexpoede, stormed it then and there, and delivered him. Walmoden then assumed command, and, resuming the retreat, took up a convex position before Hondschoote, with his right leaning on the Bergues canal, his centre just in advance of Hondschoote itself, and his left resting on the village of Leysele.

The whole of his front was covered by a maze of small ditches and hedges, through which the only access was a single dyke leading into Hondschoote; but this broken ground, however valuable for defence, deprived the Allies of the use of their cavalry, which was the arm in which above all they overmatched the French. From thence Walmoden sent urgent messages to the Duke of York for reinforcements; and it is significant that, owing to the inundation, no troops could reach him except by way of Bergues. There was therefore no reason why Freytag's corps should not have been concentrated about Hondschoote, where it would have covered the besiegers quite as efficiently and with infinitely less risk. The British commander-in-chief cannot be acquitted of neglect herein, though Freytag must bear part of the blame for extreme dispersion of his force.

Houchard tried to follow up his success on the following day by a renewed attack, but his soldiers would not follow him; and Walmoden, though he took the precaution to send his heavy baggage to Furnes, repulsed him without difficulty. On the 8th, however, Houchard advanced with fresh troops to the assault, himself leading twenty battalions, covered by several guns, to the principal attack by the dyke; while a second column on his left, under General Leclerc, tried to force its way along the canal, and a third, under Colland and Hédouville, moved up from Rousbrugge against Leysele.

The plan of attack was faulty, for by holding Walmoden in front and pushing the main force round his left flank, which stood in the air at Leysele, Houchard must have compelled him to retire or to be driven into the swamp of the Great Moor. The new French tactics, however, made good the general's shortcomings. Taking cover cunningly behind every hedge, ditch, or bush, the French skirmishers poured a deadly fire into the Hanoverians and Hessians, who stood exposed in their array of three ranks deep, discharging their volleys by platoons with perfect discipline, and pressing forward with the bayonet when the French ventured too near to them. But the volleys did little injury to dispersed and hidden skirmishers, and the charge with the bayonet was little more effective over such intricate ground; for the French did not await it, but ran back to the nearest hedge and resumed their fire from behind it.

For four hours Walmoden's brave men held their own with the greatest gallantry in spite of heavy losses, until at noon their last reserves of ammunition were exhausted, when, their left flank being seriously threatened by Hédouville, the general gave the order to retire in two columns upon Furnes. A battalion of Hessians covered the retreat with splendid tenacity; and the wreck of the force took up a position between the two canals just to the south of Furnes. The infantry had lost at least a third of its numbers, perhaps even more;

and the Hanoverians, by the confession of their own officers, were no longer to be depended upon. (Murray to Dundas (private), 9th September 1793).

It was no reproach to them that this should have been so, for no troops in the world can endure heavy punishment during consecutive days of unsuccessful fighting, and remain unshaken. Their losses had been very great, and their behaviour, by the admission both of friend and foe, most admirable.

On this same day the garrison of Dunkirk made a sally against the besiegers in the village of Rosendahl, but was repulsed, though not without loss to the Allies; and in the afternoon came the news of Walmoden's defeat. At four o'clock orders were given for the heavy baggage to be sent back to Furnes, and at eight a Council of War was held. The Duke of York hoped to carry off his siege-guns, but the French, having control of the sluices, had shut off the water from the canal, so that it was no longer of use for transport; and it was represented that delay might mean the overpowering of Walmoden's army and the cutting off of the duke's retreat by Furnes. At midnight therefore the besieging army retired in two columns, with a confusion which shows the inefficiency of the duke's staff. Transport being scarce, the waggons were so much overloaded that the animals could hardly drag them, and the columns were constantly checked by fallen horses and overturned vehicles.

Further, no orders for the retreat were sent to the two battalions in Tetteghem, and the whole of one column was delayed until they could join it. It was thus ten o'clock on the morning of the 9th before the entire force reached the camp at Furnes, fortunately without the least molestation from the enemy. (*Narrative of an Officer*; Ditfurth, i.). There the duke effected his junction with Walmoden, but took the precaution to send his heavy baggage to Ostend. He had been fortunate in escaping from a most dangerous position with no greater loss than that of his thirty-two heavy guns; but incessant fighting, a swampy encampment, bad drinking-water and fever had grievously thinned the ranks of his army. It was reported at the time that the siege of Dunkirk had cost the Allies from one cause and another nearly ten thousand men, (*ibid*); and I am disposed to think that this estimate is not exaggerated. Murray wrote:

> Our whole enterprise is defeated and our situation embarrassing in the extreme. It is uncertain whether we can maintain

ourselves behind Furnes; at all events I think we shall hold good behind the canal at Nieuport.

This letter reached Downing Street on the 11th; and on that same day Macbride's fleet appeared before Nieuport, three weeks too late.

But the troops found some consolation for their failure in the momentous news that on the 26th of August Lord Hood, by the invitation of the inhabitants, had occupied Toulon.

Indeed, Dundas's orders between the 11th and 18th of September form a notable specimen of his ideas of carrying on war. The news of the failure at Dunkirk had at first completely unnerved him; but, on realising how critical was the position of affairs in that quarter, he directed eight battalions, (3rd, 19th, 27th, 28th, 42nd, 54th, 57th, 59th), to embark for Ostend, as a temporary measure. Then he warned the Duke of York that five thousand of his Hessians must be held ready to sail to Toulon as soon as this reinforcement reached him, and that the eight battalions themselves would be required elsewhere at the beginning of October.

On the same day he wrote to Lord Hood that everything must give way to the importance of holding Toulon; that he had written to Austria for troops; and that he would send him the five thousand Hessians aforesaid, as well as two battalions out of the five stationed at Gibraltar. Four days later he warned General Bruce to be ready to receive at Barbados fifteen battalions, which were under orders for active service in the West Indies. Lastly, at the same time or very little later, he framed a design for a descent upon St. Malo and for the occupation of the Isle D'Yeu, off the coast of La Vendée.

★★★★★★

Dundas to Murray, 11th, 14th September; to Hood, 14th September; to Bruce, 18th September 1793; Pitt to Grenville, *Dropmore Papers*, ii. (the conjectural date of September attached to this last is wrong, and should be changed to October).

★★★★★★

It is now time to return to Flanders, and to follow in detail the reaction of Dundas's genius upon the operations in that quarter.

In the first peril of the retreat from Dunkirk the British commanders seem to have entertained serious thoughts of re-embarkation, (*Narrative of an Officer*, i.); but Houchard did not follow up his stroke upon the force of Walmoden. For this he has been much blamed; and indeed his failure to destroy the Duke of York's army was made the

71

excuse for bringing him shortly afterwards to the guillotine. But in truth he had lost his true opportunity through the unskilfulness of his attack upon Walmoden, wherein his troops, already half starved and less than half disciplined, had been seriously shaken by their losses.

He therefore reinforced the garrisons of Bergues and Dunkirk, and, in the hope of relieving Quesnoy, fell with thirty thousand men upon the flank of the Dutch cordon from Poperinghe and upon its front from Lille. His success was at first encouraging, for he defeated his opponents completely, Sept. 12th, 13th, with the loss of forty guns and three thousand men, and captured Menin. General Beaulieu, who had been dispatched with over four thousand Austrians to the assistance of the Dutch, for some reason refused to act with them, but checked the advance of the French beyond Menin, and occupied Courtrai.

The Dutch fled in disorder to Bruges and Ghent; and for the moment it seemed as though communication between the Duke of York and Coburg was hopelessly severed. The duke, after leaving a detachment under Abercromby at Furnes, had withdrawn to the rear of the canal between Nieuport and Dixmuyde, in order to secure his retreat to Ostend; but he now, Sept. 14th, ordered Abercromby back to Nieuport, and marched with the bulk of his force eastward to Thorout, where he was joined by two battalions, (19th, 57th, 3 cos. 42nd), from England.

From thence on the 15th he moved southward to Roulers; and on that day the situation underwent a total change. Beaulieu, being attacked by Houchard before Courtrai, waited only for a reinforcement which the duke had hurried forward to him, when, taking the offensive, he utterly routed the French, who fled in the wildest confusion, and, pursuing them to Menin, recaptured the town. The duke entered Menin on the following day, where he received letters from Coburg who was already at Cysoing, not more than eighteen miles to the south, reporting that since the fall of Quesnoy he had gained a brilliant victory over one of Houchard's divisions at Avesnes-le-Sec.

This action, which, though almost unknown to Englishmen, still remains one of the greatest achievements in the history of cavalry, was not only most glorious to the Austrians in itself, but was important as showing that the new tactics of the undisciplined French army were inapplicable to any but a strongly enclosed country. Nine Austrian squadrons, counting some two thousand men, without a single gun, had utterly dispersed seven thousand French, chiefly infantry, cut down two thousand of them, captured two thousand more, and taken twenty guns, all with a loss to themselves of sixty-nine men. These successes effectually checked the advance of the French. Houchard, after the defeat at Menin, had already given the order to retreat; and the French retired to their former positions before Cassel, Lille, and Maubeuge.

Then arose the question what should be done next. The season was advancing, but events had marched rapidly in Paris since the revolt of Toulon. Following hard upon the news of Houchard's reverse came tidings that the Duke of Brunswick had defeated the French with a loss of four thousand men at Pirmasens, on the northern frontier of Alsace; and this succession of disasters stirred the Jacobins to the ferocity of panic. On the 17th two savage laws were passed, which practically placed all lives and all property at the arbitrary disposal of the reigning faction; and then the demagogues turned with fury upon the generals. Loudest among them was Robespierre, who, profoundly jealous of any man who could do what he could not, was suspicious above all of soldiers.

Thanks to his denunciations, Houchard and his staff were recalled under accusation of treason, Sept. 21st; and thereby another blow was added to the many already struck at the army. The troops were greatly demoralised by the continual change of commanders, (Poisson, ii.), whom the Commissioners of the Convention promoted or deposed at their arbitrary pleasure; and the commanders were not less demoralised by the certain prospect of death if they failed to achieve the impossible with troops that were neither fed, nor clothed, nor paid, nor disciplined. The Allies, therefore, could still reasonably look for success from a concentration of their whole army and a vigorous offensive.

Dundas, since the failure at Dunkirk, had become suddenly an advocate for keeping the whole of the forces together, and for making an attack upon the enemy before undertaking any further enterprise, (Dundas to Murray, 13th September 1793); but with what precise object a general action was to be fought he did not say, for the very sufficient reason that he did not know. The British Government, so far as it favoured any operations at all in Flanders, would have preferred a second attempt upon Dunkirk; but it gave, or professed to give, a free hand to the commanders, flattering itself that, if the attempt were abandoned, the British troops would be the sooner released for service at Toulon and, above all, in the West Indies. Coburg, on the other hand, had already put forward what was at any rate a definite plan, though upon the old lines. He wished to besiege Maubeuge, which was certainly an important point, since it formed the chief link in the communications between the French armies of the north about Lille, and of the Ardennes about Givet and Philippeville, while its entrenched camp made it a point for a formidable concentration of the French forces at large.

Moreover, it obstructed the passage of the Austrian troops from east to west, compelling all reinforcements from Luxemburg to fetch a compass by Namur and Charleroi before they could join the army of Flanders. The Dutch agreed to come forward again to further the operations; and before the British Government, upon Murray's representation, could finally make up its mind to co-operate with the Austrians, Coburg had crossed the Sambre with forty thousand men and invested Maubeuge. (Dundas to Murray, 13th, 14th, and 28th September; 14th October. Murray to Dundas, 14th and 15th October 1793).

Thereupon there followed the usual distribution of troops into a cordon. The besieging force numbered fourteen thousand, the covering army, including twelve thousand Dutch, twenty-six thousand men; and to the Duke of York was entrusted the task of protecting Flanders along a front of some forty-five miles, from Cysoing to Nieuport. For this purpose Coburg gave him about sixteen thousand Austrian troops in addition to those in the pay of Britain; but, owing to the vagaries of the British Minister for War, the corps was exposed to the most dangerous risk.

Hardly had the eight reinforcing battalions from England joined the army in Flanders, before Dundas ordered four of them to return at once, and the remainder as soon as possible. Further, not content even with this, he gave Murray to understand that the embarkation of the Hessian corps from Flanders was only deferred, and hinted that a part of his artillerymen might also be spared for Toulon. Now Dundas knew perfectly well that the troops had passed through a very severe campaign, had fought several actions and had suffered heavy losses; he knew perfectly well that no adequate steps had been taken for filling up the gaps in the ranks; he could not have been ignorant that winter was approaching; and Murray had twice warned him that the French were rapidly increasing their forces between Lille and the sea.

Yet the minister, though he had given the generals nominally a free hand, calmly withdrew battalion after battalion, until at last Murray told him plainly of the danger of the situation. The state of the army was most distressing: the force in British pay was reduced to twelve thousand fighting men, or less than half of its original numbers; the sick and wounded of the whole army under the duke's command numbered at least nine thousand, or more than one-fourth; the troops were dangerously dispersed along a very wide front; and, though Murray did not mention this, the Austrian Government had deprecated all field-fortification, on account of the damage that might ensue to meadows and the banks of canals, (Ditfurth, i.).

Finally, he gave warning that, if the enemy made an attack, the duke would be obliged to abandon Ostend. Dundas's reply to this was very characteristic. Without a word to Murray he ordered the *commandant* at Ostend to retain the second batch of four battalions which, by his own order, had been sent there for re-embarkation to England; and he wrote an angry letter to Abercromby, a subordinate officer, first expressing horror at the idea of abandoning Ostend, and then regretting that attempts had been made to keep those same four battalions in Flanders. He wrote:

> It would be impossible to restrain the just indignation of the country, if, for the sake of feeding an army under a Prince of the blood, so substantial an interest to this country as that of the French West Indies had been sacrificed.—Murray to Dundas, 6th October. Dundas to Ainslie, 12th October; to Abercromby, 13th October 1793.

Apart from the fact that such language, especially when addressed to a subordinate concerning his chief, was utterly unbecoming a Minister and a gentleman, it was not obvious why an army should be starved, whether in the matter of empty ranks or of empty stomachs, simply because it happened to be commanded by a Prince of the blood. If its presence in Flanders were an embarrassment to the Government, the simple remedy was to withdraw it altogether, rather than leave it so weak as to be in peril of destruction; for there was no lack of employment for it elsewhere. The charitable explanation of this amazing outburst would, therefore, be that Dundas was drunk when he penned it; but this is no solitary instance of Dundas's bad taste, much less an unique example of his incapacity; and, if drunkenness be accepted in excuse of his innumerable foolish actions, the conclusion must inevitably follow that he was very rarely sober.

Meanwhile Murray's apprehensions increased; and events soon came to justify them. Jourdan, on Carnot's recommendation, had succeeded Houchard in command of the army of the north; and, with Carnot himself at his back, he now concentrated forty-five thousand men at

Guise for the relief of Maubeuge, Oct. 7th, leaving the remainder of his troops, some sixty thousand men, extended in a long line to the sea. Coburg sent pressing entreaties for reinforcements to the Duke of York, who at once moved about nine thousand men to Cysoing, and leaving half of them there, proceeded Oct 10th with the rest—chiefly the wreck of the British troops—to join hands with the Austrian advanced corps a little to the south of Quesnoy at Englefontaine.

It was, however, to no purpose, for Jourdan, having increased his force to sixty thousand men, attacked Coburg furiously on the 15th and 16th at Wattignies, and, despite very heavy loss to himself both in men and in guns, compelled him to raise the siege of Maubeuge. The Dutch, who had not behaved well in the action, retired to Mons; but Coburg moved his headquarters to no greater distance than Bavai. He was there meditating further attacks upon the French, when the Committee of Public Safety, drunk with the success at Wattignies, ordered Jourdan peremptorily, Oct. 18th, to take the offensive and to drive the hordes of the tyrant into the Sambre, which river, it may be observed, at that moment flowed between the opposing armies.

A second and still more ludicrous order, Oct. 22nd, bade him keep his force together, menace several remote points simultaneously, operate in two divisions against Mons and Tournai, and withal act with prudence.

Jourdan, however, not daring to attempt the passage of the Sambre, on the 20th sent one division to assail Marchiennes, and another under Souham against all the Allied posts from Cysoing to Werwicq, which last was held by six thousand men under Count Erbach. Both attacks were successful, though Marchiennes was retaken on the 24th; and on the 22nd Erbach was forced to fall back to Tournai and Courtrai, abandoning even Menin.

On the 22nd likewise a division from Cassel attacked Ypres, while another from Dunkirk under Vandamme captured Furnes, and, pressing northward with twelve thousand men, opened on the 24th the bombardment of Nieuport. The town had been but hastily fortified, and the garrison consisted of only two weak Hessian battalions, a few dragoons, and the British Fifty-Third Regiment, in all fewer than thirteen hundred men. For the moment it seemed certain that the British would be cut off from their base.

Murray, foreseeing this, had ordered all stores, beyond what was necessary for the moment, to be moved from Ostend. The *commandant* disembarked some of the four battalions which, pursuant to Dundas's order, were about to sail to England; and Dundas, on hearing of the situation, at once sent Major-General Grey, the appointed commander of the West Indian expedition, with four more battalions, (3rd, 28th, 54th, 59th—they had already made one voyage to Ostend and back), to command at Ostend, giving him full liberty to defend it or to bring away the whole of the eight battalions, as he might think best, without reference to the Duke of York.

Meanwhile he clamoured for information as to the intended plan of operations, and for a statement of the reasons for the possible abandonment of Ostend; for it had not yet occurred to him that the French, by attacking in overwhelming force, might compel the Commander of the Allies to conform to their plan of operations instead of pursuing his own. (Murray to Dundas, 18th October; Ainslie to Dundas, 23rd October; Dundas to Grey, 26th October; to Murray, 27th October 1793).

However, matters soon righted themselves. The French were driven back with heavy loss from Cysoing and Orchies, Oct. 24th. The garrison of Nieuport held its own gallantly, being reinforced on the 27th by another battalion of Hessians and by a few gunners from Ostend; and meanwhile the Duke of York was hastening back from Englefontaine and Tournai, while Coburg followed him westward with half of his army as far as Solesmes, midway between Cambrai and Landrecies. On the evening of the 28th Grey arrived at Ostend, and at once sent the Forty-Second and four companies of Light Infantry to the help of Nieuport.

On the same evening the Duke of York having reached Camphin, a few miles east of Cysoing, detached Abercromby with four battalions and two squadrons, (2 Aust. batts., 3rd Guards, flank batt. Guards, 1 squad. 7th L.D., 1 squad. 15th L.D.), northward against the French post at Lannoy.

The place was captured with little loss, and the British Light Dragoons did terrible execution in the pursuit of the flying enemy. On the following night, Oct. 29th, another division, under the Austrian General Kray, made a brilliant attack upon the post of Marchiennes, driving out the French with a loss of nearly two thousand men and twelve guns, at a cost to itself of fewer than one hundred casualties.

Meanwhile the French, on hearing of the Duke of York's advance upon their flank, had retired from Menin and Ypres; and early on the next morning Vandamme, fearing to be cut off, retreated from before Nieuport, leaving four guns and a quantity of ammunition behind him. So easy was it to change the whole face of affairs by concentrating a compact force against one point and rolling up a cordon from end to end. It is almost comical to observe how at first both sides used the cordon-system; how the French, after abandoning it with success, relapsed into it once more; and finally how the Allies, also abandoning it under British direction, in their turn gained the upper hand.

Throughout this anxious period the interference of Dundas with the operations had been incessant, and his tone by no means the most courteous. The incoherence and folly of his orders may best be judged from a summary of the reply which Murray at length found time to write on the 20th of October. He wrote, in effect:

> Let me point out to you, that the same messenger brought to me from you, first, advice to besiege St. Quentin; secondly, orders to keep a body of troops at Ostend; and, thirdly, strong exhortations against division or detachment of our force. As to Ostend, if Nieuport holds out, it is safe for the winter; and I see no reason why Nieuport should not hold out. As to St. Quentin, this means taking a train of artillery there in the month of November. It means also that twenty thousand out of Coburg's twenty-five thousand men must be detached, while the remaining five thousand remain quietly between three fortified towns and a forest, from which fifty thousand men may attack them from all sides at any time. Further, the detached force must draw its subsistence from a distance of forty miles across the whole French army without any other protection than that of those five thousand men.
>
> I beg pardon, for taking up your time with this kind of argument, which it was not your intention to enter into, but I think it is right to show that, perhaps, people in England are not more infallible in their judgments than those upon the Continent.

Irony so keen sped home even through the dense armour of Dundas's concei, he answered, taking refuge in bluster:

> You have not sufficiently weighed the feeling of this country if you think that any successes could have counterbalanced the loss of Ostend.

Murray hastened to soothe him by pointing out that the Duke of York, though against his military judgment, had strictly obeyed his instructions as to the protection of Ostend, and that it was not Grey who had saved it but the duke himself, who, before he knew of Grey's arrival, had forced Vandamme to retire by threatening his communications. (Murray to Dundas, 30th October and 12th November; Dundas to Murray, 8th November 1793).

This sharp passage of arms silenced Dundas for the time, though, as will be seen, it taught him little wisdom for the future. Meanwhile, after a few small affairs of outposts, the campaign came to an end. The Emperor of Austria sent orders to Coburg to fight a general action, for no particular object; and the Committee of Public Safety gave the like instructions to Jourdan, in the hope that he might be able to advance to Namur and so to threaten the Austrian line of communication. But neither was in a position to obey. The campaign had been most arduous, as a war of posts must always be, not only from the innumerable minor actions, but from the strain imposed on the troops by constant vigilance and by endless marching to and fro to reinforce the threatened points of the cordon.

The losses on the side of the Allies had been great: those of the French had been enormous, not only in men but in *matériel*, for the Allies had taken from them over two hundred guns. In brief, both armies were thoroughly exhausted; and yet the Allies had accomplished comparatively little, owing partly to the false plan imposed by England, partly to the false tactics of the Austrian commanders, not a little to the misunderstandings and jealousy that make coherent action so difficult in an army composed of many nations.

On the Rhine likewise little had been accomplished. Soon after the victory of Pirmasens the King of Prussia left his army for Posen; and, though the Austrian, General Wurmser, drove the French in utter confusion from the lines of Weissenburg, Oct. 13th, yet, in consequence partly of faulty dispositions and partly of the half-hearted co-operation of the Prussians, an advantage which might have been decisive was turned to little account. Prussia, in truth, was little anxious to aid Austria in gaining Alsace; while Poland, as always, kept the two powers in an attitude of mutual suspicion and mistrust. There was nothing, therefore, left to the Allies but to take up cantonments for the winter, which they accordingly did, while Grey and the whole of the eight battalions with him returned to England. The Allies had missed their opportunity in Flanders.

The British Government thereupon bestirred itself to frame its projects for the coming campaign. The Duke of York left Belgium for London on the 6th of February; and a few days later, 12th, Mack, now advanced to the rank of major-general, arrived there likewise to concert plans with the Ministers. The Austrian genius had shortly before submitted, (York to Dundas, 2nd February 1794—with enclosures), a scheme calculated for a force of three hundred and forty thousand men, which had been received with great satisfaction by the British Cabinet and the Duke of York; but, since there was no earthly possibility that the Coalition could put that number of men into the field, the whole of this elaborate creation was valueless.

Both Mack and Coburg, however, pressed for a concentration of forces and a march on Paris, though neither of them could conceive the feasibility of taking the offensive without leaving one hundred and twenty thousand men behind them to guard the frontier from the Meuse to the sea. The prime question, therefore, was one of men, and Pitt on his side promised his utmost endeavour to increase the British contingent to a figure which should ensure a genuine total of forty thousand fighting soldiers. As to the means whereby this force should be produced, Pitt was remarkably vague, being clear only that he could not spare the few thousand men under Lord Moira's command, since he wished to hold them ready to sail to any part of the British coast which might be threatened by a French invasion.

Moira, therefore, though one of the ablest officers in the Army and adored by the men, was kept inactive, while his troops sickened and died of gaol-fever in overcrowded transports at Jersey. (Dr. Hayes to Lord Cathcart, 1st February 1794; Monthly returns, 1st February to 1st May; Ditfurth, ii.).

However, Pitt made up his forty thousand men to his own satisfaction by naming various reinforcements, which he hoped to pour into Flanders during the summer and autumn; for it was one of the delusions of this gifted man, as also of his friend Dundas, that an army of twenty thousand men, supplemented by monthly driblets of two thousand men during ten months, is the same thing as an army of forty thousand men ready for the field at the opening of the campaign.

The next requisite was that the Austrian, Prussian, and British contingents should each of them possess a siege-train, since, according to Mack, it was essential for the Allies to master every fortress on the French frontier from the Meuse to the sea. Pitt promised this also, on behalf of the British; and then arose the question of commanders. Though well aware that the King's assent would be wrung from him only by extreme pressure, the ministers were for recalling the Duke of York and appointing Lord Cornwallis, who had just returned from

India, in his place. Herein they were undoubtedly right, for, after all allowance made for the extreme difficulty of his position, the duke did not shine in the field. The ministers, however, blamed him especially for the failure before Dunkirk, wherein they themselves were chiefly in fault; and Mack, prompted apparently by the king, found little difficulty in making excuses for the duke.

It was finally arranged that he should retain command of the British contingent, but that he should be kept always in the neighbourhood of the principal army, with a few thousand Austrians attached to his own corps, so as to subordinate him the more completely to the Austrian commander-in-chief. This compromise bears so clearly the mark of the British politician that its origin cannot be doubtful. It is of a kind that may serve for the construction of a Cabinet, but it is not suitable for war, and was particularly ill -fitted to the projected campaign. For the rest, Pitt declared himself satisfied that the command should remain with Coburg, who was deservedly most popular among the Austrian troops; and Mack rejoiced the heart of the British Cabinet by announcing that the emperor would direct the operations as *generalissimo* in person. Altogether the results of the conference were considered to be so satisfactory that the king presented Mack with a jewelled sword as a reward for his good service. (Witzleben, iii.)

The British Government's satisfaction was soon proved to be premature. The discussion of future operations with the Court of Berlin was, in fact, only a trick of Thugut to keep as many Prussian troops as possible on the French frontier; and the whole intent of the emperor's taking personal command was that Coburg and other honest men in his army, who profoundly distrusted his chief adviser, should be kept under proper restraint. Thugut now declared, in answer to Pitt's proposals, that Austria would not advance a penny towards the subsidies for the Prussian Army, being well able to dispense with every part of it beyond the twenty thousand men which formed its contribution towards the forces of the Empire. In fact, he was so madly jealous and fearful of Prussia at this time that he secretly proposed to Russia a scheme for a joint attack upon her.

On learning the emperor's decision, March 11th, King Frederick William ordered Marshal Möllendorf to begin the withdrawal of his troops from the Rhine. Coburg was in consternation, for he knew that, without Prussian help, the execution of the approved plan of campaign would be impossible. He therefore asked the Duke of York to join him in requesting Möllendorf to delay his retirement, and despatched letter after letter to Vienna, adjuring the emperor in terms of touching devotion and patriotism to send every man that he could raise to Flanders, and to work loyally with Prussia to crush the terrible power of the Revolution while there was yet time.

Möllendorf courteously acceded to his desire; but the prince's protests fell on deaf ears in the Imperial capital. There were over sixty thousand men ready for service at Vienna, but from his insane dread of Prussian aggression, Thugut would not part with one of them; and Coburg's only reward for his faithful and disinterested counsel was rude and ungracious rebuke. Just at the critical moment, however, Lord Malmesbury checked the further withdrawal of the Prussian troops, by threatening to break off all negotiation for a subsidy unless they remained on the Rhine until he could receive further instructions from London.

This brought the impecunious king to reason, for without English money he was lost. Shortly afterwards the parley was, with Pitt's sanction, resumed; and there was much haggling over the sphere wherein the Prussian troops should be employed, Frederick William declaring that for operations on the Rhine he would furnish eighty thousand men, but for Belgium not more than fifty thousand. Finally, Malmesbury succeeded in compromising matters; and a treaty was signed at the Hague on the 19th of April, whereby Prussia, in consideration of a lump sum of £300,000 and a subsidy of £50,000 a month, engaged herself to provide sixty-two thousand men, to be employed wherever Great Britain and Holland, their paymasters, should think fit. Ten days later, April 30, Fox in the House of Commons predicted that this would be a useless waste of money; and it will be seen that he was a true prophet. (Sybel, iii.; York to Dundas, 22nd March, 3rd April 1794; Witzleben, iii.).

Meanwhile Coburg was doing his utmost to prepare his army for the heavy work that lay before it; but the Austrian forces had not improved since the previous year. Heavy losses had brought many young soldiers into the ranks; and, owing to the extreme extension of his line of cantonments, the troops had gained little rest during the winter. The French delivered as many as forty-five petty attacks between the 6th of January and the 26th of March, each one of which meant the setting of many detachments in motion for long and harassing marches.

Moreover, owing to the decay of the emperor's popularity in Belgium, the people would do little or nothing for the troops; and, Coburg being unwilling to take from the inhabitants what they refused to give, the men suffered greatly from want of food, fuel, and shelter. Money would, of course, have overcome all difficulties, but, though he begged piteously for it, he could obtain none from Vienna; and the consequences were most cruel. He wrote in February:

> Some regiments have been without bread for several days, and two contractors have been driven to suicide.

On the other hand, taking a true measure of his enemy, Coburg had issued instructions that the French must be attacked at all times and in all circumstances, and that, even in the defence of a position, at least a third of the men should be kept ready for a counter-attack. But there was one clause in his orders which seems to give the key to many an Austrian defeat.

> Men defending entrenchments will sit in the banquette, arms in hand, until the enemy comes within three hundred paces, or even somewhat nearer, and then open a heavy fire.

British troops were accustomed to hold their fire until the enemy was within thirty paces; and hence it was that the French Army of Italy, when they met them in Egypt, found the red-coats tougher adversaries than the white. (Witzleben, iii.; Ditfurth, ii.).

Among the rest of the Allies matters were little better than with the Austrians. The Hessians in Flanders were far below their proper strength, sickness and constant skirmishes having swallowed up the additional recruits furnished during the winter; while the brigade which had been attached to Moira's force left one hundred dead and two hundred and fifty invalided in the Isle of Wight, over and above five hundred sick men whom they carried with them to Ostend, (Ditfurth, ii.).

As to the British, everything was, as usual, behindhand, though the Duke of York had now a more energetic Chief of Staff than Murray in Colonel James Craig, who was at Wilmington in 1781. Recognising from his American experience how serious was the duke's deficiency in light troops, Craig tried to hire some from Prussia, but without success. Then there was a difficulty about the British siege-train, for it was discovered, some weeks after the duke had made requisition for it, that the application had been mislaid at the Office of Ordnance.

Again, though Dundas made profuse promises of British drafts and reinforcements, to the number of five thousand men, not one thousand of these had arrived by the middle of March, and Abercromby's brigade was quite unfit to take the field. Next the remount-horses were discovered to be very bad. Then artillery-drivers, the dearth of which had been represented by the duke for quite six months, were found to be so scarce in England that the master-general was fain to seek them, though without success, in Hanover. Then came a fresh disappointment in the matter of foreign troops, for three thousand Brunswickers, whom Dundas had counted upon taking over from the Dutch into the British service, proved to be unobtainable.

Rapidly the forty thousand soldiers promised by Pitt dwindled away; and Craig resigned himself to the inevitable fact that the deficiency would amount to at least ten thousand men. But this was not, to his thinking, the most formidable danger. With a boldness which must have shocked Pitt and Dundas, he wrote to the War Office a very strong and damaging criticism of the cordon-system, and predicted that nothing but misfortune could attend Generals who upon principle preferred dispersion to concentration. (Craig to Nepean, 7th, 22nd, 31st March, 11th April; to York, 7th, 15th, 16th March; York to Dundas, 9th, 22nd, 26th March, 1794).

So the month of March passed away, the unhappy Coburg waiting in anxious suspense to know first, when the troops that composed his heterogeneous army would be ready; secondly, what their numbers might be when they were ready; and thirdly, what the emperor would expect him to do with them when it should please him to honour headquarters with his presence.

Meanwhile he had even in February given orders for the contraction of his cantonments; and at the beginning of April, after much shifting, his force occupied the following positions.

The Right, or western Wing of the Allied Army, covering maritime Flanders, was entrusted to Clerfaye with a force of Austrians, Hessians, and Hanoverians, who thus occupied the ground formerly entrusted to the British and Dutch. His headquarters were at Tournai, where an entrenched camp had been thrown up. In his front also Orchies and Marchiennes had been strengthened by field-works; and on his right efforts had been made to restore the defences of Menin, Ypres, and Nieuport, though, except in the case of Ypres, with little result. The effective strength of his army in the field, after deduction of garrisons for the strong places, was about twenty-four thousand men.

On Clerfaye's left, and connected with it by a detachment of five thousand men under General Wurmb at Denain on the Scheldt, stood the Centre or principal army, consisting of about twenty-two thousand men under the Duke of York, about forty-three thousand men under Coburg himself, and of about nineteen thousand Dutch, under the Prince of Orange. The duke occupied the right with headquarters at St. Amand, Coburg the centre with headquarters at Valenciennes, and the Prince of Orange the left with headquarters at Bavai. It was reckoned that, after providing for garrisons, Coburg could spare sixty-five thousand men for active operations.

The Left Wing consisted of twenty-seven thousand Dutch and Austrians under Count Kaunitz, which were stretched over the space from Bettignies, a little to the north of Maubeuge, to Dinant on the Meuse.

To these must be added fifteen thousand more Austrians under General Beaulieu, cantoned between Namur and Treves, bringing the grand total of the Allied force to something over one hundred and sixty thousand men, of which at the very most one hundred and twenty thousand were free for work in the field.

★★★★★★

Ditfurth (ii.) reckons the field force at from 120,000 to 130,000, but he includes British troops which were not on the spot, and reckons the strength of those present at too high a rate.

★★★★★★

It will be noticed that the corps of Clerfaye and of the Duke of York had changed the places which they had occupied during the previous year, pursuant to the design of the British Ministers that the Duke of York should be kept under the immediate eye of Coburg. The first result of this interference was to spoil Clerfaye's temper for the whole campaign; for he judged his force too weak for its task of defending the maritime provinces; and indeed it was only upon the positive orders of Coburg that he consented to hold the command, (Witzleben, iii.).

The whole arrangement, in fact, was calculated to cause confusion. It was bad enough that the lines of retreat for the British and Austrians should be in exactly opposite directions; and the obvious course,, upon the change of the Duke of York's station, would have been to have shifted his base to Antwerp. But far from this, not only was his base continued at Ostend, but, to make matters worse, a brigade of British was placed under Clerfaye's command, and a respectable number of Austrians under the Duke of York's; so that in case of mishap, not only must the lines of retreat for the right and right centre intersect each other, but neither corps could retire upon its base without leading several of its regiments in the wrong direction.

Meanwhile on the French side Carnot had girded himself for a supreme effort. He wrote to Pichegru on the 11th of February:

> We must finish matters this year, unless we make rapid progress and annihilate the enemy to the last man within three months, all is lost. To begin again next year would mean for us to perish of hunger and exhaustion.

He therefore decided to combine the armies of the North, of the Ardennes and of the Moselle, and to mass two hundred and fifty thousand men along the line from Dunkirk to the Meuse. Of these about one hundred thousand were to move upon Ypres, march thence upon Ghent, master maritime Flanders, and then wheel eastward upon Brussels; while at the same time another hundred thousand were to advance upon Namur and Liege, and sever communication with Luxemburg. In other words, he designed to turn and envelop both flanks of the Allied Army, leaving about fifty thousand men to stand on the defensive in the intermediate space between Bouchain and Maubeuge.

Of the many eminent critics who have passed judgment upon this plan, there is not one who has failed to point out and condemn its defects; and indeed it is obvious that if the Allies, neglecting small detachments, should fall with their full strength upon either wing of the enemy, they might annihilate it. An advance of the French in overwhelming strength upon the communications of the Allies about Namur would have been equally effective and far less hazardous. Yet Carnot prescribed the invasion of the maritime provinces as the first object, partly no doubt with a view to the ultimate invasion of England, but chiefly, as I conceive, with the political object of threatening the retreat of the British and thus overawing the most formidable power in the Coalition.

It is worth while to recall that in 1815 Wellington looked for Napoleon to turn the western flank of the Allies and cut the British off from the sea, and that he dreaded such a movement so much that he made his dispositions at Waterloo with a view to prevent it. Wellington's action has been as sharply criticised as Carnot's; and yet, when two such men agree upon such a point, their opinion is at least worth serious consideration. In any case, the threatening of the lines of communication both east and west was quite sufficient to distract the councils of the Allies, to set them quarrelling as to which among themselves should be sacrificed to the others, and so perhaps to bring about political discord and the rupture of the Coalition.

At the end of March Pichegru gave the strength of the army of the North at two hundred and six thousand, and of the army of the Ardennes at thirty-seven thousand men, making a total of two hundred and forty-three thousand present under arms, of which one hundred and eighty-three thousand were free for service in the field. The army of the North at the beginning of April was thus distributed. The Left Wing, seventy-one thousand men, extended from Dunkirk by Cassel and Lille to Pont-à-Marque; the Centre, forty-seven thousand men, from Arleux (near Douai) by Cambrai, Bouchain, and Bohain to Etreux, a little to the north of Guise; the Right Wing, thirty -six thousand men, from Avesnes by Cerfontaine, St. Rémy, and St. Waast to Maubeuge.

This made a total of one hundred and fifty-four thousand men ready for the field; one half of them, under such leaders as Moreau and Souham, standing on the frontier of maritime Flanders. As early as on the 11th of March Carnot ordered Pichegru to begin the advance on Ypres; but the general, though willing to train his troops by countless skirmishes, made no movement until the 29th of March, when he attacked the Austrian advanced posts at Le Cateau with thirty thousand men, and was beaten back with the loss of twelve hundred killed and wounded and four guns. He reported:

It is dangerous to match our young troops against the enemy so soon.

And therewith his operations incontinently ceased.

Meanwhile Coburg, still awaiting his orders, made no attempt to overwhelm any one of the scattered French divisions. At last on the 2nd of April the emperor quitted Vienna, reached Brussels in company with his brothers, the Archdukes Charles and Joseph, on the 9th, and on the 14th joined Coburg at Valenciennes. The prince then laid before him the danger of the Allied position, with both wings too weak to take the offensive against an enemy which was reported to be three hundred thousand strong; and thereupon he recommended the advance of the centre to the siege of Landrecies, for which Mack had prepared one of his usual elaborate schemes.

Thus the Austrians reverted once more to a war of petty sieges, which could produce no decisive result; and the only thing to be said for operations in the selected quarter was that the country was open and well suited to cavalry, in which arm the Allies were far superior both in quantity and quality to the French. The emperor approved the plan; and the troops were set in motion forthwith, nominally for a great review to be held in the emperor's honour near Le Cateau. Thus, despite all Carnot's efforts to take the initiative, it fell to the Allies to open the new campaign.

CHAPTER 4

The Spring Campaign 1794

On the 16th of April, 1794, as had been arranged, the whole of the main army was inspected by the emperor on the heights of Cateau. The British infantry was represented, as in the last campaign, by three battalions of Guards, with a fourth battalion formed out of their flank companies, and Abercromby's brigade of the Fourteenth, Thirty-Seventh, and Fifty-Third. These last had at length received their first instalment of recruits to make good their losses during 1793, in the shape of a draft which was described as "much resembling Falstaff's men, and as lightly clad as any Carmagnole battalion," (Calvert), of the French Army. The cavalry numbered twenty-eight squadrons, drawn from fourteen regiments and organised into four brigades, three of heavy and one of light dragoons, the last being supplemented by a picked squadron of the Carbineers under the command of Captain Stapleton Cotton, a lad of twenty, who in later years was to earn the title of Viscount Combermere, and would command Wellington's Cavalry in the Peninsular War. (*The Golden Lion* by Mary Combermere, W. W. Knollys & Alexander Innes Shand is also published by Leonaur).

★★★★★★

Three squadrons of the 1st Dragoon Guards, two squadrons each of the Blues, 2nd, 3rd, 5th, 6th Dragoon Guards, 1st Royals, 2nd Greys, 6th Inniskilling Dragoons, 7th, 11th, 15th, 16th, Light Dragoons. The 8th and 14th Light Dragoons were embarked or embarking to join the army. It has been a matter of much difficulty to discover how these regiments were brigaded.

Harcourt's Brigade. (?) 1st, 5th, 6th D.G. = 7 squadrons.

Mansel's Brigade. (?) Blues, 3rd D.G., Royals = 6 squadrons.

Laurie's Brigade. (certainly), Bays, Greys, Inniskillings = 6 squadrons.

Ralph Dundas's Brigade. 7th, 11th, 15th, 16th Light Dragoons, 1st squadron of the Carbineers = 9 squadrons.

After the death of Mansel on the 26th of April, Dundas took over his brigade, and Colonel Vyse took Dundas's. But the regiments seem to have been much shifted from one brigade to another.

Calvert. *Cannon's Records*, Royal Horse Guards.

★★★★★★

The review over, the emperor took up his quarters in Le Cateau, whither the commanders forthwith repaired to him for orders. April 17th. The French troops under Pichegru in the immediate front of the emperor consisted of three divisions, with an average strength of twelve thousand men each, extended along an entrenched position some eighteen miles long, on the wooded heights of Bohain and Nouvion. Of these Fromentin's division held Catillon on the Sambre, a village rather over four miles east and south of Le Cateau; westward of Fromentin, Ballaud's division lay astride the road from Le Cateau to Guise, at Arbre de Guise and Ribeauville; and, still further to west and south, Goguet's division held the ground about Vaux, Fremont, and Bohain. The nearest French troops to westward were fifteen thousand men under Chappuis about Cambrai; while to eastward three divisions of the French right wing, numbering some thirty thousand men, lined the Sambre from St. Waast to Maubeuge.

There was therefore an opportunity of overwhelming one or other of these isolated bodies; but the Austrians stuck religiously to their old methods. The force was divided into eight columns, three of which were directed to move north-westward toward Cambrai, so as to check any movement from that side. These need trouble us no more. Of the remaining five, two on the left were ordered to drive the enemy out of Catillon, cross the Sambre, and after clearing the forest of Nouvion to push forward their light troops. One column in the centre, under Coburg's personal command, was designed to move by Ribeauville upon Wassigny to master the heights further to southward; while two more on the right, under the Duke of York and Sir William Erskine, were to advance, the former upon Vaux, the latter upon Fremont, to drive the enemy from their entrenched positions there and at Bohain, and to press their light troops forward upon Le Catelet. All commanders were expressly ordered to halt the main portion of their troops in the captured positions, so that there was no intention of pursuing the enemy in the event of success.

It would be tedious to describe so feeble an operation. The scene of the engagement is a country much broken by ravines and hollow roads, so that the heavy artillery of some of the columns was with difficulty brought forward; but the French, being in a manner surprised, were manoeuvred out of their positions with little trouble or loss. The Duke of York's and Erskine's columns alone encountered resistance worth mentioning, but they found little difficulty in turning the French entrenchments, while the Austrian Hussars and a squadron of the Sixteenth Light Dragoons succeeded in cutting down great numbers of the retreating enemy. Altogether the Allies lost fewer than seven hundred killed and wounded, while the action was reckoned to have cost the French over two thousand men, besides from twenty to thirty guns, of which eleven were captured by the British columns.

Beyond this the French were little molested in their retreat to Guise, and the trifling success of the day was marred by disgraceful plundering and burning by the troops after the engagement. The British had already shown tendencies in this direction, but had been checked by the Duke of York, who had hanged two offenders, caught red-handed, on the spot, without even the form of a drum-head court-martial. Now, however, the Austrians showed the way in misconduct, either led astray by some of their savage auxiliaries, or in aimless revenge for their starvation during the winter; and the British were only too ready to follow the example. (Ditfurth, ii. Craig to Nepean, 18th April 1794).

On the following day the army halted between Nouvion and Prémont, pushing its outposts further to southward, while detachments of Austrians were posted also at Prisches, a few miles north of Nouvion, and at La Capelle, Fontenelle, and Garmouset to eastward, so as to cover the left flank and rear of the army. Thereupon the Prince of Orange, whose troops had been advanced towards Cambrai on the 17th, countermarched to Le Cateau, and assembling his force at Forest, about three miles to the north of it, on the 20th attacked the enemy's posts over against Landrecies on the left bank of the Sambre. After a hard struggle, which cost him one thousand men and the French twice as many, he carried the French position, and at once opened the trenches before the town.

On the following day Pichegru delivered feeble and incoherent attacks upon the positions of Prisches and Nouvion, and upon the heights to the south of Wassigny, all of which were beaten off with the loss to him of many men and four guns. Further desultory fighting at the advanced posts on the next day was equally unfavourable to him, as indeed he deserved for his folly in not concentrating the thirty thousand men, who lay ready to his hand at Maubeuge, for an overwhelming attack.

Coburg then judged it safe to proceed with the siege in earnest, and, withdrawing the covering army to the north, formed it in a huge semicircle around the besieging force. His left wing curved round from the heights that lie to eastward of Landrecies, and between it and the village of Maroilles, southward to Prisches, thence south east across the Rivierette to Le Sart, and thence by Fesmy to the Sambre, the whole line being strongly entrenched, with several bridges thrown over the Rivierette. The force allotted for the defence of this tract was thirty-two battalions, fifty squadrons, and twenty-six light companies, the left under General Alvintzy, the right under General Kinsky.

On the western bank of the Sambre the right wing completed the semicircle, with a total of twenty-six battalions and seventy-six squadrons. The first section of the defences on this side ran westward of Catillon to the Selle, from which stream the Duke of York's army carried the line north-westward to the road from Le Cateau to Cambrai. This, a broad paved way, runs straight as an arrow over the long waves of rolling ground that lie between the two towns, the undulations rising to their highest at the village of Inchy, upon which the duke rested his right. The position thus occupied by the Allies was over twenty miles in extent, following a chain of hills of easy slope but seamed to east of Catillon by deep water-courses and hollows, and broken by small copses and enclosures in the neighbourhood of the villages. Westward from Catillon, however, towards Cambrai the hills subside into a broad plain, not unlike Salisbury Plain, except that the undulations are far longer and the acclivities therefore less severe. Covered with crops but unenclosed, its gentle slopes and unseen folds present an ideal field for the action and manoeuvres of cavalry.

On the 23rd intelligence reached the Allies that fifteen thousand of the enemy had moved out from Cambrai in three columns towards the north-east, were driving in the outposts along the lower Selle, and had even crossed that river, apparently with the object of intercepting the Emperor Francis, who was returning from a visit to Brussels to rejoin the headquarters of the army. The Austrian General

Otto, receiving information of these movements from Major-General Sentheresky at St. Hilaire, between four and five miles north-west of Inchy, at once joined him there; and reconnoitring farther north he found the enemy, apparently about ten thousand strong, near the village of Villers-en-Cauchies.

Having with him only two squadrons of the Fifteenth Light Dragoons and as many of the Austrian Leopold Hussars, making together little more than three hundred sabres, Otto fell back to St. Hilaire, and sent a message to the Duke of York for reinforcements. Late at night he was joined by the Eleventh Light Dragoons, two squadrons of the Austrian Zeschwitz Cuirassiers, and Mansel's brigade of the Blues, Royals, and Third Dragoon Guards, the whole numbering ten squadrons. Early on the following morning he again moved northward down the valley of the Selle, keeping the Fifteenth and Leopold Hussars in advance and the remainder in support; and at about seven o'clock the four advanced squadrons came upon a force of French light cavalry of twice or thrice their strength in a long belt of dwarf coppice, near the village of Montrecourt, and about two miles east of Villers-en-Cauchies. Being attacked on their left flank the French horsemen at once retreated with precipitation for a quarter of a mile, when they rallied, and then retired steadily westward, covered by a cloud of skirmishers.

Finally they reformed between Villers-en-Cauchies and Avesnes-le-Sec, fronting to eastward, and masking a force of unknown strength in their rear. Otto appears to have followed up this cavalry with great speed, for, on looking round for his supports, he could nowhere discover them. He halted the advanced squadrons, but, perceiving that he had already committed them too deeply, he assembled the officers and told them briefly that there was nothing for it but to attack. The English and Austrian officers then crossed swords in pledge that they would charge home; and it was agreed that the British should attack in front, and the Austrians on the enemy's left flank towards Avesnes-le-Sec, which was already a name of good omen in the annals of the Austrian cavalry.

The Fifteenth led by Captain Aylett then advanced at a rapid trot, breaking into a gallop at one hundred and fifty yards from the French cavalry. These did not await the shock but wheeled outwards, right and left, and retired at speed, unmasking a line of French skirmishers and guns, which opened fire before their front was clear and killed several of their own soldiers. In rear of the artillery six French battalions, or about three thousand men, were massed together in quadrate formation of oblong shape, with the front rank kneeling.

★★★★★★

So say the records of the 15th Hussars. I suspect that there were two squares with the guns between them, as at Avesnes-le-Sec on 12th September 1793. Two squares side by side would give an appearance of oblong shape to the formation.

★★★★★★

A volley from the eastern face of this square, together with a discharge of grape from the guns, checked the attack for a moment; but, cheered on by their officers, the Fifteenth swept through the battery and dashed straight upon the bayonets. The French infantry seems to have stood till the last moment, for Aylett fell with a deep thrust through the body, and four other officers had their horses wounded under them; but the onset of the dragoons was irresistible. One half of the square was dispersed instantly; and the other half, after firing a volley, broke up likewise before the charge of the Fifteenth, and fled in wild disorder. In rear of the square were more French squadrons, upon which those that retired from the front had been re-formed; but these had given way before the impetuous attack of the Austrian Hussars, and for half a mile the sabres of both Austrians and British dealt terrible havoc among the flying Frenchmen.

★★★★★★

The records of the 15th Hussars for some reason seek to excuse the slaughter of the fugitives, by mentioning that the National Convention had decreed that no quarter should be given to the English; and this mistake has been copied by Sir Evelyn Wood in his excellent account of the action in *Achievements of Cavalry*. As a matter of fact the decree was not made until the 26th of May; and three hundred men need no excuse for taking no prisoners when attacking five thousand.

★★★★★★

Leaving, however, the Austrians to pursue the infantry towards Cambrai, the Fifteenth, now commanded by Captain Pocklington, passed on to the road from Villers-en-Cauchies to Bouchain, dispersed a long line of fifty guns and ammunition-waggons, which were retiring to the north-west, and continued the pursuit until the guns of Bouchain itself opened fire upon them, and a relieving force came out to save the convoy. Meanwhile not a sign appeared of the supporting squadrons which would have ensured the capture of the artillery; and

Pocklington, observing other forces of the enemy closing in upon him from every side, rallied his men and retired at a trot. The blue uniform of the Light Dragoons, however, caused the French to mistake them for friends; and it was not until they were close to Villers-en-Cauchies that Pocklington perceived that he was cut off. The enemy was, in fact, established in his front, blocking the road with infantry and artillery at a point where a causeway carried it across a valley, though to the south of the village there were visible the scarlet coats of Mansel's brigade. Wheeling about, therefore, for a short time, Pocklington checked the pursuers that were following him from Bouchain, and then, wheeling once more to his proper front, he galloped through the French amid a heavy fire of grape and musketry with little loss, and safely rejoined his comrades.

Things, however, had not gone well with Mansel and his brigade. Whether it was by Otto's fault or by his own that he had gone astray, and whether he attempted and failed in an attack upon the French who were obstructing Pocklington's retreat, is a mystery. We know only that Craig reported, with great regret, that the brigade had behaved ill; that he attributed the fault mainly to Mansel, whom after the action of the 17th he had already reported as an incompetent officer; but that the troops also were to blame, though the Royals had immediately rallied and covered the retreat of the other two regiments. More curious still, the list of casualties shows that the Third Dragoon Guards suffered the very heavy loss of thirty-eight men and forty-six horses killed, besides nine more men wounded and missing, though the casualties of the Royals and the Blues were trifling.

★★★★★★

In *Cannon's Records* of the 3rd Dragoon Guards these casualties are ascribed to the action of the 26th of April. Whether the mistake be due to accident or to design, it is to be regretted.

★★★★★★

From this I infer that Mansel led his brigade to the sound of the guns, and, being ordered to attack the fresh division of the enemy that had come upon the ground, contrived by irresolution and mismanagement to bring the Third Dragoon Guards under enfilading fire of the French cannon, and to throw the whole of the six squadrons into confusion. In any case it is certain that the brilliant attack of the Fifteenth was insufficiently supported, and that Mansel and his brigade, justly or unjustly, lay under reproach, until two days later they redeemed their good name beyond all cavil. The casualties of the French in this action were eight hundred men killed and four hundred wounded, besides three guns taken; while the Fifteenth escaped with a loss of thirty-one men and thirty-seven horses killed and wounded, and the Leopold Hussars with a loss of ten men and eleven horses killed and wounded and the same number missing.

The Emperor of Austria conferred on the officers of the Fifteenth a gold medal and the much-coveted order of Maria Theresa; and the regiment still bears on its appointments the name of Villers-en-Cauchies. (Misspelled Villiers-en-Couche, which in these days is surely unnecessary, with excellent French maps easily obtainable to give the correct spelling).

With a little more luck, or, it may be, a little better management, Otto would have achieved one of the greatest successes ever recorded of cavalry against infantry, and annihilated the whole of the force that had moved out from Cambrai.

As matters stood, however, the reverse to the French produced little effect on Pichegru. Successive reinforcements had more than made good his losses and on the 24th of April the combined strength of the armies of the North and of the Ardennes, not counting fifty thousand men employed as garrisons, was little short of two hundred thousand men free for service in the field, or nearly two to one of Coburg's force. Relying upon this numerical superiority he started for Lille, in order from thence to direct operations against Clerfaye. At the same time, however, he set his troops in motion to raise the siege of Landrecies, directing General Charbonnier with thirty thousand men of the army of the Ardennes to attack Kaunitz on the extreme left wing of the Allies, while simultaneously General Ferrand with forty-five thousand from Guise should fall on the covering army on the east and south, and General Chappuis with thirty thousand men from Cambrai should assail the Duke of York on the west.

Accordingly, early in the morning of the 26th the French engaged the covering army simultaneously at all points. On the east General Fromentin with twenty-two thousand men assailed Maroilles and Prisches, and after a long and severe struggle captured the latter position, severing for the time communications between Alvintzy and Kinsky. Alvintzy himself was disabled by two wounds, and the situation was for a time most critical until the Archduke Charles, who had succeeded to the command of his force, by a final and skilful effort recovered the lost ground and drove the French over the Little Helpe. This enabled him to reinforce the centre under General Bellegarde, who with some difficulty was defending the line from Oisy to Nouvion against twenty-three thousand men. Thereupon Bellegarde instantly took the offensive, completely defeated the French, and captured from them nine guns.

But far more brilliant was the success of the Allies on the west, where Chappuis led one column along the high-road from Cambrai to Le Cateau, while a second column of four thousand men advanced upon the same point by a parallel course through the villages of Ligny and Bertry, a little farther to the south. Favoured by a dense fog the two columns succeeded in driving the advanced posts of the Allies from the villages of Inchy and Beaumont on the high-road, and of Troisvilles, Bertry, and Maurois immediately to south of them; which done, they proceeded to form behind the ridge on which these villages stand, for the main attack. Before the formation was complete the fog cleared; and the duke, observing that Chappuis's left flank was in the air, made a great demonstration with his artillery against the French front, sent a few light troops to engage their right, and calling all his cavalry to his own right, formed them unseen in a fold in the ground between Inchy and Bethencourt, a village a little to westward of it.

★★★★★★

Going over the ground, my companion and myself fixed upon a hollow about half a mile to west of Inchy, and on the north side of the road, as the spot where Otto concentrated his squadrons out of sight of the French. The left flank of the French infantry, upon which the attack was opened, we reckoned to have stood in a hollow about half a mile south-east of Inchy. After very careful study of the ground, I put forward these conjectures with some confidence. J.W.F.

★★★★★★

The squadrons were drawn up in three lines, the six squadrons of the Austrian Cuirassiers of Zeschwitz forming the first line under Colonel Prince Schwarzenberg, Mansel's brigade the second line, and the First and Fifth Dragoon Guards and Sixteenth Light Dragoons the third, the whole of the nineteen squadrons being under command of General Otto.

★★★★★★

The establishment of an Austrian Cuirassier Regiment was six squadrons; the British regiments, as originally organised in 1793, should have made thirteen squadrons; but I imagine that

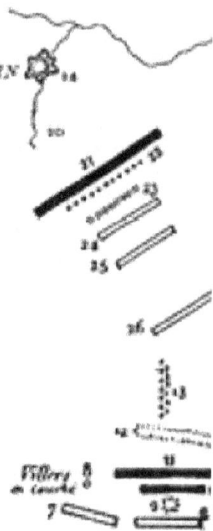

BOUCHAIN

11

24
25

26

Villers
en Couché
7

A Sketch

of the Action fought on the 24ᵗʰ of April 1794

at VILLERS en COUCHÉ

when the 15ᵗʰ Regiment of Light Dragoons

behaved so gloriously & gallantly

St Hilaire

Query

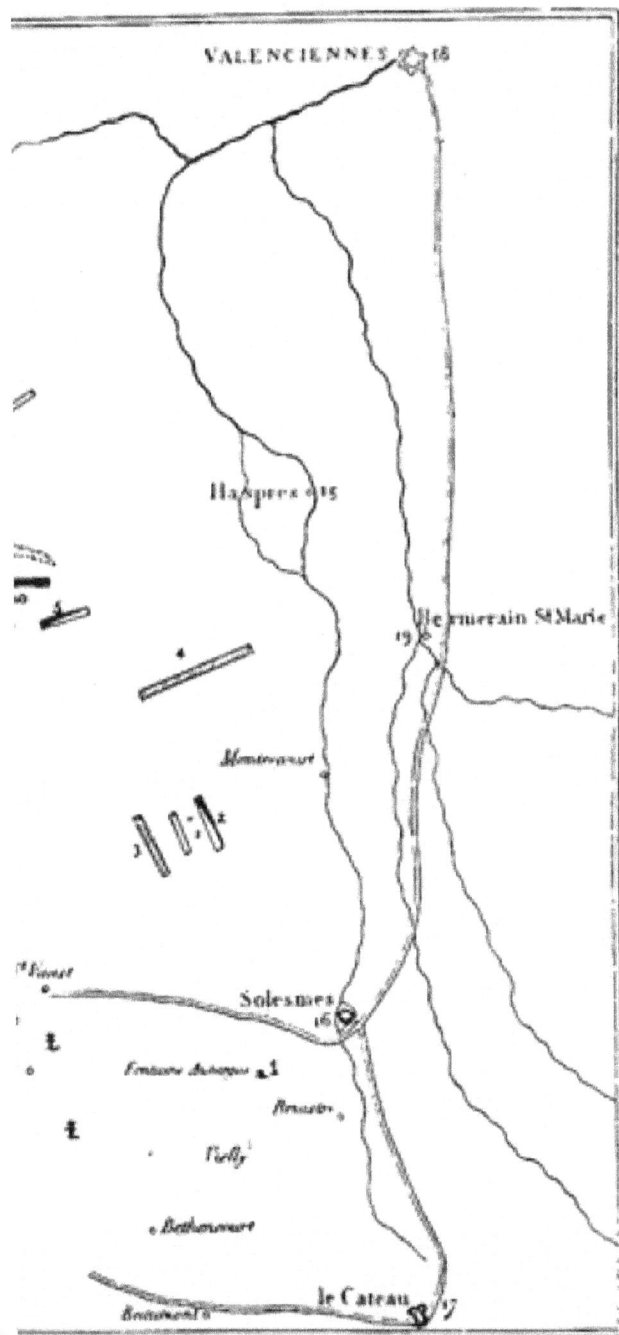

VALENCIENNES ✦ 18

HaAspres ✦ 15

4

Montenanst

3

Solesmes 16

l'Evêque

Fontaine au Evêques

Hornain St Marie 19

le Cateau 17

losses had reduced one or other of them to a single squadron, for both Witzleben (iii.) and Ditfurth (ii.) give the number as six Austrian .and twelve British squadrons. J.W.F.
★★★★★★

In this order they moved off, Otto advancing with great caution, and skilfully taking advantage of every fold in the ground to conceal his movements. A body of French cavalry was first encountered and immediately overthrown, General Chappuis, who was with them, being taken prisoner. Then the last ridge was passed and the squadrons saw their prey before them over twenty thousand French infantry drawn up with their guns in order of battle, serenely facing eastward without thought of the storm that was bursting on them from the north.

There was no hesitation, for Schwarzenberg was an impetuous leader, and the Cuirassiers had been disappointed of distinction at Villers-en-Cauchies; the Blues, Royals, and Third Dragoon Guards had a stain to wipe away; the King's and Fifth Dragoon Guards were eager for opportunity to show their mettle; and the Sixteenth Light Dragoons, being the only Light Dragoons present, were anxious to prove that they could do as well as the Fifteenth.

The trumpets rang out, and with wild cheering white coats, red coats, and blue coats whirled down upon the left flank and rear of the French. The French guns, hastily wheeled round, opened a furious fire of grape, while the infantry began as furious a fire of musketry; but the charging squadrons took no heed. Mansel, stung by the imputation of cowardice, which had been thrown out to account for his mishap on the 24th, had vowed that he would not come back alive, and dashing far ahead of his men into the thick of the enemy went down at once; but Colonel Vyse, of the King's Dragoon Guards, taking command of both brigades, led them as straight as Mansel. In a very few minutes the whole mass of the French was broken up and flying southward in wild disorder, with the sabres hewing mercilessly among them.

The misfortunes of the enemy did not end here, for one of their detachments, which had been pushed forward to Troisvilles, was driven back by a couple of British guns under Colonel Congreve, and joined the rest in flight. Meanwhile Chappuis's second column had advanced a little beyond Maurois with its guns, when the appearance of the fugitives warned them to retire; but in this quarter, too, there was a vigilant Austrian officer, Major Stepheicz, with two squadrons of the Archduke Ferdinand's Hussars and four of the Seventh and

Eleventh British Light Dragoons. Following up the French column he drove its rearguard in upon the main body a little to westward of Maretz, and a few miles further on broke in upon the main body also, dispersed it utterly, and captured ten guns.

Twelve hundred Frenchmen were killed in this part of the field alone, so terrible was the Austrian hussar in pursuit; two thousand more had fallen under the sabres of Otto's division, which likewise captured twenty-two guns and three hundred and fifty prisoners. The shattered fragments of the French infantry fled by a wide detour to Cambrai; and Pichegru's attack on this side was not merely beaten off, but his troops were literally hunted from the field.

So ended the greatest day in the annals of the British horse, perhaps the greater since the glory of it was shared with the most renowned cavalry in Europe. The loss of the Austrians was nine officers, two hundred and twenty-eight men, and two hundred and eight horses; that of the British, six officers, one hundred and fifty-six men, and two hundred and eighty-nine horses, killed, wounded, and missing. The British regiments that suffered most heavily were the Blues and the Third Dragoon Guards, each of which had sixteen men and twenty-five horses killed outright; and the determination of the Third to prove that the harsh criticism of their comrades on the 24th was unjust, is shown by the fact that five out of the six officers injured in the charge belonged to them.

Mansel, the brigadier, who was also their colonel, died as has been told. Of the captains one, his own son, was overpowered and taken in a desperate effort to extricate his father, and another was wounded. Of the lieutenants one was killed and another, if not two more, wounded. The major in command, however, had the good fortune not only to escape unhurt but to receive the sword of General Chappuis. The total loss of the covering army was just under fifteen hundred men; that of the French was reckoned, probably with less exaggeration than usual, at seven thousand, while the guns taken from them numbered forty-one.

On the following day, April 27th, the emperor ordered his army to devote itself to singing a *Te Deum* and to solemn thanksgiving, which was very right and proper, but might well have been deferred for a day or two until the full fruits of the victory had been gathered. For although there were four fortresses, Avesnes, Guise, Cambrai, and Maubeuge, within easy distance as a refuge for fugitives, another day's pursuit would assuredly have swept up many hundred stragglers, while the mere sight of the Allied troops would probably have sufficed to set the French levies running once more.

There was however better excuse than usual for inaction, for among General Chappuis's papers had been found evidence that a most formidable stroke was about to fall, if it had not already fallen, upon Flanders. It is now necessary to narrate the course of events in that quarter, namely, on the right or western wing of the Allies.

On the 23rd of April a force from Cambrai, acting in concert with that which was beaten on the 24th at Villers en Cauchies, had moved northward against Wurmb's corps of communication at Denain, and, but for the arrival of Clerfaye with some eight thousand men from Tournai, would have driven it across the Scheldt. On the 24th, 26th, and 27th the harassing of the advanced posts of the Allies about Denain continued, and meanwhile the true attack was developed, pursuant to Carnot's plans, on the extreme left of the French line.

On the 24th Michaud's division of twelve thousand men marched from Dunkirk, part of it towards Nieuport on the north, the rest upon Ypres to south-east, sweeping back the feeble posts between the two places. Simultaneously Moreau's division of twenty-one thousand men moved eastward from Cassel upon Ypres, and drove all the outlying detachments on that side to take shelter under the ramparts. Then, leaving some of Michaud's division at Messines to watch the fortress from the south, Moreau pursued his way eastward against Menin, and surrounded that fortress upon all sides.

At the same time Souham's division of thirty thousand men, under the personal direction of Pichegru, advanced from Lille north-eastward upon Mouscron, drove back upon Dottignies the weak detachment that defended it, and captured Courtrai, which was practically without a garrison. General Oynhausen, however, restored matters somewhat by collecting troops from Tournai at Dottignies and retaking the position of Mouscron, where reinforcements arrived in the nick of time, April 28th, to strengthen him.

The papers found upon Chappuis gave Coburg the key to all these movements; and on the very evening of the 26th he sent twelve battalions and ten squadrons under General Erskine from his own army to St. Amand, bidding Clerfaye to recall at once to their proper stations the reinforcements which he had imprudently hurried to Denain. Clerfaye accordingly hastened by forced marches through Tournai to Mouscron, which he reached on the 28th, raising the garrison of that place to ten thousand men, exclusive of about two thousand more in

Battle of Mouscron

the detached posts of Coyghem and Dottignies.

The relief of Menin was his first and most urgent object, and he had fully resolved to attempt it on the 30th; but Pichegru was too quick for him. On the 29th the two columns under Generals Souham and Bertin fell, the one upon his front, the other upon his left flank and rear, with a superiority of three to one, and after a hard struggle forced him from his position. Clerfaye seems to have begun his retreat in good order, but the movement speedily degenerated into a flight; and when he rallied his beaten troops at Dottignies he was the weaker by two thousand men killed and wounded and twenty-three guns. Happily six of the battalions sent from the army before Landrecies had by that time reached Dottignies, and, with these to hearten his demoralised force, he retired eastward to Espierres, on the western bank of the Scheldt.

This defeat decided the fate of Menin. The garrison consisted of rather more than two thousand men, chiefly Hanoverians, but in part French Emigrants, which latter if captured could expect nothing but the guillotine. The *commandant*, Count Hammerstein, therefore decided to cut his way out through the besiegers, and with the fortune that favours the brave, succeeded during the night of the 30th in forcing his passage northward to Thourout and thence to Bruges. Thus Menin and Courtrai, the two gates of the Lys, were lost, and a gap broken in the long cordon of the Allies. Along the whole of the right wing there was something like a panic, and the roads were choked with long trains of supplies and stores flying northward to Brussels and Ghent.

At Ostend there had lately arrived the Eighth Light Dragoons and the Thirty-Eighth and Fifty-Fifth Foot, sadly belated, since the infantry, with Dundas's usual wisdom, had been embarked at Bristol; but General Stewart, the commandant at Ostend, did not think it prudent after Clerfaye's defeat to send them down country. (Stewart to Dundas, 30th April; Craig to Nepean, 25th April; Adjutant-General to Duke of York, 22nd April, 1794. These two unfortunate battalions spent three weeks on the passage).

Happily Pichegru did not pursue his advantage as he ought. He did indeed push a detachment northward from Menin upon Roulers, May 3rd, which was attacked and defeated with a loss of two hundred men and three guns by three squadrons of the Allied cavalry; (York to Dundas, 6th May 1794), but there his activity ceased; and he solemnly sat himself down about Moorseele on the left bank of the Lys, with one flank resting on Menin and the other on Courtrai, as if to allow time for Coburg's army to come up in his front.

✶✶✶✶✶✶

It is curious to note that Jomini's account makes the French force front to the south, whereas Craig conceived of it as facing to the north; so that evidently it was prepared to face either way.

✶✶✶✶✶✶

Coburg meanwhile had passed through no enviable days. On the 28th news reached him that Kaunitz on his left wing had been forced back by overwhelming numbers to the Sambre, while on his right wing Pichegru had made his way to Courtrai; but, however serious the outlook, he was still tied for the present to the miserable and useless fortress of Landrecies. By a strange irony Mack on that very day submitted a plan of future operations, whereby Bouchain, Cambrai, Avesnes, and Maubeuge were in succession to be besieged, (Witzleben, ii. Memorandum of the 28th of April in *W.O. Corres.*); but circumstances on this occasion were too strong for pedantry. Landrecies fortunately fell on the 30th, and Coburg on the same day ordered the Duke of York to lead the rest of his force with all speed to Clerfaye's assistance, and to drive the French from Flanders.

Heavy rain, however, delayed the duke's progress; and it was not until the 3rd of May that he reached Tournai, where he reunited Erskine's force with his own and pushed forward a strong detachment three miles westward to Marquain and Lamain, releasing five thousand men, which had hitherto held those points, to join Clerfaye. The front thus occupied by the Allies, from Tournai in the south to Espierres in the north, was from seven to eight miles long and faced due west, their objective being the right flank and communications of the French left wing. The British brigade at Ostend, namely the Twelfth, Thirty-Eighth, and Fifty-Fifth under Major-General Whyte, and the Eighth Light Dragoons, were by this time on their way to Clerfaye's army; and the united force of Clerfaye and the Duke of York was now reckoned at about forty thousand men.

✶✶✶✶✶✶

Clerfaye (including the reinforcements from Ostend), nineteen thousand; Walmoden at Warcoing, six thousand; Duke of York at Tournai, eighteen thousand (Craig to Dundas, 6th May 1794). Witzleben, however, reckons the united force at thirty thousand men only (iii.), and Ditfurth gives but four thousand men to Walmoden.

✶✶✶✶✶✶

105

Pichegru, on the other hand, had from forty to fifty thousand be-tween Menin and Courtrai, and twenty thousand more under General Bonnaud (who had succeeded Chappuis) at Sainghin, about five miles south-east of Lille, to act as a reserve. On Clerfaye's proposal it was agreed that on the 5th of May he himself should cross the Lys a little below Courtrai and fall upon that place from the north, while simul-taneously the Duke of York should move eastward to cut it off from Lille. Clerfaye, however, whether from diffidence or mere frowardness, would not venture on the attempt. Appeal was made to the Emperor Francis to give him positive orders to attack, but meanwhile Bonnaud concentrated over twenty-five thousand men between Bouvines and Anstaing, a little to the west of Marquain, as if to threaten the duke's left. Finally, when the emperor's orders did reach Clerfaye, he first wasted four days in reconnoitring, and at last made but a feeble attack on the 10th, contenting himself with the capture of the outermost fringe of Courtrai.

Pichegru seems to have had good information of Clerfaye's move-ments and possibly even of his intentions, for he left Moreau's division alone to deal with him; and, having moved Souham's division to the east bank of the Lys, he on the same day attacked the line of the Al-lies in force. Souham advanced against the Hanoverians on the Allied right, but, though he forced the posts of Dottignies and Coyghem, was repulsed from Espierres. On the left of the Allies thirty thou-sand French moved out in two columns against the Duke of York's entrenched position between Lamain and Hertain; the stronger col-umn of the two, which included five thousand cavalry, following the main road from Lille to Tournai, the other turning south-east from Bouvines by Cysoing upon Bachy, as if to turn the duke's left flank.

This latter column was checked by a couple of battalions and three squadrons under command of an Austrian officer at Bachy, and was unable to penetrate further. The other and more formidable body car-ried the advanced posts of Baisieux, upon the main road, and of Cam-phin about a mile to south of it, and forming on the plain between these two villages opened a furious cannonade from howitzers and heavy guns. Thereupon the duke, perceiving a gap in the enemy's line, whereby the right of their main body was uncovered, ordered sixteen squadrons of British dragoons and two of Austrian hussars to advance into the plain of Cysoing by the low ground that lies south of the heights of Lamain, and from thence to attack.

The cavalry obeyed with alacrity; but the ground on the plain, though perfectly level and unenclosed, was much broken by patches of cole-seed, grown in trenches after the manner of celery, which checked the progress of the heavy dragoons. Moreover the French infantry, for the first time since the Revolution, threw themselves into squares and faced the galloping horsemen with admirable firmness. Nine regiments of cavalry in succession charged up to the bayonets, but with insufficient speed, and fell back baffled. (*Life of Lord Combermere*, i. The military part of this republished as *The Golden Lion* by Leonaur.)

Nevertheless they followed the French up the plain from south to north, until, a little to westward of Camphin, their left came under the fire of some French heavy batteries, established on some gently rising ground before the village of Gruson. The duke then ordered a brigade of British infantry to move forward between that village and Baisieux, at the same time sending down four battalions by the same track as the cavalry had taken, to support their attack. The French infantry thereupon retreated from Camphin in a northerly direction towards the village of Willems, their cavalry covering the movement; while the British cavalry, now reinforced by six more squadrons, hovered about them watching for their opportunity to attack.

At length they fell upon the French horsemen on both flanks, and utterly overthrew them, after which they renewed their attempt upon the infantry, but again without success. At last, however, a little to the south of Willems, the battalion-guns of the British infantry came up and opened fire, when the French, after receiving a few shots, began to waver. The squadrons again charged, and an officer of the Greys, galloping straight at the largest of the squares, knocked down three men as he rode into it, wheeled his horse round and overthrew six more, and thus made a gap for the entry of his men.

The sight of one square broken and dispersed demoralised the remainder of the French. Two more squares were ridden down, and for the third time the British sabres had free play among the French infantry. Over four hundred prisoners were taken, thirteen guns were captured, and it was reckoned that from one to two thousand men were cut down. The loss of the British was thirty men killed, six officers and seventy-seven men wounded, ninety horses killed and one hundred and forty wounded and missing, the Sixth Dragoon Guards being the regiment that suffered most heavily. It is hardly necessary to call attention to the arm which was lacking on this day, or to point out that a single battery of horse-artillery would have enabled the cavalry to break the squares at the first onset, would greatly have increased the enemy's losses, and would have made the day's operations more decisive.

Not for eighteen years was the British cavalry destined again to ride over French battalions as they rode on this day; and then Stapleton Cotton was fated once more to be present, leading not a squadron of Carbineers, but a whole division of horse to the charge at Salamanca. But the 10th of May 1794 is chiefly memorable as marking the date on which the new French infantry showed itself not unworthy of the old.

★★★★★★

The regiments engaged were the Blues, Second, Third, Sixth Dragoon Guards; First, Second, Sixth Dragoons; Seventh, Eleventh, Fifteenth, Sixteenth Light Dragoons. Which were engaged throughout and which came up as reinforcements, I have been unable to discover. The account of the action is drawn chiefly from Calvert, *Journal. Narrative of an Officer*, ii. Ditfurth, ii. *Life of Lord Combermere*, i. The first is the most important.

★★★★★★

After the action the French main body retired once more across the Lys to its old camp between Menin and Courtrai; but on the 11th Souham attacked Clerfaye in his position at Lendelede, about four miles north of Courtrai, and after an obstinate engagement forced him to retire still further northward to Thielt, with the loss of fifteen hundred men and two guns. Meanwhile the Duke of York, in spite of his success on the 10th, became anxious as to his position in presence of numbers so overwhelmingly superior, and pressed Coburg to send him reinforcements.

At the emperor's headquarters, however, there was some hesitation whether the principal army should move eastward to the assistance of Kaunitz on the Sambre, or westward for the salvation of Flanders. The first idea was to make a demonstration towards Cambrai with a part of the force; the next to make a rapid march and invest Avesnes, also with only a part of the force, in order to take pressure off Kaunitz. The idea of moving with the whole army to any given point seems to have occurred to none of the Austrian Generals. Then came the Duke of York's application for help, whereupon General Kinsky was ordered with some six thousand horse and foot to Denain, to enable Wurmb's detachment at that place to join the Duke of York at Tournai.

One day later, May 12th, arrived news. from Kaunitz that he had been compelled to fall back still further northward from the Sambre, and was attacked on all sides; the fact being that Carnot on the 30th of April had directed fifteen thousand men from the army of the Rhine to join the army of the Ardennes, so as to ensure decisive superiority on the Sambre.

Upon this, Coburg determined that the subdivision of the army into fragments must cease, and called upon the emperor to choose between the Sambre and Flanders, as the sphere of action for the entire force. Intelligence of a successful engagement fought by Kaunitz and of Clerfaye's retreat to Thielt inclined the Emperor to Flanders; and though, even then, Austrian pedantry insisted that some eight thousand men under the Prince of Orange must remain in the vicinity of Landrecies, yet the bulk of the army on the 14th commenced its march westward.

This movement, however, was by no means to the taste of some of the emperor's advisers; and it becomes necessary at this point to turn for a moment from the western to the eastern centre of European disturbance, and to glance at the influence which events in Poland had exerted upon the Imperial Cabinet. It has already been said that Thugut's only object in persuading the emperor to take personal command in the field, was that the operations might subserve his own policy. With this view the minister prepared to remove to Valenciennes, which was to be the political headquarters of the Empire during the emperor's stay in the Netherlands; but before he could leave Vienna he was startled by the news of a general rising in Poland.

This insurrection under the leadership of Kosciusko broke out on the 25th of March, and spread with a rapidity and success which left the Russians absolutely helpless. Catherine, greedy for the partition of Turkey, had already moved the best of her troops southwards; and the only force of any kind upon the spot was that of Prussia, which fact in itself was enough to kindle Thugut's jealousy. On the 20th of April Kosciusko, after two days' fighting, captured Warsaw; and five days later Catherine, while asking the emperor for the troops due to her by treaty, mentioned also how greatly she needed the help of the Prussians, of whom likewise she had claimed assistance. Meanwhile King Frederick William, growing nervous lest the rebellion should infect also his own Polish provinces, after some hesitation decided to throw the Treaty of the Hague to the winds; wherefore, withdrawing twenty thousand of his troops from the Rhine, he left Berlin on the 14th of May to take personal command of his army in Poland.

All this was gall and wormwood to Thugut, and the more so because Kosciusko had expressed a wish to place Austrian troops in occupation of Poland rather than yield it to the Prussians. He became more and more anxious to have done with France, if possible by a separate peace with the Republic, and to devote all Austria's energies to the thwarting of Prussia in the East. The embitterment of his hostility towards Prussia brought him more than ever in conflict with Coburg and Mack, who desired above all things a good understanding with the second great power of Germany; and, unfortunately, he found two officers of like sentiments with himself in the Prince of Waldeck, who held a high position on the Staff, and General Rollin, who of all men possessed greatest influence with the emperor. It was therefore with profound dissatisfaction that Thugut's ignoble clique saw the mass of the Austrian troops drawn nearer to France and further from Poland; and though outwardly they swallowed their ill-humour, yet they had every intention of compassing their own ends, even by means the most infamous. (Sybel, iii. Witzleben, iii.).

On the 15th of May the emperor joined the Duke of York at Tournai, and the Archduke Charles brought the Austrian Army from Landrecies to St. Amand, eleven miles to south of it. The field, on which the decisive action was to be fought, was one that had drunk deep of human blood. It may be described as the parallelogram enclosed by a line drawn south-eastward from Courtrai to Tournai, thence south-westward to Pont-à-Marque, thence north-westward through Lille to Wervicq, and thence north-eastward back to Courtrai. To east it is bounded by the Scheldt, to north by the Lys; and through the midst of it, flowing first from south to north past Pont-à-Marque and Cysoing to Lannoy, and thence westward into the Deule and so to the Lys, runs the Marque, a stream impassable except by bridges, owing to soft bottom and swampy banks.

The principal bridges were those of Pont-à-Marque on the great road to Paris, and Pont-à-Tressin on the road from Tournai to Lille; but there were others on by-roads at Louvil, Bouvines, Gruson, Tressin, L'Hempenpont, Pont-à-Breug and Marque, most of them fortified and strongly held by the French. Two smaller streams of the same character as the Marque, but running from west to east, form also important obstacles within this arena, namely, the Espierres-brook, which has its source close to Roubaix and flows into the Scheldt at Espierres, and the Baisieux-brook, which rising near Hertain joins the Scheldt at Pont-à-Chin. The ground is mostly level, excepting the undulating heights that rise from the Lys, the low ridge upon which stood the villages of Roubaix and Lannoy, and the group of hills about Tournai itself; but it was thickly studded with villages, linked together by chains of innumerable cottages and farmhouses, which were all of them enclosed by hedges.

The fields were cut up by swampy brooks and by a ramification of wide drains, which, with other enclosures, practically forbad the movements of troops except by road. The roads, however, even then were many; and the principal highways were nearly broad enough to permit an advance in column of half-companies, (Ditfurth, ii. He says actually that there was nearly room for the full width of a company, of course in triple rank). But all of them, as well as the waterways, were lined with trees, making it extremely difficult to see the movements of troops from a distance. Thus it was and is a country unfit for cavalry, and far better adapted in that day to the tactics of the French than of the Allied infantry.

★★★★★★

Great part of the battlefield is now built over. Lille alone covers a vast extent of it, and Roubaix and Lannoy are to all intent part and parcel of Lille. But the general character of the ground, and in particular its blindness, remains unchanged.

★★★★★★

Within the parallelogram the French were somewhat widely scattered. Osten's division of ten thousand men lay at Pont-à-Marque. To the left or northward of it the bulk of Bonnaud's division of twenty thousand men was encamped at Sainghin, with detachments occupying also Pont-à-Tressin and Lannoy, further north upon the Marque. Souham's division of twenty-eight thousand, and Moreau's of twenty-two thousand men lay on the south bank of the Lys between Courtrai and Aelbeke, a village nearly four miles south of it, with Thierry's brigade at Mouscron, and Compère's brigade at Turcoing to preserve communication with Bonnaud. In all, the French army numbered eighty-two thousand men.

Against this force Coburg could pit sixty-two thousand, twelve thousand of them cavalry. Of the Allied army, fourteen thousand under the Archduke Charles were at St. Amand; seventeen thousand under the Duke of York at Tournai; nine thousand under Kinsky at Marquain; four thousand Hanoverians under General von dem Bussche at Warcoing, on the Scheldt; and, lastly, sixteen thousand men under Clerfaye were at Oyghem, about five miles north and east of Courtrai on the north bank of the Lys.

The whole of these troops, excepting Clerfaye's corps, could easily be concentrated within twelve hours at Tournai, from which a swift and resolute attack upon the southern flank of Souham and Moreau, by Roubaix, Mouveaux and Bondues, might have cut them off from Lille, driven them into the arms of Clerfaye and overwhelmed them. The Austrians, however, were not to be weaned from their own methods, and accordingly on the 16th Mack prepared an elaborate plan, which he designed, and even declared, to be a plan of annihilation.

The army was as usual to be divided. The first column, of four thousand Hanoverians under Bussche, was to march by Dottignies upon Mouscron, detaching a third of its strength northward on the high road from Tournai to Courtrai, and, having captured Mouscron, was to open communication with the second column. The second column, of twelve battalions and ten squadrons, or about ten thousand men, under Field-Marshal Otto, was to advance by Leers and Wattrelos upon Turcoing. The third column, of twelve battalions and ten squadrons under the Duke of York, was to move by Lannoy against Mouveaux, sixteen British squadrons being held in reserve at Hertain under General Erskine.

The fourth column, of ten battalions and sixteen squadrons under Count Kinsky, was to be employed partly in covering the duke's left flank; but the bulk of it was to advance on Bouvines and there force the passage of the Marque. The fifth column, of seventeen battalions and thirty-two squadrons under the Archduke Charles, was to march to Pont-à-Marque, sending a small detachment northward by Templeuve to preserve communication with the fourth column. Having gained the passage of the Marque he was to attack the enemy on the western side of the river, and, after leaving detachments to guard the bridges, to wheel northward, unite forces with Kinsky and move up with him to join the Duke of York at Mouveaux.

Finally the sixth column under Clerfaye was to march from Oyghem on the left bank of the Lys, force the passage of the river above Menin on the morning of the 17th, and manoeuvre in rear of the enemy about Mouscron and Turcoing. Thus the design was to attack the enemy's front with half the army, turn both their flanks with the remainder, and destroy the French irremediably; but whether the surest way of attaining this object was to disperse the troops in isolated columns over a front of twenty miles in a blind and strongly enclosed country—this was a question over which Craig, at any rate, shook his head.

Miscarriages of the great plan began early. Clerfaye did not receive his orders for the movement towards Menin until late on the morning of the 16th, and did not march until the evening. His progress was much delayed by the heavy sandy roads, and, consequently, it was the afternoon of the 17th before his corps reached Wervicq, and attempted to cross the Lys by the bridge.

The French, however, had covered it by entrenchments which blocked his passage; and, when the pontoons were asked for, it was found that by some mistake they had been left behind. Several hours were wasted while they were coming up, and the pontoon-bridge was consequently not laid until late at night, when a few battalions only crossed the river, the remainder of the force bivouacking on the left bank. The general result was that Clerfaye's corps, one-fourth of the whole army, counted for nothing in the first day's operations. (Witzleben iii. considers the slowness both of Clerfaye and the Archduke Charles on this day to have been inexcusable).

The march of the remaining columns was begun in a thick fog which made concerted movements difficult, and the Austrian Staff seems to have made no allowance for the varying distances to be covered by the columns; Kinsky having little more than seven miles to traverse from Froidmont to Bouvines, whereas the Archduke Charles had fully fifteen miles from St. Amand to Pont-à-Marque. Bussche concentrated at St. Leger, a little to west of Warcoing in the night, advanced upon Mouscron, and captured it, but was driven out again with very heavy loss, and forced back to Dottignies.

For this misfortune Mack was chiefly responsible, by directing the detachment of so large a proportion of this column on a perfectly aimless errand towards Courtrai. Otto, on Bussche's left, fared better, driving Compère's troops from Leers, Wattrelos, and Turcoing; but, unfortunately, with no further result than to join them to Thierry's brigade behind Mouscron, to the greater discomfiture of the unfortunate Hanoverians.

To the left and south of Otto the Duke of York with about ten thousand men, (brigade Guards/4 batts.; 14th, 37th, 53rd Foot; 2 Hessian, 5 Austrian batts.; 7th, 15th, 16th Light Dragoons/6 squad.; 4 squad. Austrian Hussars), advanced by Templeuve upon Lannoy which, after a sharp cannonade, he attacked with the brigade of Guards in front while the Light Dragoons turned it by the left; but the enemy beat so hasty a retreat that they escaped with little loss. Leaving two Hessian battalions in Lannoy, the duke pushed on to Roubaix, where the enemy stood, with greater force both of infantry and artillery, in an entrenched position; but, in spite of a very obstinate resistance, the Guards carried this post also with the bayonet.

Having no intelligence of the columns on his right and left, the duke rightly decided to leave his advanced guard at Roubaix, and to fall back with his main body to Lannoy; when to his dismay he received a positive command from the emperor himself, who with the Headquarter-Staff had accompanied the rear of his column, to push on to the attack of Mouveaux. This order was sheer folly, unless indeed it were dictated by wanton and deliberate wickedness.

★★★★★★

Hamilton (*History of the Grenadier Guards,* ii.) says, I know not on what authority, that the pretext for this order was that Clerfaye required assistance. It is certain that the Austrian Headquarters had heard nothing and knew nothing of Clerfaye's situation at this time, so that, if General Hamilton's story be more than mere gossip, the order was probably urged by Waldeck or some other of Mack's enemies, with the object of bringing his elaborate combinations into contempt. The fact that the British would be the chief sufferers in case of mishap, would rather have encouraged this faction in the Austrian Staff to the measure.

★★★★★★

But it was reiterated in spite of all protests, and though the evening was falling and the troops were weary with a long and harassing day's work under a burning sun, the duke reluctantly obeyed. The French position at Mouveaux was enclosed by palisades and entrenchments and flanked by redoubts; but for the third time the brigade of Guards drove the enemy out brilliantly with the bayonet. The Seventh and Fifteenth Light Dragoons under Abercromby's personal direction at once pressed forward in pursuit, and galloping round the village, which had been kindled by the flying French, overtook the fugitives, and cut down three hundred of them.

Three guns were captured; and one small party of the Fifteenth actually rode into the French camp at Bondues, nearly two miles to west of Mouveaux, and set the troops there running in every direction.

★★★★★★

The *Gazette* prints this place as Bouderes; and the mistake has been copied into many regimental histories. It is only one among innumerable instances of the slovenliness of the clerks of the War Office at that time.

★★★★★★

The main body of the duke's column then bivouacked astride of the road between Mouveaux and Roubaix. With the two columns south of the duke, however, affairs had gone but indifferently. Kinsky' s advance from Froidmont was delayed by a message from the Archduke Charles, to the effect that his force could not possibly reach the Marque at the appointed hour of six in the morning; but in due time he moved forward to Bouvines, and drove the French from their entrenchments. The enemy, however, broke down the bridge over the Marque as they retired, and, until the advance of the Archduke began to make itself felt, Kinsky was unable to repair it, since the passage was commanded by a battery of heavy guns.

The archduke's column had meanwhile left St. Amand at ten o'clock on the evening of the 16th, and after driving back the French advanced posts at Templeuve, (not to be confounded with the village of the same name further north, on the road from Tournai to Lannoy), Cappelle, a little to east of Pont-à-Marque, finally succeeded in forcing the passage of the river at that point. But it was not till two o'clock in the afternoon, instead of six in the morning of the 17th, that his army had passed to the west bank of the Marque; and his troops were too much exhausted to move further than Lesquin, a little east of the road between Pont-à-Marque and Lille.

There he bivouacked on the heights between Lesquin and Peronne, a village about three miles to south-east of it; his men having been on foot for twenty-two hours, marched more than twenty miles over bad roads, and fought a sharp action for the passage of the river. His advance, however, had forced the enemy to evacuate Sainghin, and thus enabled Kinsky to repair the bridge at Bouvines; but none the less Kinsky, with excess of caution, would not cross the river, and encamped for the night on the right bank, which was for him the wrong bank, of the Marque.

At the beginning of this day the French commanders had no information of any movements of the Allies beyond the march of Clerfaye; and, accordingly, the divisions of Souham and Moreau, together with Vandamme's brigade, had crossed to the left bank of the Lys. The advance of the Allies from the east and the combats about Turcoing, however, soon undeceived them. Pichegru being, as Soult said, fortunately absent, Generals Souham, Moreau, Macdonald, and Reynier met in council at Menin; and on the evening of the 17th they decided to make new dispositions and to set their troops at once in motion.

Vandamme's brigade alone was left on the north bank of the Lys to watch Clerfaye, and the remainder of the troops on that side crossed the river to take up their appointed stations. Malbrancq's brigade was posted between Roncq and Blancfour, villages lying from three to four miles due south from Menin on the road to Lille; to the left of Malbrancq, Macdonald's brigade crowned the heights of Mount Halluin; the rest of Souham's division, under Generals Daendels and Jardon, lay some three miles away to the east of Macdonald, occupying a line between Aelbeke and Belleghem, a village lying a little to the south of Courtrai; and the gap between Macdonald and these troops was filled by the brigades of Compère and Thierry about Mouscron.

Thus the formation of the French left wing was that of a double echelon; the three divisions being arranged at the three angles of an isosceles triangle, with the van at the apex, Mouscron, and the rear before Menin and Courtrai. The right wing, consisting of Bonnaud's and Osten's divisions, some thirty thousand strong, was assembled about Flers, two miles and a half to the east of Lille; where orders arrived on the evening of the 17th from Souham that a general attack was designed for the morrow, in which the duty of Bonnaud's division would be to march upon Lannoy and Roubaix.

It was not without anxiety that the reports from the various columns of the Allies were awaited on the evening of the 17th at the Austrian headquarters at Templeuve. The failures of Bussche to capture Mouscron, and of the Archduke Charles to reach the point assigned to him, had sufficed to mar Mack's plans; and of Clerfaye there was no news whatever. Orders were therefore sent at three o'clock next morning to the Archduke Charles to march at once with his own and Kinsky's corps upon Lannoy; while the Duke of York and Otto were directed to attack Mouscron at noon, in the hope that before that time something would have been heard of Clerfaye.

But it seems to have occurred to none of the Austrian Staff that the disposition of the Allied Army, as prescribed by Mack, positively invited the French to take the offensive. On this night Bussche lay at Dottignies and Coyghem with his weakened corps of Hanoverians. On his left the main body of Otto's column, seven and a half battalions and three squadrons, was at Turcoing, with detachments of two battalions at Wattrelos, and of three battalions and three squadrons at Leers, on the line of his retreat. Thus his force was distributed in isolated patches along a length of five miles, with its right flank not only unprotected, but actually threatened by a superior force of the enemy, lying within three miles both of Turcoing and Wattrelos.

On Otto's left the Duke of York's column was as dangerously dispersed. The Guards, with the Seventh and Fifteenth Light Dragoons,

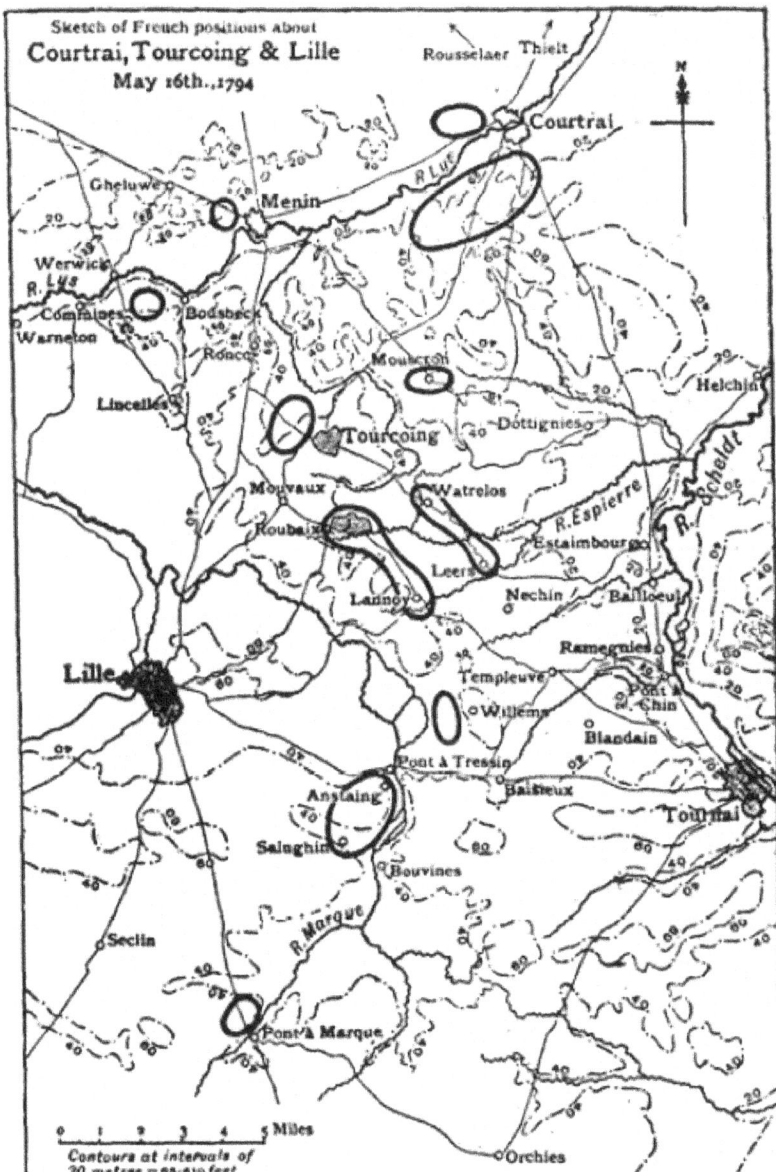

Sketch of French positions about
Courtrai, Tourcoing & Lille
May 16th., 1794

Rousselaer   Thielt

N

Gheluwe
Menin
Werwick
R. Lys
Commines
Warneton
Bodsbeck
Roncq
Linceiles
Mouscron
Helchin
R. Lys
Courtrai
Tourcoing
Dottignies
R. Espierre
R. Scheldt
Mouvaux
Watrelos
Roubaix
Estaimbourg
Leers
Nechin
Bailloeul
Lannoy
Ramegnies
Lille
Templeuve
Pont à Chin
Willems
Blandain
Pont à Tressin
Baisieux
Anstaing
Tournai
Salnghin
Bouvines
Seclin
R. Marque
Pont à Marque
Orchies

0 1 2 3 4 5 Miles

Contours at intervals of
20 metres = 65.619 feet

under Abercromby, were at Mouveaux; four Austrian battalions and the Sixteenth Light Dragoons were at Roubaix; the Fourteenth, Thirty-seventh, and Fifty-Third were on the road between Roubaix and Lille, in order to repel any attack from the garrison of the latter place; two Hessian battalions lay at Lannoy, and four squadrons of Austrian hussars were engaged in patrolling.

The duke's right was indeed covered, but his left was exposed to attack not only by the garrison of Lille but by Bonnaud's superior force about Flers; and thus both his column and Otto's practically passed the night pent in on three sides by forces of thrice their strength. To the left, or southward, there was a gap of four miles between the duke's troops and the nearest of Kinsky's detachments, which lay at Pont-à-Tressin and Chereng, with the main body still further south at Bouvines; while the Archduke Charles, with nearly one-fourth of the whole army, lay over against him at Sainghin on the other side of the Marque, with advanced detachments pushed far to the south-west at Seclin. Finally, Clerfaye, with rather more than a fourth of the whole army, was still on the western side of the Lys at Wervicq. Certainly the dispositions lent themselves to a plan of annihilation.

At three o'clock on the morning of the 18th, while Coburg was signing the orders for his troops, the French army began its march to the attack. On the south Osten's division was left about Flers and Lezennes, to watch the Archduke Charles and Kinsky; while Bonnaud, dividing his eighteen thousand men into two columns, directed them northward, the one by L'Hempenpont upon Lannoy, the other by Pont-à-Breug upon Roubaix. Simultaneously Malbrancq's brigade marched south from Roncq upon Mouveaux; Macdonald's from Mont Halluin upon the western front of Turcoing; Compère's from Mouscron upon the northern front; Thierry's, also from Mouscron, together with Daendels's from Aelbeke, upon Wattrelos; while Jardon's brigade moved from Belleghem towards Dottignies to hold the Hanoverians in check. Excluding this last brigade, sixty thousand men in all were thus turned upon the six posts in which the eighteen thousand men under Otto and the Duke of York were dispersed.

Otto's force, being nearer to the enemy, was the first to feel the weight of the attack. General Montfrault, who commanded at Turcoing, perceiving the overwhelming strength of the enemy, begged reinforcements from the Duke of York, who sent him two Austrian battalions from Roubaix, but with strict orders that they should return in the event of their arriving too late to save the town. As a matter of fact they did arrive too late, for the garrison had already been driven from Turcoing; but none the less they attached themselves, as was perhaps natural, to Montfrault, who stood fast on the eastern skirts of the town and held back the enemy for a time, until a French battery, unlimbering on ground to the north of him, forced him to retire.

Seeing himself threatened by large bodies of cavalry, Montfrault formed his troops into a large square, with four battalions and light artillery in front, one battalion on each flank, and the cavalry in the rear. In this order he fell back, his heavy artillery and waggons being enclosed in the centre of the square, and his light troops skirmishing on all four sides. It was about half-past eight when he began his retrograde movement; but already Wattrelos, the first post on his rear, was in possession of the enemy. The garrison, two Hessian battalions, had manfully resisted an attack of six times their number until eight o'clock, when, finding themselves in danger of being surrounded, they retired, and, with the help of two companies sent forward by General Otto, withdrew successfully to Leers. Montfrault thereupon found himself compelled to leave the main road for a by-way, which ran between Wattrelos and Roubaix, in order to continue his retreat.

Between six and seven o'clock, rather later than the opening of the attack on Turcoing and Wattrelos, Bonnaud's two columns came up from the south upon Lannoy and Roubaix; and shortly afterwards Malbrancq's brigade from the north fell upon Mouveaux, while a part of the French force that had captured Turcoing appeared also on the north of Roubaix. The Duke of York despatched urgent messages to recall the two Austrian battalions which he had sent to Otto, but to no effect; and meanwhile he made such head as he could with his handful of troops against overwhelming odds.

The troops at Mouveaux were disposed in two sides of a square, the left showing a front towards the east at Mouveaux, the guns stationed in the angle at the northern end of the village, and the right thrown back to the hamlet of Le Fresnoy. To the south, the British brigade of the Line under Major-General Fox, near Croix, sought to bar the way against part of Bonnaud's division from Lille; but to defend the rest of the ground there were but three Austrian battalions. Of these half a battalion was stationed in Roubaix itself, and the remainder echeloned to the right rear of Fox's brigade behind the sources of the Espierres brook, which ran along the southern skirts of the village.

These Austrian battalions seem to have been the first to give way, and one of them, by Craig's account, did not behave as it ought; but

TOURNAY

LILLE

Citadel

BATTLES OF
TURCOING & TOURNAY
(18 May) · 1794 · (22 May)

A. K. JOHNSTON F. R. G. S.

SCALES

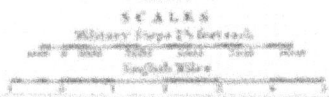

Military Steps 2½ feet each

English Miles

French · Allies

they were pressed hard both in front and on their right flank, which, owing to the absence of the two battalions sent to Otto, was wholly uncovered. One brigade of Bonnaud's division therefore succeeded in forcing its way between Mouveaux and Roubaix to Le Fresnoy; and the Duke thus saw Abercromby and the brigade of Guards absolutely cut off from him. Moreover, though he knew it not, the victorious French of Thierry's and Daendels's brigades were coming down from Wattrelos upon his rear. Seldom has a general found himself, through no fault of his own, in a more extraordinary position.

He had been assured that the Archduke Charles would join him from the south, and he had therefore ordered Abercromby to defend Mouveaux to the last extremity; but not a sign of an Austrian was to be seen whether to south or north. His first instinct was to ride to the Guards at Mouveaux; but this was seen to be out of the question. He then tried to make his way to Fox's brigade, but found that the French were in possession of the suburbs of Roubaix, and that he was cut off from this brigade also. Realising then that, his Austrian battalions being dispersed, he had not a man left to him except two squadrons of the Sixteenth Light Dragoons, he took a small escort from them and rode to Wattrelos, hoping to obtain from Otto the means for extricating the Guards. Meanwhile he sent orders to Abercromby to retire to the heights on the east side of Roubaix.

Montfrault, however, had fared ill in his attempt to withdraw. Until he reached the ground between Wattrelos and Roubaix, his square preserved good order; but being attacked at that point by overpowering numbers from the south as well as from north and west, it was broken up, and fled in disorder towards Leers. Meanwhile General Fox, finding himself absolutely isolated, at length gave the order for his brigade, which so far had held its own, to retire. The retreat began in perfect order, and the brigade, having successfully fought its way to the road at Lannoy, followed it for some distance, under incessant fire from all sides, until checked by a battery covered by an abatis, which the French had thrown up on the road.

The first shots from this battery struck down several men, and Fox for the moment feared that surrender would be inevitable; but fortunately in the ranks of the Fourteenth was a French emigrant who knew the district well, and undertook to lead the brigade across country. It pursued its retreat therefore under constant fire of artillery and musketry in front and on both flanks, and with cavalry constantly threatening its rear; but it kept its assailants at bay, and at one moment made so sharp

BATTLE OF TURCOING

a counter-attack as to take temporary possession of some French guns.

Thus partly by good luck, partly by good conduct, partly by the misconduct and mismanagement of the enemy, the three battalions contrived to reach Leers, with the loss of all their battalion-guns excepting one, and of nine officers and five hundred and twenty-five men out of eleven hundred and twenty. The greatest credit was given to General Fox for the coolness, skill, and patience with which he extricated his brigade.

Abercromby appears to have begun his retreat from Mouveaux at about nine o'clock, but of necessity very slowly, having with him a considerable number of guns. The retirement was conducted in perfect order as far as Roubaix, the Seventh and Fifteenth Light Dragoons covering the rear with great gallantry. At Roubaix the French, though in occupation of the suburbs, were not in possession of the little walled town, which was still held by a dismounted squadron of the Sixteenth Light Dragoons. The place consisted of a single long street, the direct continuation of which led to Wattrelos, while, just outside the eastern gate, the road to Lannoy turned sharply to the right, being bordered on one side by a deep ditch and on the other by the Espierres brook.

The defile through the town took necessarily much time, but the guns emerged safely and the Guards also. Next to the Guards were the Austrian Hussars, still in the street; then in rear of them a party of the Fifteenth; next to this party were the Sixteenth, who were formed up in the market-place; and in rear of all were the remainder of the Fifteenth, holding the pursuing French in check. All was still in order when a French gun posted on the Wattrelos branch of the street suddenly opened fire from the edge of the town, sending shot after shot among the Austrian Hussars. The ordeal would have been a severe one for any troops, and presently the Hussars dismounted and tried to find a way out among the houses, but in vain.

The trial became unendurable as the French pressed on and opened fire on all sides upon the horsemen thus pent in for slaughter; and at last the whole body remounted, galloped wildly down the road, swung round the corner, where the French infantry thrust vainly at them with their bayonets, and raced onward for three or four hundred yards, when the foremost troopers suddenly found the way blocked by horseless guns. The French had brought a second gun to enfilade the road to Lannoy, and the drivers of the British cannon had fled. The shock of this mass of galloping horsemen suddenly checked was appalling. In an instant the ground was strewn with men and horses, kicking and struggling in frantic confusion, while a number of bat-horses dashed into the ranks of the Guards, plunging and lashing out, with their loads turned under their bellies.

For a short time the disorder appears to have been beyond remedy, for a belt of wood surrounding the town gave excellent shelter to the French sharpshooters, who had a very easy target in the mass of struggling men and animals. Very soon, however, the Guards recovered themselves, and cleared a way for the cavalry to pass on beyond the wood to open ground. There the Light Dragoons rallied, the rear-guard was re-formed, and the retreat, always under heavy fire, was resumed towards Lannoy.

That village, which was enclosed by a low earthen rampart and a shallow ditch, had likewise been attacked early by one of Bonnaud's brigades from Lille, but had been defended with the greatest gallantry by two battalions of Hessians, who were apparently still in possession when the British troops approached it, though surrounded on the west side, and indeed nearly on all sides, by the French.

★★★★★★

The evidence upon this point is very conflicting. All the English accounts state that, when the British reached Lannoy on their retreat, the place was in possession of the French. Ditfurth, on the other hand (ii.), is very positive that it was held by the Hessians until 1 p.m., which, in his opinion, was long after the British would have reached it; and the evidence which he adduces is very strong. On the other hand, it is certain that the British would have been only too thankful to rally at Lannoy if they could, and that they were greatly disappointed to find themselves cut off from it. It is also to be noted that Ditfurth rakes up everything that he can to the discredit of the English, but was not at the pains to read a single English account of the action, except the Duke of York's letter as published in the *Gazette*, and that his account of their movements is consequently full of errors.

I incline to the opinion that the Hessians were still in Lannoy, but that the French around them were so numerous as to cut the British off from it in fact, that the French practically held it invested, with a covering force powerful enough to keep the British at a distance. The same was the case at Roubaix, which the Sixteenth Light Dragoons contrived to hold till Abercromby retreated, though the Austrians, the Duke of York, and Abercromby himself all believed it to be in the hands of the French. It still remains to be explained why the Hessians made no sign of their presence when Abercromby's column approached, for the British artillerymen actually began to lay their guns upon it in the assurance that it was in the enemy's hands.

✶✶✶✶✶✶

The British officers, however, could see no sign of a friendly garrison, and Colonel Congreve was actually wheeling his cannon round to open fire on the place, when there galloped up to them some blue-coated horsemen, who, being mistaken for Hessians, were allowed to approach without molestation, and succeeded in cutting the traces of some of the guns before they were discovered. The Guards then perceiving their retreat to be cut off, faced about against their pursuers, and, leaving the high road, made their way across country as best they could south-eastward to Marquain. The Hessians in Lannoy, either before or shortly after this, were forced to evacuate the village, and, finding the road to Leers blocked by the enemy, were likewise obliged to make their way across country in disorder, losing out of nine hundred officers and men some three hundred and thirty, of whom two hundred were cut off and captured in Lannoy itself.

Meanwhile the Duke of York, conspicuous by the star on his breast, had been hunted all over the country by the enemy's dragoons, and had escaped, as he frankly owned, only by the speed of his horse. On reaching Wattrelos he found it in the hands of the French, but passing beyond it under constant fire he found a gallant little party of Hessians still holding the bridge of the Espierres brook. These by a final attack with the bayonet gained a little respite for him, but were presently swept away from the bridge, and escaped only by fording the brook neck-deep. The duke, thinking apparently that the bridge was lost, or not knowing of its existence, spurred his horse into the brook; but the animal rearing up and refusing to enter the water, he dismounted, scrambled over on foot, and taking a horse from one of his *aide-de-camps*, at last succeeded in finding Otto.

About Leers and Nechin the fragments of Otto's force, together with some of the Duke of York's men, rallied upon the few battalions that held these places. The French did not press their advantage, and at half-past four the action came to an end. The loss of the Allies was about three thousand men killed, wounded, and missing, which was relatively slight, for, with proper management and conduct on the part of the French, not a man of the duke's and Otto's columns would have escaped alive. The brigade of Guards lost one hundred and ninety-six officers and men killed, wounded, and missing, the flank-companies being

126

the heaviest sufferers; while the Seventh, Fifteenth, and Sixteenth Light Dragoons, who by general admission behaved admirably, lost fifty-two men and ninety-two horses. The total loss of the British of all ranks was nine hundred and thirty, besides which nineteen out of their twenty-eight guns were captured.

It may be asked what the rest of the army was doing on this day, while these two columns, together less than one-third of the whole, were in process of annihilation. The answer is that, for some reason, it observed a conspiracy of inaction. Bussche sat still at Dottignies exchanging occasional shots with Jardon's brigade. Clerfaye crossed the Lys near Wervicq at seven o'clock in the morning, and turning eastward advanced between Bousbecque and Linselles, where he was met by Vandamme's brigade, which numbered eight thousand men against his sixteen thousand. He engaged the French, overthrew their right wing, took eight guns, and then sat still; until, being informed of the approach of more French troops about Bondues, he withdrew to the Lys, which he recrossed on the next day, and thence retreated northward.

The behaviour of Kinsky and of the Archduke Charles was still more extraordinary. Kinsky, on being asked by one of his officers for orders at six o'clock in the morning, replied that he was sick and no longer in command. The Archduke Charles received at five in the morning the order to move at once upon Lannoy, a distance of six miles, so that his troops might well have been upon the scene of action between eight and nine. He did not march till noon, though within sound of the guns, nor did he strike the road from Tournai to Lille until three, when he received orders to return to Tournai. The military renown justly earned later by the archduke forbids us to believe that this delay was due to ignorance; and the fact that, though the Duke of York had early informed the Emperor of his danger, not a word was sent to hasten the archduke or Kinsky, shows clearly that their torpidity was not unexpected nor disapproved at headquarters.

Jealousy of the Duke of York and of Mack are among the reasons assigned to account for the general paralysis of the Austrian commanders; but possibly the true reason was that Thugut was sick of the war in Belgium, and wished the English to sicken of it also. Why he should have chosen the slaughter of several hundred British and Austrians as the best means of forwarding his purpose, and how he persuaded Austrian officers to second him therein, are matters which only an Austrian can determine. For us it must suffice that the decisive battle of the campaign was lost by the deliberate design of the Imperial generals. Before long they were to learn that those who court defeat for dishonest ends may, when they least desire it, find defeat thrust upon them.

★★★★★★

There are few actions which I have found so difficult to describe as this of the 18th of May. I have drawn my account from Witzleben, iii.; Ditfurth, ii.; Jomini; *Narrative of an Officer,* ii.; Cannon's *Records of the Seventh and Fifteenth Hussars and Sixteenth Lancers*; Calvert's *Journal*; and Craig's letters to Nepean of 19th May 1794 (Record Office).

★★★★★★

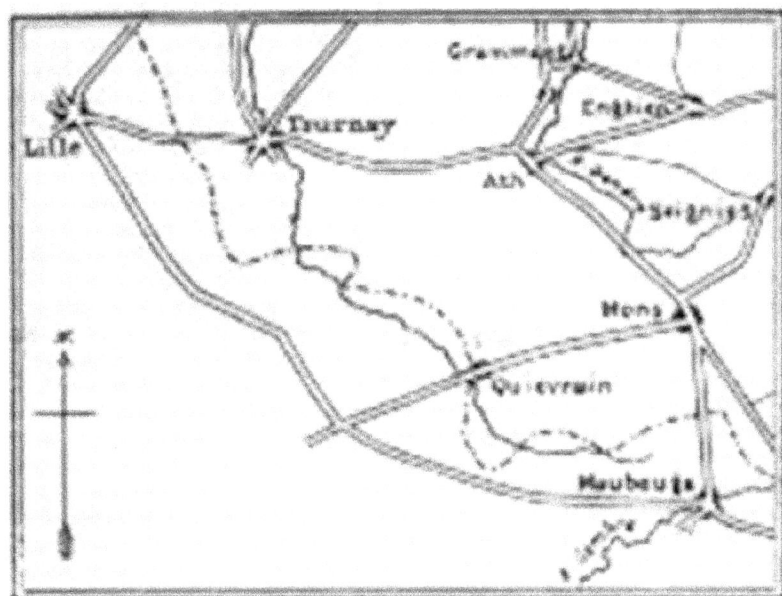

SCALE OF MILES

0   5   10   15

THE NORTH-EAST FRONTIER OF FRANCE IN 1794.

CHAPTER 5

A Parting of Ways

The entire army of the Allies, with the exception of Clerfaye's corps, was gathered into camp about Tournai in the course of the 19th May, 1794, , the emperor being received in silence when he rode into the town, while the Duke of York was loudly cheered by the inhabitants, (Calvert). The condition of the army was very far from satisfactory. The troops themselves, or at any rate the British, were not seriously shaken by the rout of the previous day; but the emperor and the Austrian commanders were much discouraged, and the animosity of the various nations towards each other was dangerously embittered. The British, above all, were furious against the Austrians for leaving them to be overwhelmed without so much as an attempt to assist them. Craig wrote to the War Office:

> It is impossible to bring the Austrians to act except in small corps. I lament that we should be destined as victims of their folly and ignorance. Do not be surprised at the word ignorance: I am every day more and more convinced that they have not an officer among them.

These were hard words, but they were true and just, though the Archduke Charles in later days redeemed himself from this reproach. However, for the moment the commanders laid aside their differences and agreed that the attack should be renewed, this time with united forces, upon Mouscron; and meanwhile Coburg dispersed the whole army in a semicircle around Tournai; the advanced posts running from Camphin on the south by Baisieux, Willems, Nechin, Leers, Estaimpuis, and St. Legers to Espierres, while the inner circle of entrenchments ran from the Scheldt on the north by Froyennes, Marquain, and Lamain to the suburb of St. Martin and the citadel of Tournai itself.

The French generals, as already narrated, made no effort to follow up their victory of the 18th, but awaited the return of Pichegru, who, on the news of the victory, hastened from the Sambre to turn it to account. On the 22nd, after a consultation with his officers, Pichegru decided to make a general attack upon Coburg's position, and directed that Souham with four brigades, (French brigades at this period were of the strength of divisions), numbering from thirty to forty thousand men, should assail it on the right or northern half of its front from Espierres to Leers, while Bonnaud's division should fall upon its left about Templeuve, and Osten's division should make a demonstration still further to the south about Baisieux.

On the following day, 23rd, between six and seven o'clock in the morning the action began; and after long and hard fighting the Allies were finally driven from three important points, namely, Blandain and the hill of La Croisette immediately adjacent to it, a little to the west of Tournai, and Pont-à-Chin upon the Scheldt, a little below the city.

To abandon to the enemy these posts, particularly Pont-à-Chin, which lay on the direct road from Courtrai to Tournai and commanded the navigation of the Scheldt, was impossible; and Coburg decided that they must be recovered at any cost. Throughout this long day's fighting the troops that had borne the brunt of the work on the 18th had been held in reserve; but at about six o'clock in the evening Fox's brigade of the British Line was called out to recover Pont-à-Chin, which had already been taken and retaken three or four times.

The brigade went into this action with fewer than six hundred men, having lost half of its numbers just four days before; but the three gallant regiments, though unsupported, carried the village unhesitatingly with the bayonet, and pressing on to the low heights to south of it swept everything before them, so far as their front extended, and captured seven guns. The day ended, after a severe struggle of fifteen hours, in the retreat of the French, with the loss of some six thousand men and seven guns; the fire, both of musketry and artillery, having been the heaviest ever remembered by the oldest soldiers present.

Both sides, however, fought for the most part in dispersed order, and inflicted, comparatively speaking, little damage upon each other. The one exception was Fox's brigade. Calvert wrote:

Had their order of attack been adopted by the Allies in general, the day would probably have ended in the ruin of the French.

But the losses of the brigade amounted to one hundred and twenty killed, wounded, and missing; and there are few troops that can be trusted, after losing half their numbers on Sunday, to storm a position held by a superior force and lose one-fifth of their remnant on Thursday. Some indeed claim that but for this handful of British soldiers the day would have been lost to the Allies, (Jones, *Campaign of 1794*, the author was a captain in the Fourteenth); but whether this be true or not, the 22nd of May should be a great anniversary for the Fourteenth, Thirty-Seventh, and Fifty-Third.

It was directly after this action that the course of events in Poland began to tell upon the councils of the Imperial Headquarters at Tournai. On the 23rd, Mack, disgusted by the failure of his elaborate plans, resigned his post as Chief of the Staff, and, having first expressed his opinion that the reconquest of Belgium was hopeless, retired for the time into private life. His successor, Waldeck, being a fellow-conspirator with Thugut, was still more eager for the evacuation of the Netherlands; and the emperor was easily tempted to share their views.

On the 24th a Council of War was held for form's sake, wherein the emperor set forth the situation in such a light as to gain a ready vote from his generals that further efforts in the Netherlands were useless. The Duke of York alone pleaded earnestly for a renewal of the attack upon Flanders; and, as fate ordained it, his representations were seconded by unexpected successes of the Allies on the Sambre and in the Palatinate. On the 24th Marshal Möllendorf and the Prussians surprised the French about Kaiserslautern and drove them back with a loss of three thousand men and twenty guns; and on the same day Count Kaunitz gained a still more important victory on the Sambre. The fact was that serious differences had arisen at Paris between Carnot on the one side and Robespierre and St. Just on the other, because Carnot insisted on keeping the direction of the military operations in his own hands. Robespierre, to whom the art of war was as incomprehensible as a Chinese manuscript, was furious with jealousy and rage.

"At the first reverse, Carnot's head shall fall," cried the despicable creature, galled by the cold contempt with which his inflexible colleague rebuffed his attempts at interference; and to re-establish civil influence at the seat of war, St. Just, Lebas, and five more commissioners set out on the 2nd of May for the army of the Sambre. There they introduced the system of terror in its worst forms, and with it, of course, confusion unspeakable. They fought with the Generals, they fought among themselves; and in the midst of this chaos St. Just took upon himself the supreme direction of the operations whereby the

Austrians were to be crushed. Four times he ordered the army to pass the Sambre, wasting the lives of his troops with indomitable imbecility. Finally he gave Kaunitz the opportunity for a counter-attack, in which, with inconsiderable loss to themselves, the Austrians routed the French completely, killing and wounding two thousand men, and capturing three thousand more, besides fifty pieces of cannon.

This heavy blow to the French right wing promised a great opportunity for the Allies to renew the offensive in Western Flanders; and the Duke of York urged this step upon his colleagues with all his might. The British Government too, reckoning that the troops, promised by Prussia in return for a British subsidy, must be nearly ready, decided to send out Lord Cornwallis to concert operations with Möllendorf, directing him also to consult the Emperor and the Duke of York on his way to the Prussian Headquarters.

But, as has already been told, King Frederick William was occupied rather with Poland than France at the moment; and he had also been much irritated by certain dispositions which had been proposed for his army by Mack in the middle of May.

"I am astonished at the fashion in which Mack thinks to make use of my troops," wrote the king.

"Does Mack imagine that we can live on air?" echoed Möllendorf, (Witzleben, iii.); both of them being secretly delighted at so good an excuse for remaining inactive. Then suddenly, on the 29th of May, the Allied Camp at Tournai was thrown into consternation by the announcement that the Emperor was about to return to Vienna. Aided by the defeat of the 18th, Thugut had succeeded in persuading his imperial master to abandon the Austrian Netherlands; and even Mack, the unpopular quartermaster-general, had supported him by recommending not only the evacuation of the country but the conclusion of peace with France.

The truth was that jealousy of Prussia had prevailed over all other considerations, and that the emperor had decided to offer help to the Empress Catherine in quelling the Polish insurrection. He hoped, however, at the same time to delude Prussia into keeping thirty thousand men upon the Rhine, and England into furnishing a subsidy for the ostensible prosecution of the war with France; and it was therefore imperative upon him to conceal his intentions. He accordingly gave out that the object of his departure was to hasten the recruiting of his forces; and in his final letter to Coburg, who very unwillingly retained the command, he gave him only vague instructions to adapt his action

MAP OF FLANDERS AND BRABANT

to the exigencies of the campaign and to save his troops as much as possible.

But this duplicity deceived no one, and the less because Waldeck, before he had succeeded Mack as Chief of the Staff, had openly declared that the war in Belgium must be ended. The Austrian troops were profoundly discouraged, and two-thirds of the officers asked permission to retire. They can hardly be blamed, for the succession of murderous actions fought by the Allies against the French on the northern frontier of France, between the 17th of April and the 22nd of May 1794, has few parallels in the history of war. For a month Austrians, British, and Germans had contended almost unceasingly against superior numbers, slaying or taking, not without heavy loss to themselves, French soldiers by the ten thousand, and capturing French cannon by the score.

Yet all had been to no purpose, partly because the leaders had deliberately chosen a foolish plan of operations, partly because they had steadily refused to follow up their successes, partly because on the 18th of May they had held two-thirds of the army inactive within sound of the guns which were overwhelming their comrades. The bravest men will not fight upon such terms. They will not be butchered to serve the intrigues of politicians whose dishonesty would disgrace a sergeant, and of potentates whose incapacity would disqualify a corporal. Austria paid dearly in Italy for the 29th of May 1794. (Sybel, iii. York to Dundas, 26th May 1794—with enclosures).

Immediately before the emperor's departure came news from Kaunitz that the French had again crossed the Sambre in force; which compelled Coburg to send him large reinforcements, and thus to weaken the right and centre of the Allies in order to strengthen their left. At the same time, for the sake of keeping the Dutch in good humour, Coburg was obliged to give the supreme command in that quarter to the Crown Prince of Orange, to the natural disgust of Kaunitz, who had shown much ability and achieved great successes. The great safe guard, however, to eastward was that St. Just insisted upon controlling the French operations; and it need not be said that against such an adversary the Prince of Orange was victorious.

But far more serious were the movements of the French on the western flank. Apprised of Coburg's detachment of troops to the Sambre, hoping still to further Carnot's projects for invasion of England, and above all conscious of the advantage offered to French tactics by the enclosed country of Western Flanders, Pichegru determined to prosecute his operations on that side. Accordingly, leaving between thirty and forty thousand men in positions about Mouscron and Menin to hold Coburg in check, he marched with about the same number on Ypres. On the 1st of June about fifteen thousand men surrounded the fortress on the west and south, and opened their first parallel; while some twenty thousand more under Souham took post under Passchendaele, about six miles to the north-east, to cover the siege from Clerfaye, who was lying at Thielt. On that same day, by a curious irony, Lord Howe defeated the Brest fleet, taking eight French ships and sinking two more. This action, in which the regiments on the fleet, and particularly the Sixty-Ninth, (Captain William Parker to the Admiralty, 3rd June 1794), played no inconspicuous part, closed for the present all Carnot's projects of an invasion.

This event, however, in no way disturbed the plans of Pichegru. On the 4th of June Clerfaye contrived to pass two battalions into Ypres to strengthen the garrison; but he declared himself unable, with the fifteen thousand men that remained to him, to relieve the place unless he were reinforced. By express command of the emperor, who had lingered at Brussels on his homeward journey, Coburg sent him some ten thousand men in two detachments, reckoning that, after the recent victory on the Sambre, he could safely draw a few troops from that quarter. Clerfaye, however, continued to display the sluggishness which had characterised his conduct from the beginning of the campaign.

On the 6th, before his reinforcements had reached him, he made a feeble advance against Souham in four columns, and was of course unsuccessful; and on the 10th, when his force had been raised to over twenty thousand men, he was assailed and defeated with loss by Souham before he could make up his mind to act. On that same day Coburg had designed to make a diversion in his favour, by an attack on Mouscron, upon a plan calculated so exactly to expose the Duke of York's column to destruction, as on the 18th of May, that the duke refused to accept it until it was altered.

This, however, was of small importance, for the French, having perfect information of the intended movements, appeared in every direction in such force that the enterprise was abandoned. The state of things at the Austrian headquarters was indeed almost beyond belief. Insensible to all ideas of duty and discipline, the young staff-officers, described by Craig as "in general the most contemptible of puppies," had talked openly of the projected movement in the coffee-houses at noon, though the Duke of York received no information of it until ten hours later, nor any orders until four o'clock on the next morning. Craig wrote:

> Mack used to keep these gentry in order, and, had he been here, the prison would have been full of them next day; but indeed it would never have happened.

Meanwhile Clerfaye remained so incurably supine that the Duke of York more than once entreated Coburg to entrust the relief of Ypres to himself, but in vain.

Roused by repeated orders to attack, Clerfaye at last, June 13th moved against Souham in five columns, gained some advantage at first, captured ten guns, and then as usual sat still, until Souham had gathered troops sufficient for a counter attack, when he immediately retired to his old position at Thielt.

This sealed the fate of Ypres, the key of maritime Flanders, the chief support of the right flank of the Allies, the bulwark which protected the British communications with Ostend. The Duke of York pleaded hard for a last effort to save it, by a march of the whole army to join Clerfaye; but without success. Craig wrote:

> The truth is that the Austrian army is incapable of further action. The men are disheartened and the officers disgusted and disunited.

It was finally decided that, to cover Ostend and the Dutch frontier, Clerfaye should take up a position between the Lys and the Scheldt about Deynse, some ten miles to the south-west of Ghent; keeping half of his force between Bruges and Ostend, and sending the Eighth Light Dragoons, Thirty-Eighth and Fifty-Fifth, which had formed part of his force, to Ostend. Craig wrote:

> We are too weak by ten thousand men to hold this defensive position, if the French see their chance and push Clerfaye, they will force us to abandon this position about Tournai and will pass the Scheldt in spite of us; and then ten to one we shall find ourselves separated from him and beaten in detail. . . . Sooner than hold the defensive position I would concentrate the whole army, eighty thousand men, march to the Sambre, attack them at any risk and march back again. . . . You may expect to hear from us soon in Holland.

Clearly there was one among the despised British officers who could have taught the Austrians a lesson. (Duke of York to Dundas, 10th, 13th, 14th June 1794. Craig to Nepean, 10th, 13th, 14th June 1794. Calvert).

The situation was indeed a desperate one. The Austrians, having taken no pains to restore the fortifications of Tournai, had thrown up an entrenched camp for its protection on the western side. These lines extended from the city southward along the Scheldt to Maulde, and required so many men for their defence that few could be spared for active operations. Some seven thousand Frenchmen at Mons-en-Pévèle kept the left of the Allies in continual alarm for the safety of Orchies, which was the key of Maulde and of the passage of the Scheldt at Mortagne; for if that passage were forced, the communication between Coburg and the army of the Sambre would be endangered.

A little to the north of Mons-en-Pévèle was the entire garrison of Lille, and still further to the north, between Lille and Menin, stood from twenty to thirty thousand more French troops. Behind this screen to westward, from fifty thousand to sixty thousand of the enemy were engaged as the besieging and covering armies at Ypres; and far beyond them to the north lay the right wing of the Allies under Clerfaye, stretched in a weak attenuated line from Ostend to the Lys, and only maintaining communication with Tournai by the circuitous route of the Scheldt. On the eastern flank the French had now some seventy-five thousand men on the Sambre, with a capable leader in Jourdan, albeit still hampered by the interference of St. Just; and this was the only quarter in which recent events had gone favourably for the Allies. Such a situation could not last long, and the strain upon Coburg must have been cruelly severe.

On the 16th, however, there came a gleam of hope. The French on that day again passed the Sambre and for the fifth time were driven back with heavy loss; and Coburg, having summoned four battalions from that quarter, determined on the 18th to march and join with Clerfaye in a final attempt to relieve Ypres.

The troops were already in motion, when in the evening the news came that the French had crossed the Sambre for the sixth time, and successfully invested Charleroi; whereupon the enterprise was abandoned. On the following day Ypres surrendered, and thus Carnot's original plan of turning both flanks of the Allies began, after two months of murderous fighting, to accomplish itself.

Enabled by the fall of Ypres to turn the whole of his attention to eastward, Coburg at once proposed that he should march with all the Austrian troops to Charleroi, and leave the Duke of York to guard the line of the Scheldt from Tournai to Condé. The duke answered that his instructions were to keep the whole of the troops in British pay together, but that, if ordered, he would gladly lead the whole of them with Coburg to the Sambre. Since, however, his force was absolutely inadequate to guard the line of the Scheldt, he insisted that, if it were left behind, an Austrian garrison should remain at Tournai, and that he himself should take up a position on the eastern bank of the Scheldt between that city and Oudenarde, so as to ensure his retreat in case of mishap.

The offer to march to the Sambre was fair, and it is difficult to understand why Coburg did not embrace it; for, if the battle on the Sambre were lost, it would obviously be impossible for the duke's troops to remain isolated in Flanders. Coburg did, however, reject it, and left behind him about five thousand Austrians under General Kray between Denain and Orchies, promising that, if he succeeded in forcing back the enemy on the Sambre, he would return without delay, but that, in the event of his failure, he should not expect the Duke of York to maintain his position on the Scheldt.

He also took the significant step of transferring the Austrian hospitals and stores at Valenciennes, as well as the magazines about Tournai, to Brussels and Antwerp; the removal of the stores at Brussels having begun some time before. (Duke of York to Dundas, 28th June 1794. Ditfurth, ii.).

Finally, on the 21st, he marched away; and the duke, since the corps in British pay had now shrunk to seven thousand men, contracted his quarters, and took up a new position closer to Tournai.

But meanwhile the news that Ostend was in danger had, as usual, stirred Dundas to unwonted exertion in England. He still made a fetish of the place, and his original intention seems to have been to defend it, without any particular reference to the Duke of York's operations. On the 17th of June, therefore, he ordered Lord Moira's force in the Isle of Wight and the Channel Islands to sail for Ostend at once, together with drafts of recruits and three fresh regiments from Ireland, making in all a reinforcement of about ten thousand men.

On the 20th Moira's troops embarked, and on the 21st the Eighth, the Forty-Fourth, and the recruits arrived at Ostend. The drafts, it must be remarked, arrived without arms or military appointments of any kind; and it was only a fog at sea that prevented a whole regiment, the Ninetieth, from being also landed there without either arms or clothing, Dundas having ordered it to embark without enquiry as to these details. (*Calvert, Life of Lord Lynedock*).

But Pichegru meanwhile did not remain idle, and leaving Ypres on the 20th marched upon Clerfaye's position at Deynse. The Austrian general, after a short defence of his entrenchments, retired, with the loss of not a few men and three guns, first to Ghent, and then beyond it, finally taking up a position on the north side of the canal that runs from Ghent to Sluys where he was presently joined by his detachments from Bruges, June 24.

On the 25th of June there arrived at Ostend, after a voyage of nineteen days from Cork, one squadron of the Fourteenth Light Dragoons and the Thirty-Third regiment, the latter under the command of an officer whose name it still bears, but who was then an impecunious younger son of five-and-twenty, possessed indeed of some skill in playing the violin, but still distinguished by no higher title than that of Colonel Arthur Wellesley. Finally on the morrow Moira with the last of the reinforcements, (3rd, 19th, 27th, 28th, 40th, 42nd, 54th, 57th, 59th, 63rd, 87th, 89th), also reached Ostend, where he found an advanced guard of the French within four miles of the town, a large force of several thousand men close behind it, and the *commandant* very wisely embarking his garrison with a view to retreat.

The whole district was in a state of panic; but Moira promptly landed the whole of his men, and having observed the difficulties of defending Ostend, and the military worthlessness of the place, quietly selected his fighting ground outside it. He wrote calmly to Dundas, 26th June 1794:

> I am not at all satisfied with my position, but since you appear to attach importance to the town I will do my best to maintain it.

He added cheerfully to Nepean same date:

> The defences are so detestable, that I shall go into the open field if we must come to blows. If you are to lose everything it does not signify if you are beaten into the bargain.

It is dangerous for a general, be he even so able as Moira, to address an English Minister of War in this strain; for, in the event of mishap, the words may be brought up as evidence against him in Parliament to prove that he was reckless, careless, neglectful, or despondent.

During these days the Duke of York remained in painful suspense at Tournai, until the news of Clerfaye's defeat on the 23rd warned him to move northward without delay. As Craig had perceived, the French by crossing the Scheldt at Oudenarde could prevent the Duke of York from joining Clerfaye, crush both armies in detail, and then, passing eastward, could annihilate Coburg.

The duke therefore called in Kray's Austrians for the defence of Tournai, June 24, and marched north-eastward on the right bank of the Scheldt to Renaix, where he learned that on the same day a French corps had summoned Oudenarde. On the morrow Pichegru crossed the Lys at Deynse with the main body of his army, and striking south from thence encamped on the 27th at Huysse, between four and five miles north of Oudenarde.

On that same night came a message from Coburg to the Duke of York that on the previous day, June 26, he had made his attack on the French about Charleroi and had failed. This was the Battle of Fleurus, which had been suddenly broken off by the Austrian commander before decisive advantage had been gained by either side; and it is still a question whether Coburg's action was dictated by the requirements of Thugut's policy or by his own military judgment.

However that may be, he retreated in good order upon Brussels, halting on the 27th in a position running from Soignies on the west through Braine L'Alleud to Gembloux on the east. This movement uncovered the Duke of York's left rear, and placed him in a most dangerous position. He had with him barely ten thousand men, nearly half of them cavalry, which in so close a country were of little service; and from the church-tower at Oudenarde he could see thirty thousand of the enemy in his front.

The French, by passing the Scheldt, could at any time cut off his retreat to the north, in which case his only line of safety lay eastward towards Grammont; and this in its turn would be closed if Coburg should continue his retrograde movement towards Namur, which was his first stage on the road to Vienna.

On the morning of the 28th the enemy appeared in force before Oudenarde, showing every sign of making the dreaded movement across the river; and the duke despatched orders to Moira to join Clerfaye immediately. For two days Pichegru continued his menaces on the Scheldt, and then suddenly on the evening of the 30th he retired, having received orders from Paris to occupy Nieuport, Ostend,

BATTLE OF FLEURUS

and the island of Walcheren in force, with a view to the invasion of England. Ostend, which, together with Nieuport, Henry Dundas had kept under his own orders, was evacuated in good time, while directions to that purport were still on their way from England.

Moira's instructions extended no further than to the defence of Ostend, but, in the critical circumstances of the case, he proposed to join his force to Clerfaye, and to act with him against the French left. Clerfaye at first welcomed the offer, but, on hearing of the misfortune of Fleurus, declared that he could make no engagement with him whatever. This was unpleasant for Moira, who had counted on the help of the Austrians in protecting the transport of his camp-equipage on the canal from Bruges to Ghent.

The situation was dangerous, for the French were in force at three different places within two hours' march of the canal, bent upon preventing his junction with Clerfaye. Without a moment's hesitation Moira sent his baggage northward to Sluys, and by a rapid march made his way to Ghent, just in time to anticipate a movement made by the French to intercept him. Thus a valuable reinforcement was secured to the Allies; and three more perilous days were passed without mishap, thanks rather to the Committee of Safety at Paris than to the Austrian commanders in the field. (Duke of York to Dundas, 28th June, 2nd July; Craig to Nepean, 27th June; Moira to Dundas, 28th and 29th June, 1st July 1794).

On the evening of the 30th the Duke of York rode over from Renaix to Braine L'Alleud to consult Coburg; and it was then agreed that Clerfaye's force should change places with the duke's, so as to bring the Austrian corps nearer to its own main army, and the British contingent nearer to the sea. At the actual conference both Coburg and the Archduke Charles declared that, having no orders from the Emperor to evacuate the Austrian Netherlands, they felt bound in honour to defend them, while Waldeck opposed even withdrawal from the line of the Scheldt. All this, however, was mere trifling, for two days later, July 2nd, Coburg wrote. that his right wing had been driven back from Soignies, and that the duke would do well to retire to a position appointed him between Brussels and Antwerp.

The fall of Mons on the 1st of July having also laid bare the duke's left flank and rear, he took the hint, and while protesting against the desertion of the country, gave his orders for retreat in the morning by way of Grammont and thence upon Alost. Tournai, through the courtesy of the French, was peaceably evacuated by the Austrians, though

Condé, Valenciennes, Landrecies, and Quesnoy were held. The line of the Scheldt was abandoned, and the Duke of York's troops withdrawn from every garrison except Nieuport.

As to this last the duke, as in duty bound, asked for Dundas's orders, July 2nd, saying that if the government wished to reconquer Flanders the place should be kept; otherwise the garrison, which included five hundred French emigrants, should not for pity's sake be exposed to the risk of capture.

Then followed a miserable tragedy. Dundas, apparently before the receipt of this letter, wrote on the 3rd of July to General Diepenbrock, the Commandant at Nieuport, promising to send transports for the embarkation of the garrison, if necessary, but adding that the government attached great importance to the retention of the place. Within two days the French had broken ground before the miserable little port, where the water was so shallow that ships could not come near the shore; and less than a fortnight later, July 16, the unfortunate garrison, which included a few British troops, was compelled to surrender. Thereupon the French massed the Emigrants in the ditch of the fort and played upon them with grape-shot until the whole of them were destroyed.

It was well known that this would inevitably be the fate of those unhappy men if they fell into the hands of the Republicans; and German authors have not hesitated to censure the Duke of York because, according to the current, though unjust, opinion, he neglected to order the evacuation of Nieuport while there was yet time. It were, indeed, devoutly to be wished that the duke had respected Dundas less, and had withdrawn the garrison without consulting him, though it is manifest that he would thereby have drawn upon himself the censure of the government. The blame, therefore, for this shameful business must remain with Dundas; and it was a very great misfortune for England that he was not called to account for it. (York to Dundas, 2nd and 3rd July; Dundas to Diepenbrock, 3rd and 7th July; Diepenbrock to Dundas, 5th July 1794).

Meanwhile the duke continued his retreat northward down the River Dendre, reaching Lombeek Ste. Catherine, about eight miles west of Brussels, on the 4th of July. On the morrow the leaders of the coalesced armies again met in conference at Waterloo, when it was decided that Clerfaye's force should pass eastward towards Brussels, and that the army of the Allies should ultimately occupy a line from Antwerp, by Louvain, Wavre, and Gembloux, to Namur, but that until the

Autrichiens.

Français.

Échelle

DE FLEURUS
Juin 1794

7th, at any rate, the line in advance of Brussels, extending from Alost by Braine-le-Comte and Nivelles to Sombref, should be maintained.

Ghent had already been evacuated; and accordingly on the next day Clerfaye's force began its march to join Coburg, while Moira moved to Alost and brought his troops for the first time under the duke's personal command. But Jourdan meanwhile was not inactive. On the 6th he attacked the whole line of the Austrians from Braine-le-Comte to Gembloux; and though beaten back after hard fighting on the east, where a concentrated attack might have given him possession of the Austrian line of communications, he succeeded in pushing Coburg's right wing back from Braine-le-Comte and Nivelles to Waterloo.

Thereupon Coburg warned the Duke of York that he must retire eastward and cancel the agreement made on the 5th. The duke answered with cold sarcasm that it was a new thing for the Austrians to retire before thirty thousand Frenchmen, and appealed to the Archduke Charles to keep Coburg to his engagements; but received from him only a sad reply that he must obey orders. On the 7th and 8th Jourdan renewed his attacks, directing the best of his strength against the Austrian left, which he forced back to the battlefield of Ramillies. He then immediately invested Namur; whereupon Coburg, fearing to be cut off from the Meuse, ordered the whole of his army to retire upon Tirlemont.

The duke meanwhile, since his left was uncovered by the retreat of the Austrians, withdrew, at Coburg's request, very slowly northward to Assche, and thence struck north-eastward to the Dyle, which he crossed at Malines, fixing his headquarters at Contich, some eight miles north of that city. A new line of defence was then taken up, which sufficiently showed the divided councils of the Allies. On the right the British contingent, now numbering some thirty thousand men, was posted on the Dyle from Antwerp to Malines.

On its left the Prince of Orange with the Dutch troops and from two to three thousand Austrians covered the line from Malines to Louvain; and from Louvain the rest of the Austrian army, between forty-five and fifty thousand men, was extended in a south-easterly direction by Tirlemont, Landen, and Waremme to the Meuse, with a detachment of four thousand more on the eastern bank of that river, and between it and the Ourthe.

Thus the British and Dutch, who desired to defend Holland, could be deserted at any moment which the Emperor should select for the pursuit of his own particular object, namely, to carry his army away to share the plunder of Poland. Craig, for his part, felt no doubt whatever that the British and Dutch would very soon be left to their own resources. (Coburg to York, 7th and 8th July; York to Coburg, 7th July; to Dundas, 7th and 10th July; Craig to Nepean, 11th July 1794).

The reader may have felt surprised that, with a force of nearly one hundred and fifty thousand men, the French should not have pressed the Allies harder, and made an end of them long before. The fact was that the Committee of Public Safety had interfered with the generals on the 4th of July, by an order that the recapture of Valenciennes, Condé, Landrecies, and Quesnoy should take precedence of any further operations; and accordingly the army in Belgium had been weakened to provide for this service.

This was the work of Robespierre, who at the time was inclined towards peace; and indeed peace appears to have been a common topic of conversation between the French and Austrian outposts from the beginning of July. (Sybel, iii.; Craig to Nepean, 4th July 1794). Thirty thousand French soldiers were accordingly withdrawn to Valenciennes, as many more were wasted in occupying ports of embarkation for England, and the remainder were ordered to push the Allies completely out of Belgium, and then to occupy a cordon from Antwerp to Namur.

Pichegru, therefore, took command in person of the left wing, and on the 12th moved with eighteen thousand men against Malines, while Jourdan on the right simultaneously advanced against Louvain, Jodoigne, and Huy on the Meuse. On the evening of the 12th Pichegru drove the Duke of York's advanced posts into Malines, where they were promptly reinforced; but the fortifications of the town were in ruins, and, on renewing the attack on the 15th, the French captured the place with little difficulty. The troops charged with the defence were Hessians and Dutch; and it appears certain that the conduct of one or the other of them was not irreproachable, though there are signs also that the duke himself was partly responsible for the mishap.

The duke then threw his left back along the line of the Nethe from Lierre to Duffel; but meanwhile Jourdan had on the same day mastered Louvain, and in the course of the two following days Jodoigne and Namur also. The Dutch troops about Louvain, upon the loss of that town, fell back northward across the Demer, while the Austrians retired eastward; and thus the line of the Allies was fairly broken by their own divergent plans. The Duke of York had already in these days concerted operations with the Prince of Orange for the recapture of Malines on the 18th, (York to Dundas, 15th, 19th, 20th, 23rd July 1794), when he received a letter from Coburg saying that, owing to the loss of that place and of Louvain, he had ordered the troops formerly stationed at the latter city to fall back to Diest, and was himself retreating from Tirlemont to Landen.

The duke begged him before doing so to essay a general forward movement, but received only a vague and unsatisfactory reply; and on the morning of the 20th a staff-officer, while inspecting the left of the Dutch position, discovered that the Austrians at Diest were already retreating south-eastward on Hasselt, Coburg having given them orders to this effect without saying a word of his intentions to the Duke of York.

With his left flank thus again laid bare, July 22nd, the duke was obliged to evacuate Antwerp and retire due north from it, July 24th, across the Dutch frontier to Rozendahl. Coburg likewise fell back to eastward, crossed the Meuse at Maastricht, and took up a position about seven miles south and east of that fortress at Fouron le Comte; and thus the British and Austrians were finally parted.

It cannot be said that either of them was sorry to take leave of the other. Even in 1793 their relations had not been too cordial, for the Austrians, in their jealousy, would never allow foreign troops to pass through their fortified towns, even during a forced march; and thus the British were frequently condemned to make long and fatiguing detours. (*Narrative of an Officer of the Guards,* ii.). But the betrayal of the Duke of York's column on the 18th of May, and the subsequent operations, deliberately contrived to hasten the evacuation of the Netherlands, converted the dislike of the British for the Austrians into the bitterest hatred and contempt.

At headquarters, again, the presence of a soldier such as Craig, with ideas far more enlightened than those of the Austrians, and with some means of insisting upon them through the medium of the Duke of York, can hardly have contributed to harmony. It may be added that the Austrian troops were as severe in their criticism of their chiefs, and particularly of Waldeck, as any of the British, proclaiming loudly that the abandonment of Belgium was due to French gold. (Craig to Nepean, 11th July 1794). In fact the Austrian Army, between heavy losses and deep distrust of its leaders, was utterly demoralised; nor is it surprising that this should have been so.

It seems more than probable that, if Coburg had wished to make a stand after the action of Fleurus, his men would not have stood by him. Of course Coburg had to bear the responsibility for all this, and to digest as best he might some very bitter reproaches from the Duke of York; yet it seems that in truth he was the person the least to blame. Though as a commander in the field he was slow, unenterprising, enamoured of vicious methods, and possessed of no military quality except that of looking carefully to the wants of his troops, yet he did not lack insight, sound sense, imperturbable calm, and the instinct of honesty and straightforwardness.

His name is forgotten in England, though his portrait is still occasionally to be found in English print-shops, showing that at one time he had gained a certain fame, which was destined speedily to perish, with his allies. It can only be said of him that he was beloved by his men, that he bore the sins of others without complaining, and that he was a faithful servant to an untrue master.

CHAPTER 6

The Road to Ruin

While the Allies in the Netherlands were thus giving way on all sides during the months of June and July, 1794, the British Government naturally bethought itself of the sixty thousand men which it had agreed to hire from Prussia for operations in that quarter. The ministers had reckoned that these troops would be ready by the end of May; and accordingly, as has been told, Lord Cornwallis was sent from England to arrange with Marshal Möllendorf as to the part to be taken by the Prussians in the campaign. Visiting the Duke of York on the way, Cornwallis agreed with him that the protection of West Flanders, and, if possible, the siege of Lille, were the matters of most urgent importance; and he formulated his request to Möllendorf accordingly. He soon discovered, June 20th, that he had been sent upon a fool's errand. Möllendorf, instead of sixty thousand, had but forty thousand men, deficient in stores and supplies, and absolutely wanting in transport, which he declared himself unable to furnish without ready money from England.

The real difficulty was that the Allies were all at variance as to the use that should be made of the Prussian troops. England wanted them to aid in recovering West Flanders. Holland would at first have preferred them to remain upon the Rhine, but presently yielded to the demands of England. The Emperor of Austria not only raised strong objections to the march of Prussian troops to Belgium, but claimed thirty thousand of the sixty thousand men for the protection of the Empire, declaring that their removal from the Rhine would expose all Germany to the ravages of the French. Between all these conflicting claims Möllendorf found little difficulty in sitting still and doing nothing, which was precisely what the advisers of King Frederick William most desired. By the 18th of June Cornwallis had made up his mind that little help was to be expected from Prussia, at any rate during the present campaign; and neither he nor Lord Malmesbury was slow to express very decided opinions as to the ill-faith of the Prussian Court. (Cornwallis to Dundas, 8th and 18th June 1794, *Cornwallis Correspondence*, ii.; *Malmesbury Correspondence*; *Dropmore Papers*, ii.).

This was the situation when the failure of the Austrian attack at Fleurus determined the Emperor to evacuate the Low Countries. That potentate thereupon reversed his language as to the Prussian contingent, and urged that Möllendorf should advance into Belgium; nor did he hesitate, on the 15th of July, to order Coburg still to defend the Austrian Netherlands, though he said nothing about sending reinforcements to enable him to do so. This despicable lying and trickery had, of course, but one object, that of drawing more money from England under false pretences. The English Government, however, though it had learned that no reliance was to be placed on Thugut's statements or promises, decided in the middle of July to send Lord Spencer and Thomas Grenville to Vienna, to urge once more the renewal of the offensive in Belgium.

So far, therefore, the emperor seemed likely to gain his point; and since the King of Prussia had shown remarkable weakness in dealing with the insurrection in Poland, he had every reason to hope that decisive action in that country would be delayed, until his own and the Russian armies could appear there in sufficient force to dictate the final settlement according to their own desires. The Prussian Ministers, on the other hand, when they learned of the despatch of Spencer and Grenville to Vienna, became nervous lest England should transfer the promised subsidy from her to Austria; and they began to turn their thoughts to the negotiation of a separate peace with France, (Sybel, iii.).

Meanwhile, through the energy of Carnot, reinforcements had been found for the French Army of the Rhine, which, after a fortnight's hard fighting on the heights about Kaiserslautern, forced Möllendorf to retire under the guns of Mainz with a loss of two thousand men and sixteen guns. The Austrian troops on the Rhine thereupon withdrew from the left bank of the river; and the miscarriage of a plan, concerted a fortnight later for recovery of the lost ground, set the generals of the two nations quarrelling more bitterly than ever.

The end of July brought yet another stroke of good luck to France in the overthrow of Robespierre and the execution of himself, St. Just, and other of his principal colleagues. Robespierre's latest achievement as a military administrator had been to decree that no quarter should be shown to British or Hanoverians in the field, an order which was disobeyed by the French troops and laughed at by the British. The supreme imbecility, apart from all other faults, of his rule had brought France to the last stage of exhaustion; and, indeed, if the Allies had succeeded in keeping the French armies out of Belgium, the latter must have perished of starvation, (Poisson, iv.). His death marked the close of the Terror and the beginning of a return to common sense in the matter of administration.

The man, however, had lived long enough to waste the energies of the armies of the North in the recovery of the four captured fortresses in the frontier, when they should have been scattering the Allies to the four winds; and thus it came about that the Duke of York enjoyed a few weeks' respite for the formation of new plans.

It was fortunate for him that it was so, for he now found himself in serious trouble with his army. This was the result of the insane system, allowed by Dundas, of raising men for rank. The regiments despatched to Holland contained only a very few old soldiers mixed with great numbers of recruits, who were utterly without training and discipline. Craig wrote:

Many of them do not know one end of a fire-lock from the other, and will never know it.

Six of the battalions had been deprived of their flank-companies, that is to say, of their best men, to make up General Grey's force in the West Indies; and no sooner did the new levies find themselves released from the crimping-house and the gaol for active service, than they fell to plundering in all directions. The duke was obliged to issue a very severe order on the 27th of July, (Ditfurth, iii.), to call the army to its senses; but with such officers as had been obtained under the new scheme, it was impossible to expect the slightest obedience. In the first place the army was lamentably deficient in brigadiers and generals of division. Moira had only accepted the command of his force on the condition that he should not serve in Flanders; and though, in view of the perilous condition of the Allies when he landed, he had waived his objections for the time, yet there was another obstacle not so easily to be overcome.

Albeit enjoying an independent command of eight thousand men, Moira was almost the junior major-general of the army. Major-General Crosbie, who was with him, also held a more important command than his seniors, such as Ralph Abercromby and David Dundas, the latter of whom joined the Duke of York at the end of July. Both Moira and Crosbie, therefore, went home, from delicacy towards the feelings of their superiors; and the loss of Moira was bitterly regretted as that of a very able officer who was idolised by his men.

The British troops now consisted of four brigades of cavalry and seven of infantry, (see list following), making altogether some twenty-five thousand men; but for all these there were, after the departure of Moira and Crosbie, only four generals David Dundas, Stewart, Abercromby, and Fox, the last of whom was fully employed as quartermaster-general.

Cavalry—
    David Dundas's Brigade—2nd, 6th D.G.; 2nd, 6th
    D. Ralph Dundas's Brigade—Blues; 3rd, 5th D.G.; 1st D.
    Laurie's Brigade—7th, 11th, 15th, 16th L.D.
    Vyse's Brigade—1st D.G.; 8th, 14th L.D.
Foreign Troops—
    Uhlans Brittaniques, Irving's Hussars, Choiseul's Hussars.
Infantry
    First Brigade—3rd, 88th, 63rd.
    Second Brigade 8th,★ 44th,★ 33rd.★
    Third Brigade 12th,★ 55th,★ 36th.
    Fourth Brigade 14th, 53rd, 37th.
    Fifth Brigade 19th, 54th, 42nd.
    Sixth Brigade 27th, 89th, 28th.
    Seventh Brigade 40th,★ 59th, 67th, 87th.
Foreign Troops
    Loyal Emigrants, York Rangers, Rohan's Regiment.

British Cavalry,	165 officers,	4,350	N.C.O.s & men.	
Hanoverians & Hessians	168 "	2,939	"	"
Total Cavalry	333 "	7,289	"	"
British Infantry,	583 "	21,170	"	"
Hanoverians & Hessians	322 "	8,722	"	"
Total	1,238 "	37,181	"	"

Total of all arms, including artillery, etc., say, 1300 officers,

40,000 N.C.Os. and men.

★ The flank companies of these battalions were in the West Indies.

This was the more serious because the commanders of the new battalions, who had been juggled into seniority by the Government and the army -brokers, were not fit to command a company, much less a brigade. Some of them were boys of twenty-one who knew nothing of their simplest duties. Though they went cheerfully into action, they looked upon the whole campaign as an elaborate picnic, for which they did not fail to provide themselves with abundance of comforts; and thus the baggage columns were filled with private waggons under the charge of insubordinate drivers.

The junior officers, who were so scarce that few regiments had as many subalterns as companies, appear in many cases to have been worse than the senior, as is always to be expected when commissions are to be obtained for the asking; and with bad examples before them they were not likely to improve. Thrust into the army to satisfy the claims of dependents, constituents, importunate creditors, and discarded concubines, many of these young men were at once a disgrace and an encumbrance to the force.

Hard drinking, which was the fashion then in all classes from highest to lowest, was, of course, sedulously cultivated by these aspirants to the rank of gentleman; and it was no uncommon thing for regiments to start on the march under charge of the adjutant and sergeant-major only, while the officers stayed behind, to come galloping up several hours later, full of wine, careless where they rode, careless of the confusion into which they threw the columns, careless of everything but the place appointed for the end of the march, if by chance they were sober enough to have remembered it. These evils, too, were extremely difficult to check, for in 1794, as in 1744, political interest rather than meritorious service was the road to promotion.

While the shameful traffic of the army-brokers and the raising of endless new regiments continued, every officer who could command money or interest was sure of obtaining advancement at home without the knowledge of his chief in the field, and had, therefore, not only no encouragement to do his duty, but an actual reason for avoiding it. Thus the men were very imperfectly disciplined; there were no efficient company officers to look after them; no efficient colonels to look after the company-officers; no generals to look after the colonels.

Craig sought a remedy in begging for more generals, he wrote, on the 5th of August:

We cannot get on without a good supply and a supply of good. The evil to the discipline of the army increases every day, and is likely to become very serious. (Craig to Nepean, 5th August 1794; Ditfurth, ii.; Memorandum of the Duke of York, 23rd December 1794; Calvert).

But the duke's difficulties did not end with the defects of his officers and men. It had lately become the practice in time of peace to issue to each regiment the materials for its clothing, to be made up by the regiment itself, a system which had probably been designed to retain for the colonels the largest possible profit. Nor must the colonels be blamed herein, for they were expected to make that profit, which in those days was practically the only emolument open to general officers. It was, of course, impossible for troops in the field to spend three or four months in making up their clothes; and the result was that the duke's army was left almost naked.

Moreover, in the hurry of raising innumerable new corps, the responsibility for such details as clothing, accounts, musters, and so forth had been overlooked; the new officers knew nothing of the extremely complex methods of military finance.

★★★★★★

No officer could hope to master these mysteries without the help of two fat little *duodecimo* volumes called *The Regimental Companion*, and a third and slighter volume entitled *Military Finance.*

★★★★★★

And the sudden vast increase of business thrown upon agents and officials was greater than they could immediately bear. Finally, quite apart from these failings in respect of the raiment of entire battalions, no effort whatever was made to clothe the recruits who were sent out to fill up the gaps in the various corps. These unfortunate men, on being drafted into the depots in England, received what was called slop-clothing, which signified a linen jacket and trousers; and it is an actual fact that many of them were sent on active service in this dress, without waistcoat, drawers, or stockings. The result was that the Duke of York's corps was in a worse state in respect of clothing than had been hitherto recorded of any British Army. (Craig to Nepean, 31st August; Craig's Memorandum of 23rd December 1794).

Another great difficulty, of which Craig had complained again and again, was the want of drivers for the artillery. Lord Moira had brought with him guns but no drivers; and there were but two captains (not enough, as Craig said, to do a fortieth part of the work) available for the superintendence of a huge mass of horses. Thus a new train of artillery, which had been sent out to replace the cannon lost at Turcoing, became a positive embarrassment. The Commissariat also, as used so often to happen with British armies, was in a very bad state. The men of the new corps of Royal Waggoners had been recruited in London, and were the worst refuse of the population. Craig wrote, in his usual pithy style:

> A greater set of scoundrels never disgraced an army, I believe it to be true that half of them, if not taken from the hulks, have at times visited them. . . . They have committed every species of villainy, and treat their horses badly.

But the very worst department of all was that of the hospitals, wherein the abuses were so terrible that men hardly liked to speak of them. In December 1793 the inhabitants of one of the English ports had been shocked by the arrival of one hundred invalid soldiers from Ostend in indescribable distress. They had been on board ship for a week in the bitter wintry weather, without so much as straw to lie upon. Some of them were dead; others died on being carried ashore. No provision had been made for their comfort on landing, and but for the compassion of the gentry, who subscribed money for their relief, the poor fellows might well have perished, (*Sunday Reformer*, 29th December 1793).

Nothing was done to amend this state of things. Dundas's idea of putting an army in the field was to land raw men on a foreign shore, and to expect discipline, arms, ammunition, clothing, victuals, medical stores, and medical treatment to descend on them from Heaven. Some kind of a medical staff was improvised out of drunken apothecaries, broken-down practitioners, and rogues of every description, who were provided under some cheap contract; the charges of respectable members of the medical profession being deemed exorbitant. Craig wrote:

> The dreadful mismanagement of the hospital is beyond description, and the remedy beyond my power. Every branch and every fibre of every branch draws a contrary way. I really doubt if there will be any way to get any good from this department

but by tying them all together and sending them to you to be changed for a new set. (Craig to Nepean, 12th and 31st August, 5th and 8th September 1794. The class of medical officer obtained by Government is described in Autobiography of Sir J. M'Grigor).

Such was the composition of the force with which the Duke of York now undertook, in concert with the Dutch, to protect Holland, or, in other words, to conduct that most delicate and trying of operations—manoeuvring with inferior numbers over a wide front to hold a superior force in check. The first difficulty arose with the Dutch, for the Prince of Orange, apparently enamoured of the Austrian methods, was for scattering the troops over a multitude of different points; but this the duke, with Craig at his back, steadily refused to do. The prince then urged that the Dutch fortresses should be garrisoned by British troops; but the said fortresses were all in bad condition, and were repairing only with that incredible slowness which was peculiar to the Dutch Government.

The duke, therefore, refused this also; feeling tolerably sure that, if he consented, his battalions would be sacrificed piecemeal for the defence of Holland, while the Dutch looked on without raising a man to help them. The two gates of Holland on the south were Bergen-op-Zoom and Breda, and on the east Grave and Nimeguen, with the fortress of Bois-le-Duc midway between Breda and Nimeguen. The two eastern gates were safe so long as the Austrians retained Maastricht and their position on the Meuse; but the Austrians were not to be trusted. Accordingly, the Duke resolved to garrison Breda, Bergen-op-Zoom, and, if possible, Bois-le-Duc with Dutch troops; and himself to take up a position on the north bank of the River Aa, with his right resting on Bois-le-Duc and his left on the great morass called the Peel. From this central point he judged that he could move to the help of any of the Dutch fortresses to southward, cover the province of Gelderland, and keep Grave and Nimeguen within reach in case of mishap on that side.

He was about to move thither from Rozendahl when the news came that Moreau, who was advancing northward along the coast after the capture of Nieuport, had driven back the Dutch posts and had besieged Sluys. The Prince of Orange thereupon besought the duke to stand fast, producing a letter from Coburg which contained not only an assurance of his ability to hold the passage of the Meuse, but even a hint of possible offensive movements. After some hesitation the duke consented to a compromise by moving to Osterhout, a little to the north-east of Breda, so as to give some countenance both to Breda and Bergen-op-Zoom. He marched, accordingly, on the 31st of July, unmolested by the enemy, who were in force around Antwerp; and the Prince of Orange then came to the wise but rather belated conclusion to evacuate all the Dutch fortresses to the south of the Scheldt. The duke, therefore, lent him a strong detachment of his men, Aug. 8th, to hold the communications between Breda and Bergen-op-Zoom, so as to release Dutch troops to cover the retreat of these garrisons and to relieve Sluys. (York to Dundas, 25th, 27th, 30th July, 1st and 6th August; Craig to Nepean, 25th July 1794).

Just at this moment Henry Dundas, hearing of Moreau's advance, and having by chance a few troops unemployed, decided to send a naval armament to Flushing, together with five battalions under Lord Mulgrave for the defence of the Dutch territories in that quarter. As was his rule in such cases, Dundas kept Mulgrave under his own immediate command, but withal instructed him not to go against any order of the Duke of York,—an arrangement admirably calculated to paralyse the force and to raise discord between the commanders. Mulgrave, who had started apart from his troops, reached Flushing on the 17th, and finding that none of them had arrived, occupied himself in examining the situation.

He soon satisfied himself that the French had no further designs for the campaign than to take Sluys and Flushing, as ports from which to ship the harvest of the Austrian Netherlands to France. Meanwhile, the Dutch no sooner heard of his coming than they suspended their operations for the relief of Sluys, in the hope that Mulgrave would do the work for them; and the French, having also full intelligence of everything, increased their force at Sluys to twenty-five thousand men, which made the relief practically impossible. Dundas, meanwhile, wrote with the greatest confidence of the success of that operation, which his own interference had condemned to failure; announcing also that Mulgrave's force, which had not yet even arrived at Flushing, would be required elsewhere in a month.

At length the five battalions sailed into Flushing on the 26th, nominally thirty-two hundred strong, and actually with the following qualifications for immediate service in the field. The Thirty-First was composed chiefly of recruits, of whom two hundred and forty were unarmed, (its flank-companies, and those of the 34th, were detained for the West Indies). The Seventy-Ninth had but one officer to each company, and but eight rounds of ball-ammunition a man. The Eighty-Fourth had twenty rounds a man, but, the regiment having never ceased marching from quarter to quarter ever since it had been raised, the men were wholly untrained. The Eighty-Fifth had thirty rounds a man, but half of the soldiers had never had arms in their hands.

The Thirty-Fourth alone appears to have been fit and ready for work. Fortunately there was no work for them to do, for Sluys surrendered on the very day of their arrival; and Mulgrave, after landing them at Flushing to learn the elements of their business, suggested that at least two of the battalions had better remain there and be made into soldiers, instead of sailing to certain annihilation in the West Indies. To this Dundas agreed, for he purposed to take from the Duke of York ten of Moira's battalions, and was well content to leave him inferior troops in their place. Meanwhile, as a specimen of utter imbecility, this despatch of Mulgrave's detachment has few equals even in English military annals. The mere promise of help was sufficient to relax the exertions of the Dutch. The troops were embarked so late as to miss the object of the expedition, and, even if they had been embarked in time, they were of quality too poor to have accomplished it. In brief, the whole enterprise bears the unmistakable mark of Henry Dundas. (Dundas to Mulgrave, 7th and 13th August; Mulgrave to Dundas, 17th, 19th, 26th, 30th August, 3rd September; Dundas to York, 22nd August 1794).

Meanwhile Spencer and Grenville had throughout August pursued their negotiations at Vienna with very indifferent success. One point Thugut was ready to concede, namely, the recall of Coburg, who indeed resigned on the 9th of August, being worn down in body and mind, and utterly disgusted with his command. But Thugut absolutely refused to order troops from the Rhine to Belgium, and demanded the guarantee of a loan of three millions for the present campaign besides a new subsidy for the next. It was necessary to refer these pretensions to the Cabinet in London; and long before the reference had even been made, the Austrian Council of War ordered Clerfaye, who was to succeed Coburg, to devote all his efforts to the defence not of Belgium but of Luxemburg, Mainz, and Mannheim.

But though the Allies were idle, the French were not; and, thanks in part to a threat of the Committee of Public Safety to massacre the garrisons unless the fortresses were delivered, they had recovered both

Quesnoy and Landrecies by the 15th of August. The fall of Sluys, and the recall of the troops detached to Walcheren also enabled Pichegru to begin a forward movement, and on the 27th he advanced from Antwerp north-eastward to Hoogstraeten, driving in all the Dutch posts, and seeming to threaten the turning of the Duke of York's left. The duke, thereupon, on the advice of a Council of War, retired on the 30th to his chosen position between Bois-le-Duc and the Peel, while Pichegru sent a strong detachment eastward to occupy Einhoven in force.

Meanwhile a message had reached the Duke of York from Clerfaye, suggesting a general forward movement to save the beleaguered cities of Valenciennes and Condé; and on the 1st of September a conference was held between the Allied commanders at Bois-le-Duc to consider the proposal. It was not yet known to them, apparently, that Valenciennes had already surrendered to the French on the 29th of August, and that Condé was at the last gasp; and there was some talk among them of an advance of the British to recapture Antwerp, while the Austrians on the Meuse protected their rear.

The news that both fortresses had fallen, and that the French forces thus liberated for the field were hastening to the front, naturally disturbed this plan; and though the duke was anxious still to make the attempt, Craig perceived little hope of success, chiefly because he could not trust the Austrians to give hearty co-operation. In truth, the Allies had let slip the favourable moment through their own dissensions, and the opportunity was not to recur again. On the 4th of September Pichegru marched northward from Hoogstraeten to Meerle, as if to threaten Breda, but on the 10th turned eastward, after leaving a detachment before that place, and on the 12th reached Oosterwyk.

On the following day he attacked the duke's advanced posts at Bokstel, and on the 14th captured them, making two battalions of Darmstadt-Hessians prisoners. This was an unpleasant mishap, for these troops had hitherto always behaved admirably; and, while they complained of the duke for not supporting them, the duke in his secret report declared them to have been panic-stricken. Alive, however, to the importance of regaining this post and the line of the Dommel, the duke ordered Abercromby forward next day with ten battalions and as many squadrons of British, to recover the lost ground.

The movement was very nearly disastrous, for Abercromby only just missed falling into the midst of Pichegru's main army, which was on march to the eastward; but quickly apprehending the situation, he

162

withdrew his troops in excellent order with the loss of about ninety men, two-thirds of them prisoners. This skirmish is notable both because it brought Colonel Arthur Wellesley of the Thirty-Third under fire for the first time, and because it led to the trial of four officers, three of them belonging to a most distinguished regiment, for cowardice. This was a healthy sign, for it showed that the older officers were bent on ridding the Army at the earliest possible moment of the worthless comrades imposed on them by Dundas. (Craig to Dundas, 19th September 1794).

On the same day the duke received information that this demonstration against Bokstel was but a feint, the main force of the enemy, reported to be eighty thousand men, being in motion to turn his left. His intelligence seems to have been extremely vague and imperfect at this time; but being dissatisfied with his position, to which, owing to dry weather, neither the Peel nor the Aa afforded adequate protection, he decided that the retention of it was not worth the risk of being cut off from his retreat to the Maas. He therefore retired on the next day to that river, crossed it at Grave and took up a position on the north bank, with his headquarters at Wychen, a few miles to the north of Grave.

It then remained for him to make his dispositions to defend the line of the river, the unprotected portion of which extended for some seventy-five miles from Fort Loevestein, at the western end of the Bommeler Waert on to the west, to Venloo on the east.

★★★★★★

The Bommeler Waert is the triangular tongue of land enclosed between the Waal and the Meuse immediately to the east of Gorkum. It is very nearly an island, the entrance to it from the east being very narrow and defended by a fort, then, as now, called Fort St. Andries.

★★★★★★

This with the forces at his disposal was impossible, and he therefore arranged that all troops in British pay should be sent to him from West Flanders, and that the Dutch, who were sitting inactive behind their fortresses, should send troops to repair and to defend Crevecoeur and Bommel.

The duke's next effort was to concert offensive operations with Clerfaye, who lay on his left; and he had the greater hopes of a favourable issue, since the new Secretary at War, William Windham, was already on his way to that officer on a mission from London. But the

Austrian commander also had been unfortunate. On the 17th and 18th General Latour's corps of seven thousand men, which guarded his left on the Ourthe, was driven back by a greatly superior force of Jourdan's right wing under General Scherer; whereupon Clerfaye, who had watched the whole process without moving a man of his forty thousand to save Latour, immediately retired behind the Roer, leaving eight thousand men as a garrison for Maastricht.

The Austrian general therefore rejected all idea of the offensive as impossible, but consented to maintain communication with the duke if he would extend his left to Venloo, which, like all the Dutch fortresses, was in miserable repair and without a sufficient garrison. The duke consented, and so the matter was arranged; Clerfaye, however, giving the duke clearly to understand that if his right was turned he would cross the Rhine. (York to Dundas, 19th, 21st, 22nd September (enclosing correspondence with Clerfaye); Craig to Dundas, 19th September 1794).

The duke thereupon made his arrangements for protecting a line of from seventy-five to ninety-five miles of river with a force of thirty thousand of all ranks, the sick list having by this time claimed close upon seven thousand men of his army. His right from the Bommeler Waert to Grave was held by about five thousand Hessians, their main body being stationed at Alfen, a little to the east of the island; Grave was held by two Dutch battalions; east of Grave four brigades of infantry and two of cavalry lay about Mook; Abercromby, with two more brigades of infantry and one of cavalry, stood higher up the river at Gennep; and six thousand Hanoverians under Walmoden prolonged the line from Gennep to Venloo, with their main body at Well.

Craig, however, did not deceive himself as to the inevitable issue, being firmly convinced that there was an understanding between the Austrians and French; wherein he appears to have been correct, Craig to Nepean, 20th September 1794. Sybel, iii.)

★★★★★★

Note. From this it appears that all documentary evidence of the agreement has been carefully destroyed, but that there is a hint of secret negotiations actually proceeding on the 18th of September 1794.

★★★★★★

He wrote:

We shall have to fall back behind the Waal depend on it, this will happen in a few days . . . and in a fortnight the Austrians will be behind the Rhine.

Jourdan followed up the Austrians, leaving Kléber to invest Maestricht; whereupon Clerfaye, who had sixty thousand men behind the Roer, forthwith called loudly on the Duke of York to relieve that fortress. Grenville at the Foreign Office, anticipating something of the kind, had already despatched urgent representations to Vienna requiring the concurrence of the Austrians in this operation, but of course to no purpose. The duke, by advice of Abercromby and Walmoden, sent Craig to stir up Clerfaye and, that the Austrians might have no pretext for complaint, moved sixteen thousand men at great risk towards Venloo. But all was perfectly useless, for Clerfaye declined to move. An attack of the French on his position on the 2nd of October gave him the excuse that he wanted; and he immediately retreated across the Rhine. (York to Dundas, 25th and 29th September, 1st and 3rd October; Craig to Nepean, 1st October; Grenville to York, 25th September 1794).

Pichegru meanwhile had, on the 22nd of September, completely invested Bois-le-Duc, and sent two divisions forward to line the Maas over against the Duke of York's position. His army was now in the greatest distress from want of provisions, which had to be brought from Antwerp in waggons, and that by long detours in order to circumvent the Dutch fortresses. It was, therefore, imperative for him to possess Bois-le-Duc as an advanced base; and the place was the more difficult for him to master since he had no siege-artillery. Unfortunately the cowardice of the Dutch yielded to him all that he wanted. On the 24th he opened a feeble bombardment with his field-pieces upon Fort Crevecoeur, which guarded the passage into the Isle of Bommel from the south; and on the 28th, the place, though amply provisioned and in a good state of defence, was yielded up by the Dutch *commandant*.

Thereby Pichegru gained not only forty-two heavy guns, but the command of the sluices whereby the inundation of Bois-le-Duc could be let flow or drawn off. The loss of Crevecoeur did not improve the good feeling of the British towards the Dutch, who, from the first entry of the Duke of York into their country, had showed the bitterest animosity against his men. Intelligence now reached the duke, Sept. 30th that a general insurrection of the French party in the United Provinces was imminent; and three days later the retreat of Clerfaye compelled him to retire northward across the Waal, over which he had already thrown a bridge of boats.

The movement was conducted with some confusion owing to the mismanagement of the duke's staff; but Pichegru suffered the Allies to shuffle themselves without the slightest molestation into their appointed positions. The Hessians held the Bommeler Waert on the south bank of the Waal, and the line of the Linge over against it on the north bank. At the village of Geldermalsen on the Linge the right of the British joined the left of the Hessians, extending from thence eastward along the Waal to the road from Nimeguen to Arnheim; where the Hanoverians carried the line to its end at the parting of the Waal and the Leek, maintaining communication with Clerfaye's Austrians at Emmerick. Nimeguen, though ill-fortified and provided for, was also held on the southern bank of the Waal.

By this time even the long-suffering Cabinet in England was growing weary of paying subsidies to Austria and Prussia for service which they never rendered. On the 4th of October Dundas advised the Duke of York that the government had resolved to give them no more money, and ordered him to cut off the allowance hitherto paid to Clerfaye unless he agreed to active concert of operations. Thugut, however, had in many respects gained his point.

The British Government, thinking that a bad ally was better than none, had consented on the 14th of September to guarantee to Austria a loan of three millions in consideration of her services during the first campaign; at the same time renouncing a project which had been put forward for placing Clerfaye's force, together with the Duke of York's, under the supreme command of Cornwallis. Thugut was jubilant; for everything was going as he wished. In Poland, Suworrof was rapidly repressing the insurrection, against which the Prussian generals had shown the greatest feebleness; Belgium was already abandoned, as he had desired; and the Cabinet of London had rewarded Austria for her treachery by financial assistance. In the circumstances he could not do less than give promises of effectual help in the defence of Holland, though of course without the slightest intention to fulfil them.

Meanwhile the behaviour of the Dutch grew more and more suspicious. Bois-le-Duc was disgracefully surrendered on the 10th of October by the *commandant*; and a regiment of French Emigrants, which formed part of the garrison, having been denied permission to cut its way through the besiegers, was massacred in cold blood. On the same day, by a curious coincidence, the British Government warned the Dutch that, unless they exerted themselves, the British army should be withdrawn; at the same time proposing to put the Duke of Brunswick in command of the British and Dutch forces in order to keep them together.

Then a week later, Oct. 18th, as if to bribe the *stadtholder* to compliance, Dundas authorised the payment of one hundred thousand pounds to the Dutch, which was simply so much money wasted; for the Prince of Orange would do nothing for the defence of the country, and wished to employ the British for the repression of his own rebellious subjects. How, in the face of the Duke of York's letters, the British Ministers in London hesitated to order the immediate withdrawal of the army is incomprehensible, except on the supposition that it still trusted to the proved ill faith of the Emperor Francis. (Dundas to York, 10th, 12th, 16th, 18th October; York to Dundas, 16th, 18th, 23rd October 1794).

The French, meanwhile, continued to follow up their advantages. Jourdan, on the east, after leaving detachments to besiege Venloo and Maastricht, had occupied Cologne on the 6th of October, and drawn up his army in face of Clerfaye's main body, which was extended along the Rhine from Duisburg to Bonn and beyond. Moreau, who had taken over the command owing to Pichegru's illness, also pushed forward seven thousand men in front of Grave, posted thirty thousand between Ravestein (a little to west of Grave) and Bois-le-Duc, and ten thousand men opposite the Bommeler Waert.

On the 18th he began to lay a bridge of boats over the Meuse at Alfen, and, being allowed by scandalous carelessness on the part of the Allies to complete it, passed a considerable force over the river. On the 19th he attacked the posts at Apeltern and Druten, to east and northeast of Alfen, carried them after a very obstinate resistance from the Thirty-Seventh and Rohan's Emigrants, and succeeded in capturing the greater number of the Thirty-Seventh, who had mistaken a party of French Hussars for the Emigrant cavalry in the British service.

★★★★★★

Craig explained that this was owing chiefly to the inexperience of a young colonel. Thus the army-brokers had contrived to lift children to the command even of regiments that had been eighteen months on active service.

★★★★★★

At the same time intelligence came that a strong French detachment had passed the Meuse between Roermond and Venloo, and was heading for Cleve, thus threatening to turn the duke's left. Accordingly, in his public despatch, the duke announced that he was about to draw the whole army to the north of the Waal; but privately he reported that he could not do so, since the Dutch, in spite of many promises, had made no effort to put Nimeguen in a state of defence. On the 20th the French threw a permanent bridge across the Meuse a little to the north-west of Ravestein at Batenburg, and two days later began a new series of attacks upon the advanced posts, at the same time making demonstrations about St. Andries on the Bommeler Waert. By the 27th the troops round Nimeguen had been driven into the outskirts of the town, and the duke, who had transferred his headquarters to Arnheim, called all of them except fourteen battalions to the north bank of the Waal. The French main body then took up a position between Grave and Nimeguen, threatening to seize the two eastern keys of Holland.

At this critical moment Clerfaye paid a visit, Oct. 28th, to the duke at Arnheim, and promised that by the 3rd of November a corps of some seven thousand Austrians under General Werneck should arrive to assist in an offensive movement from Nimeguen. At the same time some effort was made to persuade Möllendorf to move to the Rhine about Bonn, and to support Clerfaye's left. But the British Government had recently, though none too soon, cut off the subsidy to the Prussians; and Möllendorf's answer was that his orders were to send twenty thousand of his men to South Prussia and fifteen thousand men to Westphalia, so that evidently nothing was to be expected from that quarter.

On the 1st of November the French broke ground before Nimeguen, and on the same day Werneck announced that his corps could not arrive before the 7th. Meanwhile the French erected batteries a little above Nimeguen at Ooi, which, though silenced for a time by the guns of the Allies on the opposite bank, so greatly damaged the bridge of boats that General Walmoden, who was in command, thought it prudent to withdraw the greater part of the garrison to the northern bank.

On the 4th, however, he made a sortie with the troops that remained, including six British battalions, supported by seventeen squadrons of British and Hanoverian cavalry.

★★★★★★

The troops engaged were the 15th Light Dragoons, 8th, 27th, 28th, 55th, 63rd, 78th. The last-named regiment, together with

168

the 80th, had arrived at Flushing at the end of September, when Dundas intended to withdraw some of the older regiments for service in the West Indies.

★★★★★★

The British, advancing under a very heavy fire, swept the enemy out of their trenches without drawing a trigger, and the cavalry pursuing the fugitives inflicted on them heavy loss. The casualties of the Allies in this affair were over three hundred killed and wounded; but though the sortie checked the progress of the French for the time, yet by the 7th they had not only repaired the batteries destroyed by the Allies, but had erected another which brought a cross fire to bear on the bridge of boats. Moreover, a letter arrived from Werneck that his arrival at Nimeguen, which he had fixed for the 7th, would be impossible until the 16th—a message which the duke rightly interpreted to signify that, he would not come at all.

On the night of the 7th, therefore, the bridge was repaired sufficiently to enable the garrison to evacuate the place, and the troops filed across the river. Two Dutch battalions were the last to leave the place under the Dutch General Haak, who, most improperly, was the first man of his nation to set foot on the bridge. As he did so, a shot struck one of the pontoons with some effect, whereupon he immediately ran across the bridge crying out that all was lost, and reported with shameless mendacity that all of his troops had passed over except the rear-guard. Upon this the pontoon-bridge was immediately fired, since a flying bridge had already been prepared for the passage of the rear-guard.

As luck would have it, however, a shot from the French batteries cut the hawser; the flying bridge began to swing round; and, to save it from running foul of the kindled boats, the sailors dropped the anchor and so brought it up. When the burning pontoons had floated away, some British seamen, who were employed on the bridge, were for cutting it adrift, but the Dutchmen would not allow them to do so, preferring certain capture to the risk of a few cannon-shot. Thus eleven hundred of them were taken, through either their own cowardice or that of Haak—a lamentable occurrence in an army which in the past had approved itself to be of incomparable steadfastness and valour. (York to Dundas, 7th and 11th November; Craig to Nepean, 10th November 1794).

The duke, therefore, now held the line of the Waal including the Bommeler Waert, and might well hope to hold it, if the Dutch did their duty, until the army went into winter quarters. He had already put most of his cavalry into cantonments across the Yssel, but the Dutch threw every obstacle in the way of providing for the comfort of the troops. The weather too grew cold, and the men, miserably clothed and housed in open barns, began to fall down very fast from cold and typhus fever.

None of them had greatcoats except some of the Guards, Fourteenth, Thirty-Seventh, and Fifty-Third, who had received those which had been provided by public subscription in 1793, and which were now worn out. Flannel waistcoats had been supplied to the rest by their officers, who had subscribed over a thousand pounds for the purpose; and it appears that, without exaggeration, they had little other clothing. Sheer nakedness, in fact, had been the cause of much, though not of all, of the plundering that had disgraced the army; and this evil had been aggravated by the bitter hostility of the inhabitants towards the British.

Not content with resenting real outrages, which were far too abundant, they never ceased flying to the duke with frivolous and groundless complaints; and so disobliging were the authorities that Lord St. Helens, Ambassador at the Hague, tried for two months in vain to find places where the British might be allowed to establish additional hospitals. On the 27th of November the infantry in British pay numbered twenty-one thousand and the sick nearly eleven thousand; and when a man was ordered to hospital his comrades would exclaim, "Ah, poor fellow, we shall see thee no more, for thou art under orders for the shambles."

On one occasion five hundred invalids were embarked from Arnheim in barges under charge of a single surgeon's mate, without sufficient provisions, without even sufficient straw, and brought to Rhenen, where they were left on board for want of sufficient space to admit them to the hospital. A Dutch gentleman counted at one time the bodies of forty-two men who had thus perished of neglect in the barges and had been thrown out dead on to the bank.

Meanwhile the rascals who bore the name of surgeon's mates charged forty thousand pounds for wine for the sick, and, not content with robbing the State by drinking it themselves, actually plundered the helpless patients committed to their care. Such was the economy of Dundas's military administration—to obtain recruits by the offer of lavish bounties, to break down their health by giving them insufficient clothing, and to contract with scoundrels so to maltreat them, medically, that they should not recover. (*Narrative of an Officer of the Guards*, ii.; York to Dundas, 27th November 1794; Harcourt to York, 15th December 1794).

Fortunately for himself the Duke of York was summoned home on the 27th of November to hold personal communication, with ministers; and indeed it seemed as if the campaign were ended.

★★★★★★

Ditfurth, who never loses an opportunity of abusing the English, of course puts a discreditable construction upon the duke's departure, not knowing that he was sent for by ministers (ii.).

★★★★★★

Upon his departure he placed the British troops under Lieutenant-General Harcourt, and the foreign troops in British pay under Lieutenant-General Walmoden, apparently dividing the supreme command between the two. This arrangement was evidently due to the duke's unwillingness to subject the British to the Hanoverian Walmoden, who was senior to Harcourt; but, even so, it seems to be absolutely indefensible.

The French, being exhausted by the campaign, went into temporary cantonments, Moreau's division on the west bank of the Rhine over against the line from Wesel to Emmerick, Souham's in and about Nimeguen, Bonnaud's between the Meuse and the Waal, and the remainder about Bois-le-Duc and Grave. The Allies were distributed along the north bank of the Waal from Tiel eastward to the Pannarden Canal, which connects the Waal with the Leek (as the Rhine from Arnheim downward is called), the Dutch taking charge of the Bommeler Waert. Eastward from the Pannarden Canal to Wesel the Allied left was to be covered by thirty thousand Austrians under General Alvintzy, which Clerfaye, on the instance of Henry Dundas, agreed to furnish for a payment of one hundred thousand pounds a month.

The Allies' line of defence seems to have been wrongly chosen, for, owing to the Pannarden Canal, the mass of the waters of the Waal was turned into the Leek, from which cause the Leek was less liable to be frozen. Harcourt had endeavoured to establish a second bridge over the Rhine besides that of Arnheim, but the Dutch, from malice or negligence, obstructed the forwarding of the materials, as indeed they obstructed everything that might help the British. Altogether the situation was not a pleasant one, for, though rain had fallen continuously from the beginning of November, there was no saying when a frost might set in and turn the rivers into stable ice. Moreover, Moreau, roused by orders from Paris, became active again. On the 11th of December the French crossed the Waal in boats at several different points to the attack of the Allied posts, and, though beaten back, left behind them an unpleasant sense of insecurity. (York to Dundas, 27th and 29th November; Harcourt to York, 11th and 15th December 1794. Ditfurth, ii.).

On the 16th Pichegru returned and resumed the command, and on the 18th the weather changed from rain to a severe frost. In a very few days the Maas and Waal were full of floating ice, which began to pack together, threatening to cover the whole breadth of their streams; while on the Leek the rapidity of the current swept away the bridge of boats at Arnheim. Harcourt, foreseeing that before long the ice on the Waal would become passable by the enemy, prepared to retreat northward. Just at this most critical moment, moreover, there came orders from Dundas that seven British battalions of his army were required for service elsewhere; that of these seven the Fortieth, Forty-Fourth, and Sixty-Third must march to Helvoetsluys at once; and that Alvintzy, who so far had thrown every possible difficulty in the way of co-operation with the Allies, must find troops to take their place. Further, it was now ascertained that the Dutch had gone far in negotiation with the French, and there were strong rumours that an armistice had been concluded between them.

Meanwhile the cold increased; sentries were frozen at their posts; and the ice on the Waal, in front of the Allies, became strong enough to give passage to the French, while that on the Leek in their rear, though thick enough to prevent the passage of boats, was too thin to bear cavalry or artillery. Harcourt's anxiety was extreme; and he begged Dundas urgently for some further instructions as to the duty expected of him, since the order to weaken the force by sending home seven battalions was not in itself of any great assistance.

Affairs were in this condition when, on the 27th December, the French crossed the Meuse on the ice to the Bommeler Waert, surprised the Dutch posts there, and pushed on by Bommel over the frozen Waal to Tuil. The Dutch at this place fled instantly without firing a shot, some of the fugitives running on even to Utrecht. At Meteren, a few miles north of Tuil, the French were checked by the Hessians; but, with their right flank exposed by the flight of the Dutch, it was doubtful whether these could maintain their position. Their commander, however, General Dalwigk, decided to stand fast, and ascertained by reconnaissance next day that the French did not exceed two thousand men; whereupon Walmoden ordered ten battalions and six squadrons of British and Emigrants under David Dundas to Geldermalsen, a short distance north of Meteren, in the hope of annihilating this foolhardy French detachment.

Accordingly, at one o'clock on the morning of the 30th, the force moved out from Meteren in three columns, two of them to move direct upon Tuil from the north and north-east, while the third, under Lord Cathcart, fetched a compass to close in upon the enemy from the west. Cathcart's column unfortunately found the roads impassable and never came into action; but Dundas nevertheless attacked without him, and drove the French, after a sharp fight, from their entrenchments and across the Waal, with the loss of four guns and many killed and wounded, while his own casualties did not exceed fifty. This checked the ardour of the French for the moment, and during a few days there was peace upon Waal. (Dundas to Harcourt, 13th and 24th December; Harcourt to Dundas, 23rd December; to York, 25th and 29th December; Walmoden to York, 22nd, 25th, 29th December 1794, 1st January 1795. The regiments engaged in the action were the 19th, 33rd, 42nd, 78th, 80th).

Walmoden now reinforced his right about Tuil, for the news had now reached him that the fortresses of Gertruydenburg and Heusden, on the extreme right of the Allied line, were in serious danger; and on the 3rd of January 1795 he shifted his quarters to Amerongen, due north of Tiel, and on the north bank of the Leek. Grave also capitulated, and released a large number of French troops for the field. Moreau's division therefore took up cantonments over against Alvintzy's corps from Xanten down the Rhine to the Pannarden Canal. Souham's division, now transferred to Macdonald, occupied the space between the Meuse and Waal as far as the point opposite to Tiel; two more divisions were in the Bommeler Waert, and yet two more about Gertruydenburg and Breda.

On the 3rd of January the weather again became intensely cold, and at noon on the 4th two French detachments from the Bommeler Waert marched over the ice, drove in the posts before Tuil and at Hesselt, a little to the east of it, after hard fighting, and thus gained a passage by which they could move westward on the north bank of the Waal. On the following day the French attacked Tuil itself, whereupon the Dutch gunners at once fled from their batteries on the river; but, advancing from thence against Geldermalsen, the enemy was repulsed with some loss by the Thirty-Third, Forty-Second, and Seventy-

173

Eighth, under the direction of General David Dundas.

It was, however, plain that these posts could not be held against a strong attack while frost practically neutralised their natural defences; and Walmoden recalled Dundas and all the troops in that quarter to the north side of the Leek, in order to take up a new line of cantonments extending from Arnheim on the east by Wageningen, Reenen, Amerongen, and Wykby-Duurstede to Honswyk.

A sudden thaw on the 6th offered hopes of re-establishing the old position on the Waal, and orders were issued on the 7th for a reconnaissance in force of the whole line of the French posts on the following day; but on the morning of the 8th the frost suddenly set in again, though not before the troops were already in motion beyond power of recall. On the right, Dundas succeeded in driving the enemy from their posts on the Linge to the Waal, and in recovering Buren and Tiel.

The brunt of the work fell upon the Fourteenth, Twenty-Seventh, and Twenty-Eighth under Lord Cathcart, who drove the enemy in succession from the villages of Buurmalsen and Geldermalsen and captured a gun, not, however, without a loss of one hundred and thirty men to themselves. On the left the orders seem to have miscarried, probably owing to the confusion of divided command. Before the operation could be carried any further, Pichegru, finding that the ice on the Waal was stronger than ever, on the 10th fell upon the Allied line in great force at three different points between the Pannarden Canal and Tiel. The attack was repulsed upon the right, but the Austrians were forced back on the left flank, and Walmoden ordered the whole force to withdraw once more behind the Leek.

This was effected with little loss; Colonel Coote's brigade of the Fortieth, Fiftieth, and Seventy-Ninth being the only British forces severely engaged. Walmoden had fully intended to continue the retreat eastward across the Yssel; but Lord St. Helen's, at the Hague, unfortunately protested against this, and a sudden thaw enabled Walmoden to acquiesce. But on the night of the 12th frost again set in more severely than ever, and on the 14th the French attacked along the whole line from Arnheim to Reenen. They were beaten back with heavy loss; but Walmoden, feeling that he was unable to hold his ground, on the following morning gave the order for a further retreat.

The days that followed are amongst the most tragical in the history of the army. During November and December the discipline of the troops in Holland had greatly improved, but with the coming of the frost and the hardships that attended the constant alarms and marches on the Waal, it had broken down completely. Certain regiments of French Emigrants, which had joined the army late in the year, were the worst offenders; but it seems certain that some of the British were not far behind them. The country to the north of Arnheim is at the best of times an inhospitable waste, and there were few dwellings and few trees to give shelter or fuel after a dreary march through dense and chilling mist over snow twice thawed and refrozen.

Marauders from the regiments of all nations swarmed round the columns; the drivers of the waggons freed themselves from all control, and the line of march was disorderly beyond description. When the day was ended, the troops of different nations fought for such scanty comforts as were to be found; and there was a pitched battle between the Guards and the Hessians, who had been on bad terms with each other from the beginning of the campaign. Day after day the cold steadily increased; and those of the army that woke on the morning of the 17th of January saw about them such a sight as they never forgot.

Far as the eye could reach over the whitened plain were scattered gun-limbers, waggons full of baggage, stores, or sick men, sutlers' carts and private carriages. Beside them lay the horses, dead; around them scores and hundreds of soldiers, dead; here a straggler who had staggered on to the bivouac and dropped to sleep in the arms of the frost; there a group of British and Germans round an empty rum-cask; here forty English Guardsmen huddled together about a plundered waggon; there a pack-horse with a woman lying alongside it, and a baby, swaddled in rags, peeping out of the pack, with its mother's milk turned to ice upon its lips, one and all stark, frozen, dead. Had the retreat lasted but three or four days longer, not a man would have escaped; and the catastrophe would have found a place in history side by side with the destruction of the Army of Sennacherib and with the still more terrible disaster of the retreat from Moscow. (Jones, *Campaign of 1794*; Ditfurth, ii.; *Narrative of an Officer of the Guards*, ii.).

By the 19th the surviving fragments of the battalions reached their destination on the Yssel, where they were cantoned on the west side of the river from Zutphen to the sea. But there was no hope of long repose for them there. Harcourt perceived clearly that the re-embarkation of his force was now the only resource left to him, and that the place of embarkation must be on the Weser, since the lack of supplies and the incapacity of his commissariat officers would inevitably forbid him to remain long on the Ems.

Within a week, want of victuals and the hostility of the inhabitants compelled him to continue his retreat from the Yssel; and on the 27th the march eastward was resumed, the main body of the British retiring towards Osnabrück, the Germans upon Münster. One detachment of British, (Light Dragoons, 27th, 28th, 80th, and 84th Foot), however, was sent northward under Lord Cathcart's command to fetch a compass through West Friesland and along the borders of Groningen, in order to ascertain whether the people of these provinces were as disaffected as their fellows towards the House of Orange.

By whose orders this isolated force was despatched upon this errand is uncertain; it is only known that it was followed up and incessantly harassed by the enemy, and that it was not very successful in discovering friendly sentiments among the Dutch. Upon reaching the Ems, the army halted, and on the 5th February took up cantonments on the western bank of the river, Cathcart on the extreme north guarding the passes of the Bourtanger Moor from the Dollart southward, while Abercromby fixed his headquarters further to south and west of the river at Bentheim, and the Hanoverians retired to Münster.

The state of the troops, however, was now worse than ever, for thousands of sick had perforce been left behind on the Yssel. Walmoden wrote to the Duke of York:

> Your army is destroyed, the officers, their carriages, and a large train are safe, but the men are destroyed. The army has now no more than six thousand fighting men, but it has all the drawbacks of thirty-three battalions, and consumes a vast quantity of forage.

A more terrible reproach was never yet levelled against any force; and yet it was rather the politicians than the military commanders who had made such a reproach possible, by flinging commissions broadcast to any man or even child who could afford to satisfy the crimps. Upon entering German territory the men found kindlier treatment from the inhabitants; but the infamous conduct of the French Emigrant Corps threatened to turn the Germans also into enemies. It now became abundantly clear that most of these regiments were simply frauds, imposed upon the English Ministers by a band of unscrupulous adventurers; but the English Army, of course, had to bear the burden of their sins; and the Hanoverians and Hessians, naturally espousing the cause of their countrymen, turned upon the British with a bitterness which destroyed all cohesion between the nations of the Allies. (Walmoden to York, 3rd February; Harcourt to York (three letters),

11th February 1795).

Meanwhile the French, after leaving their opponents to retreat unmolested from the Leek, resumed their advance, and at the end of January occupied Kampen and Zwolle on the Yssel. They made, however, no attempt to hinder the further retirement of the Allies; and their movements for the next fortnight were of the most leisurely description. Then, however, came rumours of a French understanding with Prussia, of the neutralisation of North Germany, and of a line of demarcation to be drawn according to the actual territory occupied by the opposing armies.

The French at once woke to the importance of gaining immediate possession of Groningen and East Friesland, and General Macdonald's corps was detached to invade Groningen, while Moreau's and Vandamme's remained in observation on the Yssel. On the 19th of February Macdonald occupied the town of Groningen, and thence turning eastward he, on the 27th, attacked Cathcart's fortified posts at Winschoten. He was repulsed; but two days later the attack was renewed with success by General Reynier, and Cathcart was forced to retreat, which he did with great dexterity, crossing the Ems upon the 3rd. The entire British force then fell back to the east bank of the Ems to hold the line from Emden to Rheine, headquarters being fixed at Osnabrück.

Five days later the British Cabinet at last decided to withdraw its troops from the Continent, and on the 11th Harcourt, to his infinite relief, received intimation that transports for twenty-three thousand men were on their way to him. The Hanoverians were in consternation over the danger to which Hanover was exposed by this measure, but there was no help for it. A few days later, 16th, Prussian troops arrived to hold the line of the Ems, and on the 22nd the British began their march to Bremen for embarkation.

The Prussians did their utmost by obstruction, discourtesy, and insolence to disoblige them on their passage through the country; but this was natural, for they had always professed contempt for the British as a nation of traders, and a tradesman is never so despicable to a dishonest customer as when he refuses to grant him further credit. Finally, on the 14th of April, the infantry and part of the artillery took ship for England, leaving the remainder of the artillery and the whole of the cavalry behind them under Lord Cathcart and David Dundas. The number embarked was nearly fifteen thousand, some proportion of the sick having been recovered; so that the losses after the retreat from the Leek must have amounted to about six thousand men, of which not a tithe were killed or wounded in action. Thus disgracefully ended the first expedition of Pitt and Dundas to the Low Countries.

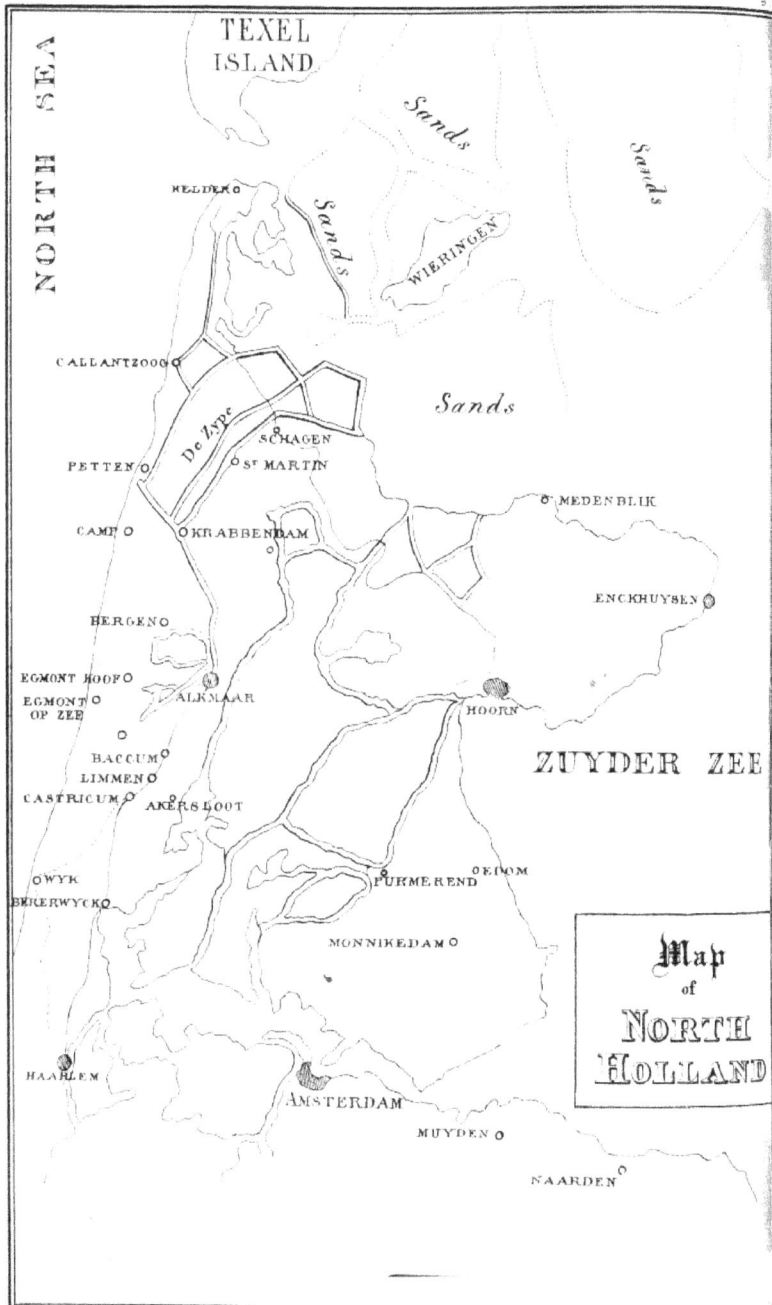

NORTH SEA

TEXEL ISLAND

Sands

HELDER o

Sands

Sands

Sands

WIERINGEN

CALLANTZOOG o

Sands

De Zype

SCHAGEN o

PETTEN o

o St MARTIN

o MEDENBLIK

CAMP o

o KRABBENDAM

BERGEN o

ENCKHUYSEN o

EGMONT HOOF o

ALKMAAR

EGMONT
OP ZEE o

HOORN

o
BACCUM o
LIMMEN o

ZUYDER ZEE

CASTRICUM o   AKERSLOOT o

o WYK
BEVERWYCK o

o EDOM
PURMEREND o

MONNIKEDAM o

Map
of
NORTH
HOLLAND

HAARLEM o

AMSTERDAM

MUYDEN o

NAARDEN o

CHAPTER 7

The Second Round

As the 18th Century drew to a close there was little sign of improvement in the British Army and, by the end of the year 1797, the ordinary sources for the supply of recruits had failed. This was owing not a little to mismanagement, but partly also to the rapid development of the manufacturing industry in England through the removal of all competition in France and the countries which had been overrun by the armies of the Revolution. Since the voluntary system had broken down, it followed necessarily that a compulsory system must be substituted for it. The ballot for the Militia provided a form of compulsion for service at home, and the only resource was to convert the Militia if possible into a fountain of recruits for service abroad.

The first step was taken in this direction in January 1798, when an Act was passed to enable any person duly appointed by the commander-in-chief to enlist a certain proportion of militiamen for an appointed number of regiments of the Line; the proportion not to exceed one-fifth of the Supplementary Militia in any county, and the total number enlisted to be limited to ten thousand men. This, however, in the circumstances of the time, was a measure adopted rather for the reinforcement of garrisons in Ireland and elsewhere than for any other service. No particular inducements were offered to attract recruits from the Militia; no exemption from the dreaded and detested service in the West Indies was promised; and men were shy of condemning themselves to death by yellow fever.

Only in Norfolk did the Supplementary Militia come forward in numbers to fill the ranks of its county regiment, the Ninth Foot; and it was rewarded for its patriotism by a gratuity which raised the bounty granted to the men to ten guineas apiece. Elsewhere the Lords-Lieutenant set their faces against the scheme; and it was a total failure.

(*C.C.L.B.*, A.G. to Sir Charles Grey, 8th June 1798; *ibid.* 22nd and 25th June).

After the suppression of the Irish rebellion and the victory of the Nile, however, all danger of invasion disappeared; and the ministers, rightly deciding to reassume the offensive, found themselves crippled by the want of a striking force. They had no hope of raising one by the time-honoured methods which had served, though only indifferently well, for the past century; and yet without such a force it was practically hopeless to attempt to bring the war to a satisfactory close. There was, however, one encouraging sign.

From the 9th of January 1799 onwards there came from Ireland a succession of offers from British Fencible Regiments and Irish Militia to serve abroad; and it was not the least satisfactory feature in these offers that the great majority emanated originally not from the officers but from the men. In the first six months of 1799 eleven battalions of Fencible Infantry, two regiments of Fencible Cavalry and seven battalions of Irish Militia volunteered for service in any part of Europe; seven other battalions of Irish Militia volunteered to serve in Great Britain; and one battalion of Militia, one of Fencibles and two regiments of Fencible Cavalry nobly offered to go wherever the King might choose to send them.

The condition, made by so many corps, that their wanderings should be confined to Europe, showed plainly that they would have nothing to do with the West Indies, and gave ministers a valuable hint for future guidance. Meanwhile, however, time was passing, and the government's preparations for the united movement of Europe to crush France had been confined so far entirely to the sphere of diplomacy.

As has already been told, Thomas Grenville's mission to Berlin had proved abortive, King Frederick William having signified in May his definite refusal to join the Coalition. But early in June the government received intelligence that Prussia might at any moment call upon France to evacuate Holland upon pain of an immediate invasion; in which case she would certainly summon the English to co-operate with their fleet and to seize the island of Walcheren. Sir Ralph Abercromby was thereupon summoned, by a letter of the 8th of June, from Edinburgh, to take command of the troops which were to be held ready for this purpose. Moreover, Lord Grenville's weapons of persuasion were not yet exhausted; for in that same month he flattered the *tsar's* vanity by proposing a joint expedition of Russia and England to recover Holland, hoping that Prussia, whose prize that country was designed to be, might thereby be still further tempted to move.

Tsar Paul readily accepted the proposal; and on the 22nd of June a treaty was signed whereby England engaged herself to provide thirty thousand men, and to pay for eighteen thousand Russians more for the recapture of Holland.

It is extraordinary that Pitt should so boldly have promised thirty thousand men for this expedition, when he knew that he had not more than ten thousand ready to his hand. The means for supplying them had, however, been already considered; and on the 12th of July an act was passed to reduce the numbers of the Militia in all counties, as could now safely be done, and to increase the army by allowing militiamen to enlist in certain regular regiments. (The regiments named were the 4th, 5th, 9th, 17th, 20th, 31st, 35th, 40th, 42nd, 46th, 52nd, 62nd, 63rd, 82nd. *Circular of Commander-in-Chief,* 17th July 1799. *Grey Papers*).

It was stipulated that these regiments should not serve out of Europe during the continuance of the war and for six months after, nor in any case until the lapse of five years; that the men could choose their own corps and not be drafted from them against their will; and that they should receive a bounty of ten pounds. Any man volunteering for service on these terms was entitled to discharge from the Militia, provided that the number of such volunteers did not exceed one-fourth of the full quota of each county. The king was further empowered to disembody the Supplementary Militia or any part of it, in which case the men so discharged might enlist in the regulars.

If any man did so voluntarily, no ballot was to be held to fill his place, though if he failed to do so he might be recalled to the Militia. Such was the first enactment in the direction of compulsory service in England, passed, as has been said, on the 12th of July in order to make up a force which was to take the field in September. The ministers, after all the bitter experience of the past six years, had not yet learned the difference between an army and an assembly of men in red coats.

Meanwhile, such few regiments as were in some degree fit for service were collected together on the Kentish coast, July; and their numbers were made up to some ten thousand men by volunteers, attracted from other battalions by a bounty of a guinea and a half. (*C.C.L.B. Circular of Commander-in-Chief,* 11th July 1799).

Sir Ralph Abercromby assumed command of this force; and upon him devolved the duty of planning the campaign in concert with the strategists of the Cabinet, Pitt and Dundas, both of whom took up their residence for the time at Walmer Castle. The avowed object of the expedition was clear enough, namely, the reconquest of Holland north of the Waal and the restoration of its independence under the House of Orange; but how those objects were to be attained was another question, for the best of the campaigning season was already far spent. Abercromby reviewed the situation and quickly came to a conclusion. The most advantageous point of attack, in the abstract, was undoubtedly the mouth of the Meuse, for from thence the British could take in rear the lines of the Yssel and of the Vecht, which July, defended Holland against attack from the south and east; and the conquest of that province, thus made easy, would probably lead to the submission of the Dutch Netherlands.

But the two mouths of the Maas were barred, the northern channel by the fortress of Brielle, the southern by the fortress of Helvoetsluys, both of them situated on the island of Voorne, which lies between the two channels. If a sufficient force were provided to attack Voorne and effect a landing on the mainland simultaneously, then all might be well; but, if no disembarkation could be accomplished without previously gaining possession of Voorne, then the operation would be hazardous; for the enemy could collect his force while the British were engaged with the sieges of Brielle and Helvoetsluys, and throw grave difficulties in their way.

Finally, Abercromby expressed a decided opinion that no attempt should be made upon Holland until the first division of the Russian contingent was on the spot and ready to cooperate in the field, (*Memo, of Abercromby*, 6th July 1799).

This blunt and practical opinion was by no means to the taste of Pitt, who was eager for action; and it was all the less so since the Russians were not expected until the end of August. A variety of schemes was now put forward, the first of them being a return to the original idea of seizing Walcheren. Abercromby freely conceded that this island would be most valuable, if the Prussians crossed the Rhine and Meuse and penetrated into Brabant; but without Prussia's cooperation it was useless to Great Britain, would require a large garrison and a squadron to protect it, and was, moreover, extremely unhealthy. It was then proposed that the force should land at Scheveningen, a few miles to north of the Hague, on an open beach where ships would be unsafe in a strong west wind, and where the troops, after disembarkation, would find the whole army of Holland upon their left flank and rear.

This plan was summarily dismissed by Abercromby. Another idea was to occupy Walcheren, Goree, an island immediately south of Voorne, and Ameland, a spit of sand off the north coast of Friesland, to support an insurrection. Abercromby, suppressing his contempt, declared quietly that such support would be worthless. The next suggestion was to land fifteen thousand men from the Ems on the shore of Groningen. This being the district where the feeling for the house of Orange and against the French was strongest, the plan had no doubt something to commend it.

It was very probable that the force might succeed in recovering Groningen, Overyssel and part of Friesland and Drenthe; but, before it could proceed to attack the Western Provinces, it must necessarily capture the fortress of Koevorden, on the Vecht, which could hardly be accomplished before the winter set in. In that case there would be a danger not only lest the troops should perish of cold, but also lest communication with England should be interrupted by ice, which would be absolutely fatal to the expedition.

Abercromby therefore pronounced decidedly in favour of the attack on the Maas as the only really serviceable plan, whether the Prussians should cooperate or not. For the success of the invasion in that quarter, however, the possession of Voorne was a preliminary that could not be dispensed with; and the capture of the island promised to be an extremely difficult and hazardous operation, for the water on the western shore was too shallow to admit ships large enough either to cover a disembarkation or to carry materials for a siege.

Abercromby did not conceal these difficulties, which he evidently judged to be insuperable by the force that was to be employed; and he did not dissemble his opinion that the object of the whole expedition was not worth the risk. Pitt, who had evidently not forgotten the part played by Abercromby in Ireland, became more and more impatient. "There are some people who have pleasure in opposing whatever is proposed," he remarked upon one occasion; but Abercromby with quiet dignity suffered this petulant rudeness to pass unnoticed, and continued to insist upon his opinion.

The root of the whole matter was that Pitt was about to commit again the old, old blunder of invading a country with an inadequate force, relying upon an insurrection of the inhabitants to do the work which could really be accomplished only by an army. Herein strangely enough he was abetted by Grenville, usually the least sanguine of men, who for some reason had formed extravagant hopes of Prussian assistance and of an immediate desertion of the Dutch troops from the French service to the British, he wrote to Dundas:

> The operation will be rather a counter-revolution than a conquest. Make your preparations to *preoccupy* the Netherlands.

Dundas, however, for once took a wise and sober view of the situation, he answered:

> Unless the Dutch co-operate with us cordially and actively, I do not think it possible to do as much by mere force of arms in this campaign as we flatter ourselves. I cannot forget the American war (of Independence), and the disappointment of our hopes.

But, in spite of this belated recollection of past experience, he yielded to Grenville, whose ideas he knew to be shared by Pitt, and consented to write to Abercromby that he was going out, not to conquer a country, but to aid a counter-revolution ready to burst out in it. More than this, though he himself had no faith in these words, he added that they were meant to serve for Abercromby's justification in case "he should be led to dash more than military rules and tactics would warrant."

Thus weakly and against his better judgment did Dundas suffer his colleagues to embark upon a dangerous enterprise upon the strength of a mere phrase. Moreover, not content with choosing one loose corner-stone upon which to build the conduct of a campaign, Pitt must needs add a second in the shape of a visionary Prussian Army; not realising, in his intense ignorance of war and of the world at large, that an edifice balanced between two such tottering foundations must inevitably collapse. Abercromby had not fought through the campaigns of 1793 and 1794 without learning something both of the Dutch and of the Prussians; and in this instance, as formerly in Ireland, his political as well as his military judgment was far sounder than that of Ministers. (Grenville to Dundas, 30th July; Dundas to Grenville, 29th and 31st July 1799. *Dropmore MSS.* Abercromby's *Memo.*, 20th July 1799. Dunfermline's *Life of Abercromby*).

Nor were these Abercromby's only difficulties, for he was anything but satisfied with the preparations for his force. His troops, even on the 1st of August, were far short of their estimated strength. The volunteers which were arrived or arriving to fill his battalions needed some days for their equipment, and three of his regiments were judged unfit for immediate service. The naval preparations were behindhand; the tonnage required for the embarkation had not yet been obtained; and the naval force itself—eight ships of sixty -four or fewer guns, and five frigates—was insufficient to carry the number of flat-boats required for disembarkation. Above all, he was uneasy upon the question of transport, no sufficient provision of horses having been made even for the large train of artillery which he had rightly judged to be essential for such operations as were enjoined upon him. He wrote at the end of July:

> The British troops want the means of conveyance for artillery, sick, baggage and provisions, and you know we have not a foot on the Continent till we acquire it. I hope it is not a crime to state such facts.

A return of the Russian troops, with an enormous train of waggons, gave him the text for a second discourse upon the same subject two days later:

> The Emperor of Russia may make a general into a private man by his fiat, but he cannot make his army march without their baggage. It is only in a free country like ours that a minister has absolute power over an army. We are too inconsiderable to resist. . . . It is self-evident that an army is not a machine that can move of itself; it must have the means of moving. . . . As our numbers increase so must our arrangements; and rest assured that an army cannot move without horses and waggons.

In his anxiety Abercromby represented the matter to the Duke of York, who brought it before Pitt and received from him full powers, that is to say, full powers to make his requisition to the Treasury and to hope that it might be timely fulfilled. But Abercromby still retained his doubts whether the importance of the question was really understood by the Government; and he was right. (Abercromby to Huskisson, 29th July and 1st, 3rd, 4th August 1798).

Dundas was so far impressed by Abercromby's representations as to the insufficiency of his numbers that he inclined for a moment to delay the expedition unless a larger force could be despatched with him. But political considerations, both domestic and foreign, prompted him, according to his own account, to urge the departure of the first division of the army as soon as possible; and on the 3rd of August he issued to Abercromby his instructions. Herein, ignoring the general's strong recommendation that nothing should be done in Holland until the arrival of the Russians, he declared it to be expedient and necessary for divers unspecified reasons, that the expeditionary force should sail in several divisions, of which Abercromby's ten thousand men had been appointed to be the first.

The duty assigned to it was to secure on the mainland of the United Provinces a safe rendezvous and a favourable position for future operations, which of course should permit of free communication with England. With this object the instructions suggested the capture of Goree and Overflakkee to south of Voorne, of Rosenburg to north of it, and of Voorne itself, as a means towards obtaining some place on the mainland where reinforcements could land without opposition, and where Abercromby could maintain himself until their arrival. Maassluis, Schiedam, Rotterdam and Dordrecht were named as places suitable for the purpose; and a reinforcement of four thousand British troops was promised to him immediately upon the capture of any one of them.

If, on the other hand, he should secure the islands above named but fail to establish himself on the mainland, the reinforcements would be delayed until the arrival of the Russians should enable them to proceed in great strength. Dundas further hinted that the operations might be furthered by naval diversions both northward towards the Texel and southward about Zealand; and to this end he enclosed a proclamation and an address from the Prince of Orange, which were to be published as earnest of England's honourable intentions. But he was careful to add that Abercromby was at liberty to abandon these projects altogether if, on arrival in the Meuse, he should think them impracticable or unduly hazardous or costly. (Dundas to Abercomby, 3rd August 1799).

All this was in the highest degree unsatisfactory, for there seemed every probability that the expedition would reduce itself to a voyage to the Meuse and back again. Goree and Overflakkee had been suggested as landing-places, apparently, by some Dutch refugees of the Orange party; but not one of them could give the slightest intelligence respecting these islands. In fact, the only information which Abercromby could obtain to guide him was that of a Dutch prisoner of war. On the 6th of August Dundas, Abercromby, and the Naval *commandant*, Vice-Admiral Mitchell, met in council to talk over the matter, with the help of Captain Flyn of the Royal Navy and a foreign officer, both of whom were supposed to be well acquainted with the navigation of the Meuse. Abercromby was very ill pleased with the result.

The admiral talked blindly of the fleet forcing its way through every obstacle; while Flyn was cautious, and afraid of committing himself. Ultimately, it was agreed that to gain possession of Voorne the island of Rosenburg must first be taken, though it was plain that, from the difficulties of navigation and other causes, the success of the operation must be most precarious.

At this stage matters remained until the 10th of August, when Abercromby again complained of his want of intelligence, and warned the government against building too much on the exertions of the Orange party. His letter was crossed by a fresh set of instructions. Dundas, though somewhat infected by the sanguine hopes of Pitt and Grenville, still mistrusted the success of the operations already contemplated, and was unwilling to let the general sail without offering him a further choice of alternative enterprises. He, therefore, directed him still to make the capture of Goree his first business, and, after effecting it, to proceed to the attack of Voorne; but, if this should prove to be impracticable, he urged upon him, as the object next in importance, to obtain possession of Texel Island and the Helder at the extreme north of Holland.

Should this operation likewise prove impracticable, he was to enter the Ems, disembark in the neighbourhood of Delfzyl, and take possession of Groningen, Friesland and Drenthe. But the capture of the Helder was set down as far more desirable, if it could be attained, as securing alike a footing in Holland, the navigation of the Zuider Zee, and probably the control of the Dutch fleet at the Texel. None the less, it was urged as essential that troops should, it possible, be left at Goree, since it was upon the presence of such a force that the loyal inhabitants had "probably" built their plans of co-operation. Finally, after recounting all these alternatives, the instructions left it to the discretion of the general and admiral to do practically whatever they might think best for the king's service. (Dundas to Abercromby, Abercromby to Huskisson, 10th August 1799; Dundas to Grenville, 3rd and 11th August. *Dropmore MSS.*).

It has been judged necessary to set forth all these orders at some length, so as to show the extreme vagueness and indecision of the ministers' intentions in despatching this expedition. They professed to count upon a rising of the Dutch, yet could give the general no certain intelligence of the designs of the insurgents. They had, when seeking Abercromby's advice, made the co-operation of a Prussian

Army a principal factor for the guidance of his calculation; yet that factor vanished altogether before the expedition put to sea. Finally, they hurried the general and his ten thousand men out of England with no definite plan of action, but merely with a hazy purpose that he should go to Holland and do something.

Abercromby sailed accordingly on the 13th of August, having evidently already made up his mind to go to the Helder. On the following day he announced his intention to Dundas, saying that an attack on the Maas was absolutely out of the question, and that he abandoned it the more readily since the persistence of Prussia in her neutrality had removed the principal reason for advocating it. Dundas at once approved cordially of his decision, though he made no effort to explain why the Government had saddled the General with a responsibility which it ought to have taken upon itself. In his usual breezy fashion he assumed that Abercromby's sphere of attack embraced not only the Helder itself, but Texel Island and the mainland south of the Helder as far as Haarlem, or, in other words, a coastline of from fifty to sixty miles; and already he had visions of an early fall of Amsterdam. (Abercromby to Dundas, 14th August, three letters; Dundas to Abercromby, 16th August 1799).

Bad luck, however, dogged the expedition from the very beginning. The fleet was overtaken by a westerly gale of unusual violence, which was ominously noted by Abercromby as certain to delay the arrival of the Russians. Happily, the transports were able to keep company, thanks to bright moonlight, and on the 21st the whole armament approached the coast of the Texel. Preparations were made for disembarkation, but on the next day a second gale forced every sail again to sea; nor was it till the 26th that the transports could be anchored in the stations appointed for them opposite the shore a little to the south of the Helder, between Kycksduin and Kallantzoog.

Water and provisions were already so short in the fleet that, had not the gale moderated on the 26th, Abercromby and Mitchell had determined to abandon the attempt on the Helder and to sail for the Ems. However, at two o'clock on the next morning, the signal was made to prepare for disembarkation, though the surf was still high, and the enemy, having had sight of the fleet for six days past, could not have failed to make preparations for defence. Moreover, owing to his ignorance of the precise duty required of him by the government, Abercromby had been unable to arrange every detail of his attack before sailing, as he had wished; and, since the ministers had failed to provide the flat-bottomed boats for which he had asked, he was obliged to rely upon the boats of the men-of-war only, which could not convey more than three thousand troops at a time. Lastly, the operation of disembarking a force in presence of an enemy was strange to the navy, whose officers hardly understood the importance of keeping companies and battalions together, and of landing them in the order which they were to preserve on shore.

In such discouraging circumstances did Abercromby approach his adventure. Behind him were the orders of an ignorant and negligent Cabinet; before him a long row of sand-hills concealing he knew not what enemy behind them. North Holland is indeed no ordinary country. Lying below the level of the sea, it is preserved, about its northern extremity, only by a gigantic dyke some five miles in length from inundation and destruction by the German Ocean. Along the western coast the part of this dyke is played by a chain of sand-dunes, varying from half a mile to four miles in width, which runs, with but a single break, all the way along the shore from the Helder to the mouth of the Maas. The break in question occurs about fifteen miles south of the Helder at Petten, and extends for some three miles southward to Kamp, between which points the waves are shut out by another huge dyke.

From Petten for some five miles northward the dunes are high, and gradually widen out from a breadth of half a mile to a mile and a half at Kallantzoog. North of that point they suddenly contract once more to a breadth of eight hundred to a thousand yards, and, rapidly decreasing in height, present, opposite to the village of Groete Keten, an absolute gap in the barrier of sand. At this point the beach is wide, and the outer bank of the dunes little more than ten feet high, so that from the main-top of a frigate a man could obtain a narrow glimpse of the reclaimed fen called the plain of North Holland.

The nature of that plain is well known to travellers. To the eye a perfectly open expanse of meadow land, it is in reality as strongly enclosed country as there is in the world. At every hundred yards, or less, it is intersected by broad ditches or canals, some of them created to carry off the water, others to mark boundaries and do the duty of fences; for the northern corner of this strange territory is almost entirely grazing land. Military movements are practically impossible, except on the roads, which without exception are carried along the dykes. With such a description of country Abercromby had become familiar during the campaign of 1794; but the sand-dunes, which were all that he could see, were an unknown quantity, and he had not the slightest idea what force the enemy might keep hidden behind them. Marking, however, the gap before Groete Keten and the low dunes to north of it, he determined, in default of better guidance, to make that part of the shore his place of landing.

Meanwhile General Brune, who held supreme command in Holland, had, of course, been apprised of the approach of the British fleet, and, thanks to the weather, had found ample time to reinforce the troops in the north. On the 27th of August there were at the disposal of General Daendels, the actual commander about the threatened point, ten thousand men; but his was no easy task.

Though the gap at Groete Keten was the obvious place for a disembarkation, and the shore to the north of Petten far more favourable for the purpose than that to the south, there was still no natural obstacle to prevent an enemy from landing at any point between the Helder and Alkmaar. He therefore decided to disperse his force along the whole of that line.

Apart from the garrisons in the forts of the Helder, one brigade lay between Kallantzoog and Petten; two battalions, with a third in reserve, were stationed in the middle of the dunes opposite to the hamlet of Kleene Keten; two more were between the village of Groete Keten and the sea, facing to north, and three more, with two squadrons of cavalry and four guns, stood before Huisduinen, a little to the south of the Helder itself, facing to south-west. Recognising that the cannon of the fleet could scour the whole beach with shot, Daendels had decided to refuse his centre, and to attack the British upon both flanks when entangled in the dunes. The position of Kleene Keten was probably chosen for the reserve, because at that point the plain east of the sand-hills is dry for a few hundred yards, and gives a little space for the massing of troops on the open ground.

At five o'clock in the morning the men-of-war, at a signal from the flagship, opened a tremendous fire upon the beach; and the whole line of boats, carrying Coote's brigade and apparently a part of Macdonald's, under the command of Sir James Pulteney, (see list following), pushed off together for the shore about the gap and to north of it.

The force was brigaded thus:—

1st Brigade.—Massed grenadiers of the Guards, 3/1st Guards—Major-General D'Oyley.

2nd Brigade.—1/Coldstream Guards, 1/3rd Guards—Major-

General Burrard.

3rd Brigade.—2nd, 27th, 29th, 69th, 85th—Major-General Coote.

4th Brigade.—2/1st, 25th, 49th, 79th, 92nd—Major-General John Moore.

Reserve.—23rd, 55th—Colonel Macdonald.

This differs slightly from the brigading as shown by Bunbury (*Great War with France*), but is taken from the return enclosed by Abercromby to Dundas in his report of the action. The full strength of the infantry on 4th August was 497 officers and 11,820 non-commissioned officers and men, of whom 753 were sick. There were also on board:—

18th Light Dragoons.—13 officers, 208 N.C.O.s and men.

Royal Artillery.—26 officers, 417 N.C.O.s and men, and 157 drivers.

The guns requested by Abercromby (20th July) were 36 6-prs. (battalion guns), 20 12-prs., 30 24-prs., 18 5½-inch mortars, 8 8-inch mortars, 19 10-inch mortars.

The landing was effected in much confusion. Several boats were upset by the surf, and not a few of the seamen and soldiers were drowned. The men had to scramble through the waves as best they could; companies and battalions were intermixed, and there was much trouble in disentangling them. Nevertheless, Daendels, doubt-less dreading the effect of the cannonade, kept his men under cover, and made no attempt, except by distant and dropping fire, to molest the disordered British soldiers as they hurried to and fro to find their places in the ranks.

Abercromby had been careful to select for his disembarkation a slight curve in the strand, where the sand-hills, drawing closer to the sea both to north and south, gave some protection to his flanks. But it should seem that, in the general confusion, the right of the land-ing force did not extend itself far enough to southward, being pos-sibly blown from its right course by the south-west wind; and for this reason a number of troops were cramped within an unduly confined portion of the beach. This increased the confusion; and the formation of the British was still, apparently, incomplete when Pulteney, possibly in order to gain more room for the rear battalions, gave the order to advance.

The forward movement must have begun a little to north of the gap, for it instantly brought down a very heavy fire of musketry and light artillery from the enemy, showing that Daendels had brought down his detachment from Kleene Keten to meet them. Thereupon it seems that the British, after climbing the outer ridge of sand-hills, charged straight upon the two leading battalions, forced them gradually back upon the third, which formed their reserve, and finally drove all three to southward in confusion upon Groete Keten.

★★★★★★

For some distance north of Groete Keten the dunes consist of an outer ridge towards the sea, and an inner ridge at the edge of the plain, with practically open ground between them.

★★★★★★

Hotly pursuing them, the British came upon the gap in the dunes, where there is a curious pan of flat sunken ground, measuring about five hundred yards north and south by one hundred east and west, from which they scrambled up a steep bank some ten feet high, in no very good order, to debouch upon the plain beyond.

★★★★★★

This hollow is so sudden and abrupt that a superficial observer would declare it to be the worked-out clay-bed of an old brickfield.

★★★★★★

No sooner, however, did they emerge from the sand upon the grass than they were met by a withering fire of grape from the guns, hitherto concealed, of a French detachment on the two roads which lead inland from this outlet. Thereupon they fell back hastily into the sand-hills; and Daendels at once launched the two battalions, which he held concealed from view at Groete Keten, upon Pulteney's right flank, called up more troops from Kallantzoog to support them, and sent orders to his regiments at Huisduinen to fall forthwith upon the British left flank. This counter-attack from Groete Keten was most dangerous and formidable.

Pulteney's troops seem to have been huddled together in the pan above described, where he tried to change the front of his right-hand battalion to meet the flanking attack, but, owing to the narrowness of the space, could only do so with difficulty, and could form no second battalion for its support. The British right was therefore borne back in great disorder; and the consequences might have been most serious had not the enemy forsaken their shelter to pursue them, when, being

BATTLE IN THE DUNES

enfiladed by the guns of the men-of-war, they were forced to retire with very heavy loss.

★★★★★★

The position of the regiments can be fixed only by conjecture, for the action was extremely confused. From the casualties I guess that the 23rd and 55th were on the right, and Coote's brigade immediately to left of them.

★★★★★★

Abercromby, however, now landed with D'Oyley's brigade of Guards to support Pulteney; while on the left Moore, who had at first been set ashore with only three hundred mixed men from every regiment under his command, was gradually reinforced by the disembarkation of the greater part of his brigade. Taking up his position opposite the Helder, his skirmishers engaged the enemy's riflemen, and seem to have checked the attack ordered by Daendels upon the British left flank.

Elsewhere the two armies were engaged in a long and confused struggle among the sand-hills, which lasted until five o'clock in the evening; the French and Dutch making effort after effort to force the British back, and the British, though without artillery, refusing obstinately to give way. At last the enemy on the centre and right, being fairly worn down, gave up the contest, and retired in good order to a position some four miles to the southward.

Thus the landing was won, but there still remained some two thousand Dutch in the batteries of the Helder, which needed to be mastered without delay. Abercromby accordingly ordered that they should be attacked at daybreak on the following morning by the brigades of Moore and Burrard.

Moore, however, noticed some movement about the Helder in the evening, and keeping careful watch, saw the enemy's troops march off at nightfall by the eastern coast, as if making for the road to Alkmaar. Pushing forward his patrols, he learned that the batteries were evacuated and the guns spiked; and in the course of the night he took possession both of the forts and of the town. At daylight the Dutch men-of-war, which were lying close under the guns of the Helder, weighed anchor and retired eastward, with the exception of seven lying in the Nieuwediep, which surrendered at once.

Admiral Mitchell employed the two following days in buoying a channel by which to approach the main body of the Dutch fleet, and, sailing in on the 30th, summoned the Dutch Admiral, Story, to hoist the Orange flag and transfer his ships to the service of the Allies of the British Crown. Story thereupon yielded up his fleet, alleging that his men refused to fight; and twenty-five more men-of-war, seven of them ships of the line, together with the naval arsenal of Nieuwediep, with all its stores and ninety-five guns, passed into possession of the British without the firing of a shot.

So great and speedy a success exceeded the wildest expectations alike of those who projected and commanded the expedition. Abercromby, in announcing his intention to hazard a disembarkation, had warned the government that to anchor two hundred sail upon an unsheltered beach, exposed to the prevalent winds, and then to throw a large force upon a hostile shore, was an operation beyond the rules of prudence and common sense. Six days' warning had given the enemy ample time to prepare for resistance; the means for landing troops were, through no fault of Abercromby, inadequate; the disembarkation had consequently been disorderly; the first advance, whether through the eagerness of the troops or the fault of Pulteney, had been too precipitate; and the action, after long wearing an ugly aspect, had terminated finally in no very decided success.

Moore, who, it is true, was always something of a pessimist, looked for a re embarkation as almost inevitable if his attack upon the Helder on the morning of the 28th should have failed. Yet, by miraculous good luck, all had gone well, and the first great object of the expedition had been secured with, in the circumstances, comparatively small loss. Three officers and about sixty men were killed, and twenty men drowned; twenty-four officers and three hundred and eighty men were wounded or missing.

The regiments that suffered most heavily were the Twenty-Third and Fifty-Fifth, upon whom fell nearly one half of the total casualties. Among the wounded officers were Pulteney, Abercromby's second in command, and John Hope and George Murray, his two principal staff-officers. (Pulteney was hit in the arm, which afforded him the satisfaction of having been wounded in both arms and both legs. Bunbury's *Great War with France*). The losses of the enemy appear to have been far greater, though it is not clear why they should have been so; but they are set down by French historians at not fewer than fourteen hundred men—an enormous proportion to the total number engaged.

Meanwhile throughout the month of August the recruits from the militia had been pouring into the appointed camp at Barham Downs in the uproarious condition which, in those days, was inevitably produced by a large bounty. Such a sight has rarely been seen in England, even after the paying off of a fleet. The possession of ten pounds filled the majority of the men with a pride which forbade them to walk to the rendezvous. They rolled up to the camp, riotously drunk, in post-coaches, post-chaises and six, caravans, and every description of vehicle, leaving the officers to plod on foot with such few luckless men as had already lost or spent their money.

Even when arrived at their destination they were utterly intractable, for, as gentlemen who rode in post-chaises, they thought it beneath them to attend drill or parade. They knew that they were to embark almost immediately for active service, and they were determined to be happy while their riches lasted. It was only with difficulty that their names and the regiments from which they came were ascertained, while all the efforts of the tailors failed to alter such a multitude of facings in time for embarkation.

Upon the news of Abercromby's success, Pitt and Dundas very injudiciously announced that they would visit the troops on the following evening, to witness a march past and the firing of a *feu de joie*. The officers spent the next twenty-four hours in a raid upon Canterbury and the surrounding villages, and by three o'clock on the appointed afternoon had swept into camp every man who could stand or walk. Not more than one man in twenty was sober, and the *feu de joie* was, in consequence, so outrageously jubilant that it was judged prudent to dismiss the troops without venturing upon a march past.

Yet these men, knowing nothing of their comrades, nothing of their sergeants and officers, nothing of their regiments, were in a few days to stand in face of an enemy in the field. A month before they had been well drilled, orderly militiamen; with three months' training in their new corps they would probably have been good, and with six months' training, excellent troops. Every soldier knew this, and there were undoubtedly soldiers who mentioned it to ministers; but it was vain to urge such matters upon Pitt and Dundas.

The first reinforcement of these new levies reached Abercromby on the 28th of August. It consisted of seven battalions organised in two brigades, and counting altogether rather over five thousand of all ranks, but with only fifty-seven lieutenants and fourteen ensigns among the whole of them. (Major-Gen. Don's Brigade: 17th and 40th/each 2 batts. Major-Gen. Lord Cavan's Brigade: 20th/2 batts., 63rd. 147 officers, 4967 N.C.O.s and men, of whom 204. sick. The 2/17th and the 40th had not a single ensign. Return, in Dundas to

Abercromby, 22nd August 1799).

With them very soon after, came the Eleventh Light Dragoons. The arrival of these troops was welcome, for it offered Abercromby the hope of improving his success. He was extremely anxious to advance, but an army, as he had said, cannot move without horses and waggons; and he had neither the one nor the other. For four days the troops bivouacked in their chosen position in the sand-hills, exposed to constant wind and rain, without any camp-equipment, and, in Abercromby's words, labouring under a precarious subsistence from want of horses to draw their provisions from the Helder. At length a few horses and waggons were found, and, on the 1st of September, Abercromby moved southward and took up a strong defensive position, with his right at Petten on the German Ocean, and his left at Oude Sluis on the Zuider Zee.

Following the bank of the Zype Canal, the line of defence ran from Oude Sluis obliquely south-westward for about twelve miles to the hamlet of Krabbendam, from which point it turned back sharply north-westward along the bank of a branch canal which ended at Petten. Thus the front was covered for its whole length by a canal; but a great dyke beyond it was presently made the first line of defence, additional bridges being constructed over the Zype to facilitate the access to it. The principal approach to the position was at the salient angle of Zype Sluis, with its adjacent post of Krabbendam; for it was at these points that the great northern canal from Amsterdam and Alkmaar, and the high road upon the great dyke, entered the lines.

Accordingly, the two hamlets were placed in a state of defence, strengthened by redoubts, and committed to the charge of the Twentieth Regiment. To westward of it, along the branch-canal to Petten, there were transverse dykes which gave access to the main dyke; and this space being the right of the line, was occupied by the two brigades of Guards. North eastward from Krabbendam, the next passage of the Zype was by the village of St. Maarten, which also was fortified and held by the Fortieth Regiment under Colonel Spencer; and the remainder of Moore's and Don's brigades, less two battalions left to guard the Helder itself, were stationed either between Krabbendam and Oude Sluis or as a reserve in rear of the centre. Every important point was covered by field-works; the troops were quartered under good shelter in Schagen, Harenskarspel, and other villages in advance of the Zype; and, thus secured, Abercromby resolved, until reinforcements should reach him, to stand on the defensive. (*Diary of Sir John*

Moore, i. Bunbury's *Great War with France*).

For this inaction he has incurred severe censure from the French historian, General Jomini, yet it is difficult to see what else he could have done. He had, it is true, from sixteen to eighteen thousand men with him, but, with the exception of the Guards and Ninety-Second Highlanders, the regiments that he had brought with him were imperfect in coherence and discipline. One and all had been hastily completed by drafts, and Don's and Cavan's brigades were simply unformed militia. The force was very ill-equipped in every respect, and the only transport that had been shipped to him so far consisted of thirty-five bread waggons, with four horses apiece, and a single forge-cart. In the country itself the waggons and teams were few, and the inhabitants unwilling to part with them.

The government had counted on water-carriage to supplement these defects; but a series of southwesterly gales made it so difficult for boats to pass from the Helder through the narrow channel which led to Oude Sluis and so into the Zype Canal, that it was impossible to form magazines even along the length of the chosen position. Moreover, even if such magazines had been formed, the boats of the Zype Canal were too large to enter the great northern canal, and the enemy had been careful to destroy or remove all the smaller craft as they retreated. Lastly, the country itself presented every possible difficulty to an advancing force. No corn was grown on the land, which, being given up wholly to grazing, produced no supplies beyond a limited quantity of meat.

Again, the maze of dykes and canals, interspersed at every hundred yards with wet ditches, rendered the movement of troops impossible except by a few roads, which could easily be obstructed either by breaking down the bridges or, in some cases, by inundation. Thus every advantage lay with the defending force, which could with comparatively few troops cover a very wide front, extending practically from sea to sea, and therefore affording no chance for a turning movement. An invasion of North Holland from the Helder signified, in fact, a campaign of frontal attacks along parallel lines of causeways. (Abercromby to Dundas, 4th September 1799).

General Brune naturally used the respite granted to him by Abercromby's halt to summon every man from the eastern provinces, to call up the National Guard, and to provide for the defence of Amsterdam by collecting a flotilla of gun-boats in the Zuider Zee, and by covering with batteries the peninsula of Buiksloot, over against the town. On the 2nd of September he joined Daendels, who had taken up a position from Alkmaar eastward nearly to Hoorn, with the outposts on his left pushed forward to within a mile or two of those on the British right. On the 8th he was strengthened by a reinforcement which raised his total numbers to twenty-one thousand men, two-thirds Dutch and one-third French; whereupon he resolved to attack Abercromby at once before more troops could reach him from England.

His plan was to turn the British right, for which purpose seven thousand French under General Vandamme were to debouch from Schoorl, a village about five miles north of Alkmaar, and advance through the dunes by Groet and Kamp upon Petten. On Vandamme's right a second column of six thousand Dutch under General Dumonceau were to march by Schoorldam, a little to eastward of Schoorl, up the great canal upon Krabbendam, master the bridge and carry the salient angle of the lines. On Dumonceau's right a third column of almost the same force under Daendels was to assemble at St. Pankras, about three miles north-east of Alkmaar, and thence advance northward upon Eenigenburg.

The attack was fixed for daybreak on the 10th, but Abercromby had been warned of Brune's intention to take the offensive. The French movements on the night of the 9th also were not conducted so silently as to escape the attention of the British picquets, and Moore's patrols were ready to move forward as soon as it was light. Vandamme's column came first into action while it was still dark, covering its attack, as usual, with a cloud of skirmishers, while the grenadiers rushed forward with the bayonet. Nothing could exceed the impetuous gallantry of this assault—four companies of the grenadiers actually gaining the edge of the small canal at the foot of the dyke which was lined by the British. But the fire of Burrard's brigade was cool and steady, the French column was completely shattered, and the four intrepid companies were killed or taken to a man. After an hour and a half Vandamme's column retired, beaten, with very heavy loss.

Further to eastward the attack was delayed by some mismanagement which brought part of Dumonceau's column on to the same road with that of Daendels, and caused much contusion. Fearful of losing precious time, Dumonceau launched one of his brigades at Eenigenburg, and, leaving Daendels to turn his force further northward against St. Maarten, hurried toward with the rest of his men to the storm of Krabbendam. Here again the vehemence of the assault and the gallantry of the assailants were conspicuous. The brigade was parted into two columns, of which the smaller dashed forward along the road, despite the enfilading fire of two British guns, gained the first houses of the village and filled them with skirmishers, while the main body made a rush to seize the entrenchments on the dyke.

Misled by the attack on Eenigenburg, Abercromby had detached the Second battalion of the Twentieth to that quarter; and consequently the whole brunt of Dumonceau's onslaught fell upon five companies of the First battalion. For a short space these were borne back, and the situation wore so serious an aspect that Abercromby dismounted and placed himself at their head. But, though hastily composed of militiamen from half-a-dozen counties besides Devon, to which the regiment was by title affiliated, the Twentieth had an excellent Colonel, George Smyth, who had already made it worthy of its old reputation. The five companies behaved with the steadiness of veterans, repelling attack after attack until the Second battalion returned to their assistance, when Dumonceau's men broke and fled, and Colonel Macdonald pursuing them with the Reserve captured a gun, pontoons, and several prisoners.

At St. Maarten, Daendels was met with equal firmness by the militiamen of the Fortieth under Brent Spencer, and soon retired. At Eenigenburg the enemy carried the village but dashed themselves in vain against the entrenchments. In brief, Brune was repulsed all along the line, and retreated with a loss of over two thousand killed, wounded, and prisoners. The casualties among the British barely exceeded two hundred killed, wounded, and missing of all ranks; and of eleven officers wounded six belonged to the First battalion of the Twentieth. Brune's chances of success, unless by singular favour of fortune, were in fact remote; though the extraordinary advantages promised by a victory may be held to have justified him in hazarding the attempt. (Lieut.-Col. Anstruther to Colonel Calvert, 11th September 1799. Notes on the expedition in *W.O. Orig. Corres.*).

The prosperous issue of this day greatly strengthened the confidence of the British troops in themselves and in their officers; and it was with high hopes that they welcomed the arrival, within the five following days, of three more brigades of British infantry, a few more squadrons of British cavalry, and two divisions of Russians. In all, the reinforcements numbered thirty-three thousand men, with the Duke of York for commander-in-chief, David Dundas as a General of Division, and Lord Paget, who is better known by his later titles of Earl of

Oxbridge and Marquis of Anglesey, in command of the Seventh Light Dragoons. (These troops were: Lord Chatham's brigade, 4th/3 batts., 31st; Maj.-Gen. Manners's brigade, 9th/2 batts., 56th; Prince William of Gloucester's, 5th, 35th/each 2 batts.; also the 7th Light Dragoons, a detachment of the 18th Light Dragoons, and Artillery).

As to the quality of these troops it can only be said that the British infantry were, like most of the regiments already on the spot, militiamen of excellent but unshaped material. The Russians, who numbered twelve thousand men, were also imperfectly trained and disciplined; for, though the Tsar Paul had busied himself immensely with military improvements, the results had not been commensurate with his spasmodic energy, and the Muscovite soldier was not yet such a man as he proved himself later to be at Eylau.

Of General Hermann, who commanded the two divisions in Holland, it can only be said that, with a great deal of boasting and pretension, he was no better than his men. As regards the Duke of York, his deficiencies in the field had been sufficiently shown in 1793 and 1794; and his appointment was beyond doubt chiefly due to the imperative need of a commander-in-chief whose rank and authority the Russians could not venture to question. But, though it may well have been essentially necessary (as in Abercromby's opinion it was), the choice of the duke was unfortunate; and the methods selected by ministers for making good his defects were more unfortunate still. For he was required by his instructions to guide himself upon all important occasions by the advice of a Council of War, consisting of Abercromby, David Dundas, Pulteney, the Russian commander, and Major-General Lord Chatham.

★★★★★★

Bunbury, *Great War with France*. I have found no trace of these instructions as to a Council of War in the papers (otherwise very perfect) in the Record Office; but there is confirmation of the statement in a letter of Lord Grenville to Lord Buckingham (*Court and Cabinets of George III.*, ii): "The Duke of York has, I really believe, had no other fault than that of following, perhaps too implicitly, the advice of those whose advice he was ordered to follow." There is no sign, however, of any share taken by Lord Chatham.

★★★★★★

The three first of these were thoroughly competent soldiers, the fourth might or might not be so; but the addition of Lord Chatham, a man of notorious indolence and incapacity, was nothing short of an insult. Still even if one and all had been Heaven-born generals, the arrangement could not but have been utterly vicious; and it would have been far better to give the duke absolute control, with Abercromby or Moore for the chief of his staff. As regards the operations to be undertaken, the government wisely left to the duke a wide discretion, merely prescribing the recovery of Holland and of Utrecht southward to the Waal, as the principal object, and hoping that his force would enable him to send detachments also to the eastern provinces, (Dundas to York, 5th September 1799).

The duke had now some forty-eight thousand men under his command, of whom three-fourths were British; but the first sight of many of them filled him with dismay. In the haste to despatch the troops from Deal and the scarcity of tonnage, many necessary articles had been left behind. Some of the men were almost naked; two whole brigades did not possess a great-coat among them; and the result, in a season of incessant wind and rain, was that seventeen hundred of Abercromby's force were already in hospital. The arrangements for transport and supply gave him even more anxiety.

In respect of land-transport the full allowance ordered by the government for a force of practically fifty thousand men was one hundred bread-waggons, as many forage-carts, twenty hospital-waggons and ten forge-carts—an allowance which, on the scale of the present day, would be wholly insufficient for a division of infantry and a brigade of cavalry, counting together less than thirteen thousand men. Moreover, these waggons were not yet on the spot, fully half of them being in England and quite possibly still in course of construction. In the matter of ammunition-waggons, again, the Office of Ordnance, from motives of economy, had sent out a number of the old pattern which had been so strongly condemned by the Duke of York himself in 1793. So cumbrous, unstable, and unmanageable were they, that the success of the action of the 10th of September was imperilled by the difficulty of bringing forward ammunition; and men and officers rejoiced to see half-à-dozen of these "vile and ridiculous" vehicles knocked to pieces.

To add to these difficulties, not a single sutler had joined the army, and there was consequently not a drop of spirits to be obtained for the men. Fuel was wanting and was only supplied, pending the despatch of coal from England, by breaking up some of the captured Dutch ships. There were no store-houses for the housing of the supplies accumulated at the Helder, and it was necessary to substitute store-ships for them. Again, the Treasury had contrived to reduce itself to hopeless confusion over the provision of bread for the army. On the 9th of September there was but six days' supply in store, and the Chief Commissary could think of no better remedy than to write a long and solemn letter to Abercromby explaining why his forces must starve. Lastly, the medical arrangements were absolutely chaotic. The authorities had not taken the trouble even to form a hospital in England for the reception of invalids from Holland; and, when requested to appoint a place for it, they named Deal, where all the unfortunate wounded must have been landed from small boats on the beach with infinite torture and risk to broken limbs.

Fortunately, a leading medical authority, Sir Jerome Fitzpatrick, interposed, and insisted upon the choice of a port where hospital-ships of large draught could come alongside a jetty. But it is abundantly evident that the ministers and the Public Departments, with the single exception of the commander-in-chief's office, were as hopelessly incompetent for the conduct of war as in 1793. The ministers were so busy planning campaigns, of which they understood nothing, that they could spare no time for the humble details whereby an army is kept efficient in the field.

There was yet one more burden laid upon the commander-in-chief—that, namely, of arming and organising the Dutch who were to bring about the counter-revolution in favour of the House of Orange. High hopes had been built by Pitt and Grenville upon such a national movement, owing to the representations of the British Agent in the United Provinces, Mr. Bentinck, whose name sufficiently explains the reasons for his appointment. The Greffier Fagel, to whom Lord Grenville at the end of 1798 had submitted some of Bentinck's letters, declared that he had never heard the names of the persons whom the agent put forward as men of influence and leading, and said plainly that little was to be expected unless the Orange party were favoured by the principal men in the actual province of Holland. (Dropmore Papers, iv.).

The British, when they landed, found the people if not actually hostile, certainly not friendly; but, none the less, the Hereditary Prince of Orange, with the encouragement of the British Government, attached himself to Abercromby and plagued him with projects of every description, the sagacious old man reported:

I listen, but follow what to me appears to be our interest. . . .

I believe the prince has been deceived in thinking that he has more friends than enemies in this country. If we can advance, everyone will be on our side, but there are few who will risk anything.

There was the root of the whole matter. A successful campaign would undoubtedly regain the people of the United Provinces for the House of Orange, not because it was the House of Orange, but because it was the winning side; and, until the British arms had reconquered Holland, all negotiations with the Dutch were premature.

Such, however, in spite of a dozen lessons within half as many years, was not the belief of the British Ministers. Emboldened by their promise of pay for any levies that he could raise, the Prince of Orange produced a list of nearly three thousand Dutch sailors and deserters, demanded wages and levy-money for them, and proposed to attach them to Abercromby's army with himself at their head. The old General positively refused to encumber himself with such a rabble; but, none the less, the British Government expressly directed the Duke of York to co-operate with the Prince in raising such levies, so that the British troops should be free to go where they were most wanted.

Moreover, Thomas Grenville was sent Ambassador to the Hague to act as the prince's political adviser; so that the Duke had every prospect of being hampered not only by the Russian Commanders and his own Council of War, but also by the Prince of Orange, and possibly by the brother of the Secretary of State for Foreign Affairs. Not yet had British Ministers learned, and not yet for ten years were they to learn, that in war all secondary considerations must be postponed to the first and greatest object of military success.

★★★★★★

Abercromby to Dundas, 11th September (two letters with enclosures from the Prince of Orange). York, to Dundas, 14th (three letters), 16th, 18th September; Dundas to York, 5th and 15th September 1799, enclosing letter from Sir Jerome Fitzpatrick.

★★★★★★

CHAPTER 8

The Ill-Fated Alliance

Owing to the time consumed in disembarking the troops, the Duke of York was unable to advance immediately; and meanwhile Brune had employed the respite thus gained since his defeat on the 10th of September in strengthening his position. He now occupied an oblique line running from the little town of Bergen, which lies about three miles north-west of Alkmaar, north-eastward for six miles to Oukarspel. Bergen itself, nestling close under the highest and steepest range of the dunes and surrounded by little woods and copses, was strongly entrenched; in advance of it the villages of Schoorl, Groet and Kamp were fortified; and commanding positions were taken up on the sand-dunes, so that every inch of the ground on his left should be defensible.

To eastward of this, his centre barred the road southward along the Great Northern Canal by the occupation of the hamlet of Schoorldam and of the village of Warmenhuizen, a little to north-east of it; and his right, posted at Oudkarspel, lay astride the great causeway which leads to Alkmaar from the north. At each and all of these points he had multiplied the many natural obstacles of the country by breaking up the roads, making abatis and palisades, and constructing redoubts at the heads of the dykes; but, though outnumbered by nearly two to one, he omitted as yet to inundate the country to east of Oudkarspel for the protection of his right flank.

In a country which was accessible only by a few causeways, the Austrian system of attack by isolated columns was the only possible one; and the Council of War laid its plans accordingly. It was agreed that the Russians should take the place of honour on the right, and that General Hermann, with twelve Russian battalions, Manners's British brigade and the Seventh Light Dragoons, should drive the enemy from the sand-hills at Bergen. (See list following).

For the reader's convenience I repeat the list of brigades:—

Cavalry.—7th Light Dragoons, 11th Light Dragoons, detachment of 18th Light Dragoons, 1 troop R.H.A.

First Brigade.—Guards grenadier battalion, 3/1st Guards—Major-General D'Oyley.

Second Brigade.—1/Coldstream, 1/3rd Guards—Major-General Burrard.

Third Brigade.—2nd, 27th, 29th, 85th—Major-General Coote.

Fourth Brigade.—2/1st, 25th, 49th, 79th, 92nd—Major-General Moore.

Fifth Brigade.—1/17th, 2/17th, 1/40th, 2/40th—Major-General Don.

Sixth Brigade.—1/20th, 2/20th, 63rd—Major-General Lord Cavan.

Seventh Brigade.—3 battalions 4th, 31st—Major-General Lord Chatham.

Eighth Brigade.—1/5th, 2/5th, 2/35th—Prince William.

Ninth Brigade.—1/9th, 2/9th, 56th—Major-General Manners.

Reserve.—23rd, 55th—Colonel Macdonald.

In garrison at the Helder, 1/35th, 69th.

This was the First Column. On its left the Second Column, consisting of the two brigades of Guards, Prince William's brigade, and two squadrons of the Eleventh Light Dragoons, under David Dundas, were to force the positions of Warmenhuizen and Schoorldam and to co-operate with Hermann. On Dundas's left the Third Column, composed of Don's and Coote's brigades, with the two remaining squadrons of the Eleventh, were to carry Oudkarspel. Finally, a strong detached column, consisting of Moore's, Cavan's and Chatham's brigades, the Reserve, two composite battalions of Grenadiers and Light Infantry, and two squadrons of the Eighteenth Light Dragoons, under Abercromby's command, were to move wide to the left upon Hoorn, some twelve miles south-east of Oudkarspel, and, proceeding thence southward by forced marches upon Purmerend, to fall on the enemy's right flank and rear.

It is plain that the nicety of combination required for the success of this movement was excessive; and indeed the whole plan bears the mark of a compromise or, in other words, of a Council of War. The object of the Allies was to penetrate as speedily as possible to Amsterdam, and for that end the first thing requisite was to clear the passage between Alkmaar and the North Sea, so as to reach Haarlem and the Y. It may be affirmed with certainty that Brune could not be ousted from his position except by forcing one or the other of his flanks; and it therefore followed that in any attack the function of the Allied centre must be chiefly to contain the enemy, while the bulk of their strength was concentrated against a flank. Undoubtedly, the eastern flank, in the direction of Hoorn, was vulnerable; but a turning movement from that side was so wide as to require a corps of sufficient strength to act independently. Moreover, such a corps would need to be concentrated at Hoorn beforehand, so as to move up on Alkmaar simultaneously with the army on the Zype; and to this there was the objection that its appearance at Hoorn would betray the design, and cause Brune to check it by inundating the country.

All considerations, therefore, dictated the massing of an overwhelming force at Petten so as to force Brune's left or western flank, which would have led the army straight upon Haarlem and Leiden. Instead of this the Council of War, apparently halting between two opinions, concentrated considerable bodies of troops on both flanks and overwhelming force on neither. The attack was appointed to begin at dawn of the 19th; and accordingly, on the evening of the 18th, Abercomby marched with his division, about ten thousand men, for Hoorn. The distance to be traversed did not exceed thirteen miles as the crow flies, but was increased to more than twenty by the deviations of the road, which, moreover, was in an extremely bad condition.

Hence his column had a long and fatiguing march, but on reaching Hoorn at two in the morning found the *commandant* and his petty garrison asleep in their beds, and the sentinels asleep at the gates. The place was therefore occupied without difficulty, and one hundred and sixty Dutch soldiers were captured, which was all to the good. But the troops were so much jaded by their exertions during the night, and the roads were so execrable, that Abercromby did not feel justified in making a forced march upon Purmerend until he heard how the day was going on his right. And things on the right, as must now be told, were going anything but well.

At two o'clock, or still earlier, in the morning of the 19th some Russian light infantry and a battalion of grenadiers under General

Schutorff crossed the canal before Petten, for no reason, apparently, except their own caprice, and advanced along the sea-shore straight upon the French lines at Kamp. General Hermann was apprised of the fact by half-past two, but made no effort to stop or recall them; and, on the firing of one or two shots an hour later, he declared that, since Schutorff had begun the attack, he must be supported. Thereupon, he ordered his first line of Russians to advance from Petten along the Slaeper dyke, parallel to Schutorff and about two thousand yards east of him.

At the same time he directed two squadrons of the Seventh Light Dragoons to support Schutorff and two more to act as escort to a troop of British Horse-Artillery, at the same time moving Manners's brigade a little to the eastward from Petten to wait in reserve. It was still too dark to distinguish any object when he ordered the gun to be fired as the signal for attack, being fully aware, as he confessed, that he was beginning his work too soon, but unable longer to restrain the impatience of the troops.

The first line of the Russians therefore advanced in very fair order along the Slaeper dyke till they reached the first breastwork erected by the French, when they sent up a savage yell and rushed forward. The enemy gave way without firing more than half-a-dozen shots, but the whole of the Russians, from front to rear of the column, responded with a tremendous and irregular fire, destructive to none but themselves. In this tumultuous state they pressed on in the dark, carrying the second of the breastworks as easily as the first, but suffering heavily from their own fire.

Meanwhile, Schutorff's column could be heard advancing as rapidly on the right through the sand-hills, and Hermann's men raised a wild cry for artillery. This was brought forward, and, though the darkness still forbade all distinction of any definite object, the guns likewise opened a furious and aimless cannonade. Pressing on to the end of the dyke the column parted itself into two divisions, one of which joined Schutorff's force, and with it poured from time to time a heavy fire upon the other division, which followed the road to Groet.

This village also was carried with little difficulty, but it was evident that the main force of the enemy was on the east side of this road; for a heavy though irregular fire was directed upon the Russians from that quarter, which was answered both by Hermann's column and, though far out of range, by Schutorff's, the latter firing indiscriminately both upon the enemy and upon their comrades. Hermann's horse was

Battle of Bergen

struck by a French bullet from the east, and he now ascended the dunes towards Schutorff's corps, leaving his own column without directions of any kind. However, both divisions still blundered on in the same irregular fashion.

The Russian light infantry had exhausted its ammunition and was thenceforth useless; but their second line of infantry came up, promptly mingled with the first, and by its impetus carried the whole body forward. The Russian colonels could not find their regiments and had lost all control of their men. From time to time they shouted the order to cease fire, but no one took the slightest notice. The men of the French advanced posts had been rallied upon three battalions before Schoorl; but the Russians in the road, though still under the fire of their comrades on the sand-hills, brushed them aside and floundered on blindly towards Bergen.

The road now passed through a chain of scattered houses and narrow copses of very thick underwood, with occasional openings towards the east, from which a steadily increasing volume of fire poured upon them from the French infantry and artillery.

★★★★★★

The character of the road, though the houses are far more numerous than a century ago, is little changed; and the course of the action can be well traced by the traveller who traverses it at this day.

★★★★★★

For Brune had already begun to reinforce his left by calling detachments from Dumonceau's troops across the bridge at Schoorldam. Captain Taylor, the British staff-officer who had accompanied the Russian column on the road, now entreated the commanding officers to deploy their regiments and extend them to eastward; but they seemed utterly helpless and incapable of more than a wild advance along the highway, with indiscriminate firing to front and flanks. They were now within a mile of Bergen, and plunged into an avenue with dense underwood on each hand, which screened them until they were within two hundred yards of the town. There the underwood ceased on the eastern side, and their advance was checked by a tremendous fire of musketry and artillery on their front and left flank.

Crowded together in a confused mass, they again yelled for guns, which were with great difficulty brought up, the horses being scarcely able to crawl. Then, covered by their fire, the mob of men again surged forward, still under a terrible rain of bullets and grape, when General

Capture of General Hermann

Essen, Hermann's second in command, at last appeared and gave the order for the troops to halt and form.

A battalion was then extended to the left, with guns, to keep down the French fire; the crowd of men on the road was re-formed; and more infantry came up in the rear under Hermann himself, who apparently had brought them down from the sand-hills. The column then advanced again, but was immediately thrown into confusion by the battalion which had been extended to the left, and which now fell back in disorder upon the road.

However, though Hermann had now lost all control of his men, they struggled on to Bergen, and actually occupied it in a helpless and apathetic fashion for about twenty minutes, without the slightest idea as to what they should do next. But by this time Brune's reserve from Alkmaar had arrived upon the scene; whereupon Vandamme, sending forward his *chasseurs* to drive back such few Russians as remained in the sand-hills, attacked the village both from east and west, and, as the main body fell back along the road, closed in upon it on all sides. The Russian retreat now became a rout.

Hermann was taken prisoner. Essen, collecting a few troops, forced his way back through the avenue under the fire of the French, who had lined the underwood alongside it, and succeeded in reaching a small body of men on the sand-hills. Upon these he rallied his troops, at the same time despatching Taylor in hot haste to bring up Manners's brigade to his support.

Meanwhile, Dundas's column, which was accompanied by the Duke of York, had advanced as soon as the light permitted upon Warmenhuizen, throwing out one battalion towards Schoorldam to cover Hermann's left flank, and two more to eastward to preserve communication with Pulteney. His progress was necessarily slow, owing to the need for throwing flying bridges over the innumerable waterways that barred his advance; but at six o'clock the village was smartly stormed by the simultaneous attack of three Russian battalions from the east, and of the First Guards from the west.

Supported by three gunboats in the great canal, Dundas moved next upon Schoorldam; but, the enemy having destroyed the roads, he could advance to it only over a network of canals, and did not reach it until nine o'clock. He carried that village also, however, taking several hundred prisoners; soon after which an *aide-de-camp* came galloping up at the top of his speed to the Duke of York. He brought the news of the utter defeat of the Russians upon the right.

The duke at once ordered Manners's brigade to advance upon Schoorl; but the French had followed up their counter-attack with astonishing rapidity, and the Russians were utterly demoralised. They were scattered in scores about the villages which they had taken—drunk, insubordinate, and pillaging upon all sides. Major-General Knox, who entered their camp at nine o'clock, found it full of stragglers wounded and unwounded; while on the sand-hills Russian riflemen were in sight, with the French *chasseurs* in hot pursuit.

Seeing; that there was nothing' to check these chasseurs, Knox sent two squadrons of the Seventh Light Dragoons to rally the Russian riflemen, if possible, and galloped back to the Helder to fetch the Thirty-fifth, which formed part of the garrison. Returning to Kamp with this regiment at about eleven, he met the Russian general, Essen, who entreated him to stay his drunken, plundering troops; whereupon he handed the Thirty-Fifth to him to cover their retreat. A more trying and difficult duty for a battalion of raw militia, which had evidently been left in garrison because it was worse fitted than the rest for the field, it would be difficult to imagine; and it is not surprising to find that it suffered heavily.

★★★★★★

A militiaman, whom I presume to have been of this corps, left a journal in which he recorded his impression of our Allies as he first saw them. "The Russians is people as has not the fear of God before their eyes, for I saw some of them with cheeses and butter and all badly wounded, and in particklar one man had an eit days clock on his back and fiting all the time which made me to conclude and say all his vanity and vexation of spirit."—*Recollections of the British Army, Colburn's Military Magazine,* February 1836.

★★★★★★

Thus it was that when Manners's brigade reached Schoorl it found the village already abandoned by the Russians and set on fire by their plunderers, and was soon fully occupied, if not overtasked, with the duty of checking the counter-attack of the French. Great efforts were made to rally the Russians, but without success. They streamed away into their own lines, and dispersed, both officers and men, without the slightest effort to re-form; and the danger that the French might force the western extremity of the Allied line became pressing. Meanwhile, the bridge over the great canal at Schoorldam had been broken down, and Dundas was unable to send a man to Schoorl until it had been repaired, which took a full hour. Battalion after battalion was then withdrawn from his force to reinforce Manners, while Dundas himself maintained his position at Schoorldam under a very heavy fire with indomitable tenacity. But it was too late.

The British were forced back from Schoorl; and Dundas then retired in good order, covered by the gunboats in the great canal. This seems to have taken place between four and five o'clock in the afternoon, by which time the British had been on foot for thirteen or fourteen hours; and the retreat, as was natural with weary, half-trained, and incoherent bodies of men, was anything but orderly. Many of the brigadiers, as well as the regimental officers, were without experience, and several battalions filed through the all important post of Krabbendam without an order to any one of them to take up positions for its defence. In fact, there were no troops to be trusted except the four battalions of Guards and the artillery; and the Guards, having been heavily engaged all through the day, had lost many men, had expended nearly all their ammunition, and were quite worn out with fatigue. These old soldiers, however, were still unbeaten, and, thanks to their spirit, the French did not venture on an attack upon the lines.

★★★★★★

According to Bunbury the situation was saved by a grenadier of the Guards, who, when his colonel hesitated to march the weary battalion back to Krabbendam (through which it had already passed), said, "Give us some more cartridges, and we will see what can be done." Thereupon the colonel gave the order to march. *Great War with France.*

★★★★★★

Meanwhile, Pulteney, after struggling with infinite difficulties before Oudkarspel, had at last contrived to carry the redoubt which barred his progress along the great causeway. Coote's brigade, which he had detached to turn the French position, had found it absolutely impossible to make its way over the obstacles presented by the marshy meadows. In front, he himself could advance no further than to a cross-dyke, from behind which he engaged in a savage duel of musketry and artillery with the Dutch, hoping that time might yet give him a favourable opening. At length, after the lapse of many hours, the enemy imprudently attempted a counter-attack, which was heavily repulsed; and the British, pursuing, entered the redoubt upon the backs of the fugitives, and drove them from it, with the loss of sixteen guns and seven hundred prisoners.

The Dutch retreated in confusion south-westward to Koedyck, and Pulteney, after advancing for a short distance in that direction with the hope of renewing the attack on the morrow, bivouacked for the night. At eleven o'clock he received an order from the Duke of York to retreat without delay to the lines of the Zype, which he did, after first destroying the captured guns; and thus the whole of the advantage which he had gained was thrown away.

Abercromby's division never moved nor fired a shot throughout the day. The first message which he received from the Duke of York came at noon and announced Dundas's success at Warmenhuizen, but added that nothing was known of Pulteney. The general thereupon took steps to ascertain whether he could march across country to the westward, but found that such a step was impracticable owing to the breadth of the canals that barred the way.

At four o'clock in the afternoon a second messenger arrived with the news that Pulteney had captured Oudkarspel, but that the Russians had been beaten, and that the division was to return to its original station immediately. Leaving the Fifty-Fifth to occupy Hoorn, where the inhabitants had been very friendly, he started at dusk along the road by which he had come. The rain began to fall in torrents directly afterwards; the road became one mass of mud, and the march was terribly arduous.

The two battalions of flank-companies from the Line, being composed entirely of militiamen, left an enormous number of stragglers on the road, one company returning to quarters with only twenty men out of one hundred and ten.

★★★★★★

Of these twenty, fourteen were old soldiers, of which there were only fifteen in the company. The remaining six were rebels captured at Vinegar Hill. Colburn's *Military Magazine*, Feb. 1836.

★★★★★★

At every point was proved the danger of throwing half-trained men suddenly into active service.

The casualties of the British were six officers and one hundred and twenty-seven men killed; forty-four officers and three hundred and ninety seven men wounded, and four hundred and ninety men missing, exclusive of three hundred and fifty men of the First battalion of the Thirty-Fifth, whose fate was stated to be unknown, but who were certainly taken. This was the unfortunate battalion that had been hurried forward from the Helder, when the retreating Russians first began to stream into Petten.

The total of casualties was therefore rather over fourteen hundred of all ranks, of whom five hundred belonged to Manners's brigade; from which it is evident that the covering of the Russian retreat cost far more men than the attacks of Dundas and Pulteney. Against this the Duke of York could show three thousand prisoners captured, the bulk of them by Dundas in his capture of Schoorldam, and sixteen French guns destroyed. The loss of the Russians was set down at between two and three thousand men, the latter figure being the more probable; and they left twenty-six guns in the hands of the enemy. The loss of the French and Dutch can have been little if at all smaller than that of the Allies; and, altogether, neither side had very much to boast of.

None the less, the moral advantage gained by the French was immense. The British had lost all confidence in the Russians; and the Russians, though their misfortunes were entirely of their own making, of course attributed them to the backwardness of the British in giving them support. Since the Duke of York had sacrificed nearly a thousand men to save them, their complaints did not render the British feeling towards them more cordial. Beyond all doubt, the Russians were responsible for the day's failure, for, if they had but gone through their antics two hours later, as had been arranged, the duke's plan, faulty though it was, might have proved successful. Even so, however, their plunder and destruction of the Dutch villages would have done, as it actually did, untold mischief by alienating the inhabitants; for, in this respect, the behaviour of the British had so far been exemplary.

Lastly, the British had lost confidence in their commander-in-chief, and the commander-in-chief had lost confidence in his troops—in neither case without good reason. The duke's hasty recall of both Abercromby and Pulteney, instead of holding on to Oudkarspel, and using a part of Abercromby's force to support it, showed that he had lost his head for the moment; and this was not calculated to encourage the troops. On the other hand, the disorder of the retreat on the right and the helplessness of the brigadiers in that difficult duty were enough to discourage any general.

Two days later, Sept. 21st, Admiral Mitchell took a flotilla of gunboats into the Zuider Zee, and paid visits to Medemblick and Enckhuisen, where the inhabitants hoisted the Orange standard; while another detachment of the like craft sailed across and made a raid upon

Lemmer, on the west coast of Friesland. There was, however, little profit in these operations, and, indeed, the admiral seems to have been no very enterprising officer, or he would long before have prepared his gunboats, as Abercromby had urged, and have threatened Amsterdam. (Abercromby to Dundas, 4th September 1799).

However, on the 24th of September a new corps of from three to four thousand Russians from Kronstadt was disembarked, and at about the same time there arrived also three troops of the Fifteenth Light Dragoons, and a company or two of riflemen from the Sixth battalion of the Sixtieth—a battalion not yet two months old, and, of course, composed of foreigners. The Duke of York, therefore, lost no time in making preparations for a second attack.

The plans which he submitted to Abercromby and Dundas were three. The first was to detach a strong corps to eastward to threaten the French right, and in co-operation with the fleet to alarm Amsterdam. This Abercromby rejected on the ground that this detachment, if raised to a proper strength, would leave too few men to hold the lines of the Zype. A second proposal, to hold the present position, and send seven thousand men to hearten the Orange party in Friesland and Groningen was rejected both by David Dundas and Abercromby, as promising no certain result and giving the enemy time to gather reinforcements.

It was, therefore, decided to adopt the third plan, namely, to make a second general attack upon the enemy's position, directing an overwhelming force upon his left, and entrusting the hardest of the work, namely, the advance along the sea-shore from Petten, to the best of the British troops with Abercromby in command.

The attack was fixed for the 29th of September, and the columns were actually formed up at daybreak; but a heavy south westerly gale made the march of troops along the beach impossible, and drove the sand so furiously before it in the dunes that no troops could have fought against it with success. Further operations were therefore unavoidably delayed for three days, which Brune did not fail to turn to account by perfecting his defences. Warmenhuizen was indeed abandoned, but Oudkarspel was further strengthened by inundations.

Koedyck, a village on the great canal about three miles to south east of Schoorl, and Schoorl itself were fortified by additional entrenchments; and the reclaimed fens called the Schermer, Beemster and Purmer, to east and southeast of Alkmaar, were flooded, thus effectually covering his right flank and rear. Finally, a reinforcement of four French squadrons, four French and several Dutch battalions made good to him his losses in the last action, and raised his force to about twenty-five thousand men.

The Duke of York laid his plans for the attack in four principal columns.

The First or Right Column consisted of D'Oyley's, Moore's, and Cavan's brigades, and Macdonald's Reserve, in all about eight thousand bayonets; together with one troop of Horse Artillery and nine squadrons of the Seventh, Eleventh, and Fifteenth Light Dragoons, making seven hundred and fifty sabres, under Lord Paget. It was ordered to march along the beach against Egmont-aan-Zee, (more familiar as Egmont-op-Zee, but I adhere to the name as given on modern Dutch maps), and to turn the enemy's left flank.

The Second Column was composed wholly of Russian troops, eight thousand of them infantry, and two hundred Cossacks, under their own General Essen. It was directed to follow the road under the eastern face of the sand-dunes, which Hermann had traversed on the 19th of September, through Groet and Schoorl upon Bergen, keeping a detachment under General Sedmoratzky on its eastern side so as to cover its left flank and maintain communication with the next column.

This, the Third Column, under command of David Dundas, was formed of Chatham's, Coote's and Burrard's brigades, with one squadron of the Eleventh Light Dragoons; in all about forty five hundred bayonets and one hundred sabres. Of these, Coote's brigade was to follow the advanced guard of Abercromby's column to Kamp, and there turning eastward to take in reverse the defences which barred the advance of the Russians, and to cover Essen's right flank. Chatham's brigade was to follow in support of Essen's corps for the attack on Bergen, and in conjunction with Coote's to endeavour to maintain communication with Abercromby. Burrard's brigade was to move on the eastern side of the Great Northern Canal and combine with Sedmoratzky's corps in the attack on Schoorldam, being assisted by seven gunboats, specially prepared and protected for the purpose, upon the canal itself.

The Fourth Column, under Pulteney, consisted of Prince William's, Don's, and Manners's brigades, two battalions of Russians, and two squadrons of the Eighteenth Light Dragoons. It was posted so as to cover the left of the British position to the Zuider Zee, threaten the enemy's right, and take advantage of any favourable opportunity that might offer itself. It numbered forty-eight hundred bayonets and one hundred and fifty sabres, and was stationed chiefly at Schagen. (I have taken the numbers from the plan enclosed in the Duke of York's letter to Dundas of 25th September, corrected by the slight alterations that are shown in his despatch of 6th October).

The attacking army, excluding the Fourth Column, was reckoned at twenty -two thousand bayonets and sabres, or, making allowance for officers and sergeants, about twenty-five thousand of all ranks.

It will be observed that the greater part of this force was to act in the sand-dunes, the one space unbroken by dykes, ditches, and canals in Brune's line of defence; and it is therefore necessary to describe them somewhat minutely. From Kamp southward to Bergen, a distance of about four miles, the dunes rise to a larger scale than at any other point on the coast. Beginning with a breadth of two or three hundred yards at Kamp itself, they widen rapidly to more than a mile opposite Groet, to about three miles opposite Schoorl, and to close upon four miles midway between Schoorl and Bergen. In this last space they attain to the dignity of true hills, with a height of fully one hundred and fifty feet, and with unbroken ridges, four or five hundred yards in length, covered with heather and stunted coppice.

On the seaward side they rise abruptly, like cliffs, for some eighty feet sheer above a broad beach. To landward they descend, for the most part, as abruptly to the level plain of the fen, covered with long strips of dense scrub and coppice, chiefly birch, which, where fully sheltered from the westerly wind, grows to a respectable height. Between the two outer ridges to seaward and to landward lies a chaos of lower sand-hills, for the most part bare or held together by coarse grasses, but frequently presenting narrow valleys of nearly level ground, dotted with heather and low creeping shrubs, and broken by occasional patches of dense stunted birch from a quarter to a half of an acre in extent. These little valleys are in places fully half a mile long, and from fifty to one hundred yards broad; and it is important to note that they are to be found, for the most part, immediately within the two outermost ridges. Hence, if a force were advancing in line through the dunes, the two flanks, unless constantly checked, would inevitably soon outstrip the centre.

It must be remarked also that, once within this confusion of sand-hills, a man is practically shut off from the world without. A company advancing just within the seaward ridge, and another company advancing along the beach within three hundred yards of it would be out of sight, and, from the roar of wind and sea, out of hearing of each other. The only means for preserving communication between them would be for one man, or a few men, to follow the comb of the outermost ridge itself, ascending and descending knee-deep in loose sand, along a surface where hardly three consecutive steps would be upon the same level. Troops summoned from the beach to the dunes would equally have to climb up a sheer ascent of eighty or a hundred feet knee-deep in sand, no very easy matter to men burdened with a heavy musket and a pack.

Finally, within the dunes themselves, an officer could rarely see to any distance either to front or flank without a laborious scramble to the summit of some ridge or hummock, where his figure would stand clear against the sky-line, an easy mark for sharp-shooters, who even within a few yards of him could find ample means of concealment. It will, therefore, be gathered that it was difficult to move infantry, and quite impossible to move artillery through the dunes. Hence, Abercromby could take no guns with him except a single troop of horse-artillery and two six -pounders, which were practically tied to the beach; and freedom of movement even on the beach, owing to quicksands and other obvious causes, was dependent on the state of the tide.

So much for the difficulties of the advance and the maintenance of communication between the beach and the dunes. Scarcely less formidable were those that beset the communication between the dunes and the reclaimed fen to landward. The road from Kamp to Bergen runs at first about five hundred yards distant from the foot of the sand-hills, draws closer to them at the village of Groet for a few hundred yards, recedes again for a short distance, and finally returning to them at the village of Schoorl hugs them closely all the way to Bergen.

At Groet there begins on the eastern slope of the sand-hills a chain of rough coppice, which continues almost unbroken to Bergen; while that slope itself from Schoorl southward is often for many hundred yards so steep that a man could hardly ride, and could only with difficulty lead, a horse from the road to the summit. A blinder country, and one more difficult for scouts, it would be difficult to find. But this is not all. Immediately to south of Bergen the width of the dunes suddenly contracts from four miles to two, and continues to shrink steadily to southward, until at Egmont-aan-Zee it hardly exceeds a mile.

The hills themselves also become easier and lower, while the plain immediately to east of Egmont itself, though perfectly level, is for nearly a mile in width sound, firm ground, enclosed by banks and free from the ditches that make the plain of North Holland impassable. It is, in fact, ground where troops can deploy, where artillery can move, and where cavalry can act. There is also a gap in the dunes at Egmont-aan-Zee, and a road running eastward from it to Egmont-aan-den-Hoef whereby guns could be easily moved to or from either flank of the sand-hills.

To south of Egmont-aan-Zee the dunes, though low and scattered, broaden out once more, while a great number of little copses on each side of the road afford additional facilities for a force retiring southward to cover its retreat. A reserve of French troops about Egmont-aan-Zee and Egmont-aan-den-Hoef could either prevent an exhausted enemy from debouching from the dunes on to the plain, and cut them off from water, or, if forced back, could effectually harass, if not actually prevent, their further advance. (I feel constrained to apologise for so lengthy a description of this little strip of country; but without it any conception of the difficulty of the Duke of York's task is impossible).

The morning of the 2nd of October broke fine and warm, though the wind still blew too strongly from the south-west to permit the flotilla on the Zuider Zee to make a demonstration, as had been intended, on the right flank of the French. About six o'clock the tide was at ebb, and Abercromby's column moved out of Petten, the advanced guard being formed by a squadron of the Seventh Light Dragoons with two guns of the Horse Artillery. The French picquet at Kamperduin retired without resistance, merely firing a signal-gun as it went; and Abercromby's column, with the other brigades that followed it, passed on to the sand hills and deployed. Coote's brigade, pursuant to its orders, turned sharply to eastward, making for the road to Schoorldam.

Macdonald's Reserve, strengthened by two composite battalions of the Grenadiers and Light Infantry of the Line, and by three hundred Russian Light Infantry, also turned to the east, its duty being to cover the left flank of Abercromby's main column. Moore's brigade, which formed the advanced guard, likewise entered the sand-dunes, keeping its right flank on the hills that rise immediately from the beach, while the rest of the column followed the beach itself, the right flank of the cavalry being constantly in the water.

★★★★★★

The *British Military Library*, ii. ill, says that Cavan's brigade (which was commanded by General Hutchinson) followed

Coote's brigade and advanced along the heights overlooking the road to Schoorl. All other authorities point to its having been on the beach, but I can find no trace of the part that it took in the action, and its casualties were slight.

★★★★★★

The enemy was visible in small bodies both on the shore and among the dunes; and a few skirmishers presently engaged and annoyed the Reserve. Thereupon Macdonald, who has been described by one of his contemporaries as a "very wild warrior," strayed away to eastward in pursuit of them, leaving the flank of Abercromby's column uncovered. Unable to discover what had become of the Reserve, and finding his flank galled by the French light troops, Abercromby was obliged to delay and weaken his advance by throwing out a flank-guard. Moore accordingly detached the Twenty-Fifth and Seventy-Ninth for this duty, taking command of them in person.

He had scarcely formed them before the French attacked them in earnest, but were driven back by a charge with the bayonet, though not before Moore had been struck in the thigh by a bullet. He continued however, to command his brigade, and the advance was resumed, the French light troops retreating before him, but skilfully using all the innumerable advantages of the ground to harass and oppose him. Gradually more battalions were thrown out to bear back the pressure on Moore's left flank and rear,—first the Royals and Fortyninth, and later the Grenadier battalion of Guards from the beach; and thus it came about that, the difficulties both of the ground and of the enemy's attacks being greatest upon his left, Moore's whole brigade was drawn out into a long irregular echelon, the Twenty-Fifth leading it on the right at a considerable distance in advance of the other battalions. However, after five hours' march in these trying circumstances, Abercromby's column arrived within about a mile of Egmont, where the enemy stood in force in a strong position.

★★★★★★

After close examination of the ground I and my companion came to the conclusion that this position was exactly opposite the village of Wimmenum, where a transverse ridge of very steep sandhills, with a multitude of little copses, cuts across the dunes from east to west. But, in truth, the whole of the dunes form one continuous defensive position.

★★★★★★

Their officers quickly noticed Moore's disordered battalions, and forthwith launched upon them their own fresh and unwearied troops. The Twenty-Fifth was struck heavily in front and flank, and three companies of the Ninety-Second, coming to their assistance, were clumsily led straight through the hottest of the fire. The whole began to give way, and at this critical moment Moore was struck down by a bullet behind the ear, and fell to the ground stunned and helpless.

The rest of the Ninety-Second, however, backed by the First Guards, came up on the right of the Twenty-Fifth; the Royals, Forty-Ninth, and Grenadiers of the Guards hastened to close up to their left; and the fight was renewed. A confused struggle followed, which lasted the best part of an hour; small bodies of men on both sides closing with each other, and, unable to use their weapons in the unstable sand, betaking themselves to their fists. At length, wearied out, the French retired to their first position, the British halted over against them, and, as if by tacit agreement, the contest ceased in this part of the field, (*Narrative of a Private Soldier in the 92nd Foot*).

In this situation Abercromby found himself as the sun began to decline. Moore's brigade, the only one except the Guards which was composed of trained soldiers, was utterly exhausted by fighting, and weakened by the loss of nearly seven hundred men and of forty-four officers, among whom was Moore himself, the best officer of all. To renew his attack he had no trained soldiers except the two battalions of Guards, of which the first had lost nearly seventy officers and men in the struggle to rescue the Twenty-Fifth, while the grenadiers, though they had suffered far less, had shared in the distressing march through the sand-hills.

To support them he had only three battalions of Militia, numbering fewer than eighteen hundred men. The enemy in his front was in great force; reinforcements were visible marching to join them; and their artillery, far surpassing his own in weight and number of guns, had already made itself felt among the troops on the beach. Of the rest of the British army he could see nothing and hear nothing. From Macdonald he had received not a word except one note written some hours before, to say that he was at Groet, which was at least three miles from where he ought to have been. Weary in body, for two horses had been killed under him, perplexed and harassed in spirit, Abercromby was fain to halt, and, while making a show of a bold front, to look for a position against the coming of night.

Nor had the other columns fared much better. Coote's brigade duly scoured the sand-hills on the right of Essen's column, while Sedmoratzky and Burrard cleared the plain on their left; but though the French retired without much resistance from Groet and Schoorl, they stood for some time at Schoorldam, until driven out at about eleven o'clock by Sedmoratzky and Burrard. At this point, however, Essen halted the whole of the Russians and declined to budge further, thus preventing Burrard from moving forward against Koedyck, and leaving only Coote's and Chatham's brigades to Dundas for the capture of Bergen. Coote's battalions were at the time above Schoorl, extended at wide intervals into the sand-hills and making little progress. Dundas therefore passed Chatham's brigade to the right of Coote's, and moved it forward so as to threaten the left flank of the French, who retired to the heights above Bergen itself, from whence they opened a heavy cannonade upon Dundas's line.

The British, easily finding shelter among the dunes, suffered little; and an attempt at a counterattack from the French along the avenue that led into Bergen was repulsed with heavy loss by the Eighty-Fifth. Dundas now passed three battalions of Coote's brigade to the right of Chatham's; and these unexpectedly found their right in contact with Macdonald's Reserve, which had been floundering aimlessly among the sand-hills all day. The whole were therefore formed in line, Coote's and Chatham's brigades to east of the road from Bergen to Egmont, and Macdonald's battalions to west of it. A general advance swept the enemy from the sand-hills on the right front; and the eleven battalions established themselves astride of the road, thus cutting the direct communication between the French on the beach and their comrades in Bergen.

Meanwhile Abercromby, though remaining halted, had pushed his troop of Horse Artillery well in advance, its escort of dragoons standing dismounted a little in rear of it and hidden from the enemy's view by a sand-hill. General Vandamme, who had just brought up two battalions and a squadron of hussars from Alkmaar, perceiving the guns to be unprotected, sent forward the hussars to make a swoop upon them; and so swiftly and cunningly did these French horsemen advance that they were actually in the midst of the battery before they were discovered.

But a dozen English sergeants and officers, among whom were Paget, Robert Wilson, and Colonel Erskine of the Fifteenth, had remained in the saddle; and this handful of horsemen galloping straight at the hussars engaged them so vigorously as to gain time for the escort to mount. The British Light Dragoons speedily came up to their assistance and every man of the French squadron was cut down or captured.

This closed the action on the western flank. Far away to eastward Pulteney had played his part in threatening Oudkarspel and the French right with sufficient skill and prudence; and at nightfall the divisions of Dundas and Abercromby bivouacked on the ground that they had won, Macdonald bringing his weary and jaded men into Abercromby's lines at dusk. The action had lasted for over twelve hours, and the men were terribly fatigued. They had by the Duke's order left their packs behind, and carried only a blanket or a great-coat and three days' provisions; but, parched by the wind and by the salt and sand with which it was loaded, the men had emptied their water-bottles by noon, and there was no water in the bivouac.

Suffering agonies from thirst, they were unable to touch their salted rations, and lay down in misery until, as had already happened in every twenty-four hours of this campaign, the rain presently came down in torrents and gave them relief. Wringing their dripping clothes into their hats they drank the water greedily; and when the morning came, it was found that Brune had withdrawn his army from its position between Oudkarspel and Egmont and retreated. He retired, however, at his leisure and in perfect order, only to take up a shorter and more formidable line from Wyk-aan-Zee on the west through Beverwyk to Purmerend. The action had not accomplished much towards the conquest of Holland.

However, the Duke of York could justly claim a victory, and the name of Egmont-op-Zee is still borne on the colours of the regiments engaged. But it was the kind of victory which ruins an army. The loss of the British amounted to over fifteen hundred officers and men, and of the Russians to over six hundred officers and men killed, wounded, and missing, making over two thousand casualties altogether. (11 officers and 226 men killed; 74 officers, 1033 men wounded; 5 officers and 218 men missing; 125 horses killed, wounded, and missing).

Considerably more than half of this loss fell, as has been said, upon Abercromby's Division, and chiefly upon Moore's brigade, wherein the Ninety-Second Highlanders alone counted fourteen officers and two hundred men fallen, besides forty more missing. Macdonald also had contrived in the course of his foolish wanderings to throw away nearly three hundred men of the Reserve; his raw troops having suffered heavily from the French riflemen.

★★★★★★

226

Surtees, *Twenty-five Years in the Rifle Brigade*. The author at the time was in the light company of the Fifty-sixth. From his account it is plain that the Reserve became broken up, and that there were companies of it scattered along the whole line from Bergen to the sea.

Surtees of the Rifles, a soldier of the 95th (Rifles) in the Peninsular campaign of the Napoleonic Wars by William Surtees and *The 95th (Rifles) in America* the experiences of two soldiers during the war of 1812, by Harry Smith and William Surtees are also published by Leonaur.

★★★★★★

The loss of the French was at least as great; and they left seven guns, besides a few hundred prisoners, as trophies to the duke. But there can be no doubt that the British in the sand-hills were outfought throughout the day by the enemy, for the simple reason that the French had an active and well-trained light infantry, whereas the British had none.

Moore himself was obliged to drive off the French skirmishers with the bayonet, having no skirmishers of his own with which to meet them; and the huge militiamen of the massed grenadier-companies exhausted themselves in rushing up sand-hills after the nimble little Frenchmen, who indeed always retired, but were seldom if ever overtaken. This was one cause of the general failure of the attack. Others, which chiefly contributed to it, were the sulky refusal of the Russians to advance, and the powerlessness of Abercromby upon his arrival before Egmont owing to the vagaries of Macdonald. But, in truth, even the most highly -trained troops under the best of officers might easily have come to misfortune over a plan of operations which was necessarily complicated owing to the enormous difficulties of the country.

On the days following the action Abercromby moved forward to the south of Egmont-aan-Zee, the Russians to Egmont Binnen on Abercromby's left, Dundas to Alkmaar and to Heiloo on the road to Haarlem, and Pulteney to the space between Alkmaar and Schermerhorn, with Prince William's brigade detached to Hoorn. But these dispositions were made in the most careless and slovenly fashion, and for two days Abercromby remained isolated at Egmont without a man between him and Alkmaar. (*Diary of Sir John Moore*, i. Bunbury, *Great War with France*).

Meanwhile Brune, having been reinforced by six French battalions from Belgium, had fortified a triple line of posts, the foremost running from South Bakkum through Limmen to Akersloot and the

Lange Meer, the next from Heemskerk to Uitgeest, and the third from Wyk-aan-Zee to Beverwyk; while Daendels held the passes through the inundations to eastward at Knollendam and Purmerend, with a reserve in rear of the latter at Monnikendam.

The Duke of York, somewhat elated by his victory and in difficulties over supplies for his army, was anxious to force the position of Beverwyk before Brune could fortify it effectually; and, ignorant of his true dispositions, ordered the advanced posts on his right to move forward on the morning of October 6th and to occupy the villages in their front. Accordingly, so far as can be gathered, a part of Abercromby's division advanced through the sand-hills on the coast, Essen's Russians moved upon South Bakkum, and Coote's and Burrard's brigades upon Limmen and Akersloot respectively.

All three of the villages were captured with little difficulty, five companies of the Coldstream and Third Guards making a brilliant charge at Akersloot and capturing two hundred prisoners. But Essen, not content with this, insisted upon wandering still further south, unaware that Brune had been concentrating upon his second line of defence; and upon reaching Kastrikum, on the road a little to southward of South Bakkum, the Russian General found his easy progress arrested by a sharp resistance from three French battalions. Instantly he sent for reinforcements. Battalion after battalion of his own troops hurried forward to join him; Abercromby also came forward on the west; and the French commander, finding that Abercromby was gaining way and likely to outflank him, evacuated the village and fell back to a position in the sand-hills.

From Egmont Binnen southward to Kastrikum and beyond it, the dunes again widen out to a breadth of fully three miles, no longer separated by a hard line from the cultivated plain, but gradually merged in it, in a tangle of little hills, enclosures, and copses. Here, therefore, the French held their own till Brune came to their support with the greater part of a division; and then for three hours a stubborn conflict was maintained with little advantage to either side, until Brune observed British troops, presumably Burrard's brigade, moving from the east to the help of Essen. Thereupon he detached three battalions to hold Burrard in check, and, massing the remainder in close columns, fell upon the Russians with the bayonet, and drove them headlong back to Kastrikum.

Here Essen rallied his broken battalions, calling urgently to Abercromby for help; but hardly had he succeeded in forming about four thousand men and posting his guns to command the approaches to the village, when the French division came upon him in pursuit. A sharp struggle followed; but Brune's men, pressing on with the impetuosity of success, speedily captured his guns and again drove him back along the two roads to South Bakkum and Limmen. The French cavalry followed them up keenly on the western road, until a small party of British horse, apparently of the Seventh Light Dragoons under Lord Paget, crashed in upon their left flank from an ambush in the dunes and sent them galloping back in wild confusion upon the French infantry.

★★★★★★

This charge of the Seventh Light Dragoons (for, putting the various accounts together, I think it certain that the credit of the action belongs to them) must have taken place where the road passes actually through a belt of the dunes a little to the north of South Bakkum. There is a small open space, just large enough for a couple of squadrons, adjoining the road but invisible until actually entered, where they were probably formed.

★★★★★★

The effect of this unexpected charge of a few score of resolute men was astonishing. The panic of the French horsemen communicated itself to the French foot, and the whole, some two or three thousand strong, gave way and ran back to Kastrikum. It was but just in time, for an unbridged stream lay in the rear of the Russians, and their destruction was almost inevitable. The attack of the dragoons, however, gave them breathing-time and recovered for them their guns. Abercromby appeared in person with one brigade from the west, and two of Dundas's battalions from the east. The bridge was repaired; the stream was passed; and the fight ended at the villages of Bakkum and Limmen, whence both sides retired in the darkness to their first positions.

It is difficult to know what to make of this strange scramble of an action. It seems certain that the Duke of York had intended only to drive in the French outposts on the 6th, and to advance in force on the following day; and the British blamed Essen for carrying his troops too far forward in contempt of the duke's orders. Since Essen, by all accounts, refused to have any dealing with the duke and made a point of disobeying his commands, this may well have been the case; but the fact remains that the duke allowed the whole of his force to drift into a general action for no particular object, without the slightest idea how to control it.

BATTLE OF KASTRIKUM

He was, in fact, in Alkmaar, with one of his staff perched on the top of the church-spire and with *aides-de-camp* flying in all directions to discover what had become of his army. The country, as has been told, was extremely difficult and intricate; the rain was falling in torrents; the smoke hung thickly among the trees; and in all directions were bodies of troops engaging whatever enemy came first to hand, and advancing or retiring, sometimes in great disorder, according as they were the weaker or the stronger party. (See the account of the rout of the grenadier-companies before Egmont Binnen in Surtees).

Yet it seems that the duke had notice of the first serious encounter of the Russians with the French from Abercromby, with a warning that the enemy seemed to intend a general attack. No notice, however, was taken of this; and the duke being at dinner, only invited the messenger, a certain Major James Kempt, to join him at table. Fortunately Brune did not meditate a general attack; but the engagement was sufficiently costly. The Russians returned a loss of over eleven hundred of all ranks, and the British casualties amounted to over eight hundred killed and wounded, and over six hundred prisoners. (4 officers, 91 men killed; 36 officers, 696 men wounded; 19 officers, 593 men missing).

The brigade that suffered most severely was Chatham's, in which the three battalions of the Fourth lost nearly one hundred and fifty officers and men killed and wounded, and over five hundred, including thirteen officers, prisoners; while the Thirty-First lost over one hundred killed and wounded and thirty-three prisoners. In what part of the field these battalions were engaged I have been unable to discover, but under so incompetent a brigadier they were likely to come to misfortune in any position. According to one authority Chatham himself was wounded, but not, apparently, in time to save him from wrecking his unfortunate troops.

Far heavier work fell upon Hutchinson with the Twentieth and Sixty-Third, who was left to hold his own against superior forces in the dunes while Abercromby was extricating Essen's disordered battalions. Hutchinson himself was struck in the thigh by a bullet; the Sixty-Third lost nearly two hundred of all ranks, one-fourth of them missing, and the two battalions of the Twentieth over one hundred and eighty more; but the brigade did its difficult duty well. The loss of the French was probably somewhat smaller than that of the Allies, though they too left five hundred prisoners in the hands of the British. But there could be no question that with them lay the advantage of the day.

BATTLE OF KASTRIKUM

★★★★★★

Few modern actions are so obscure as this last, not a single English person present, apparently, having left any account of it. The above account is drawn chiefly from Jomini, iv. Moore was not present. Bunbury's narrative is as vague as the Duke of York's despatch of 7th October, wherein he reported the action. Maule, the *Military Library*, and Colburn's *Military Magazine* give few or no particulars.

★★★★★★

On that night Abercromby, David Dundas, Pulteney, and Hulse, the four lieutenant-generals with the army, went to the Duke of York, and told him that he must retreat; and both they and he wrote to Henry Dundas their reasons for the necessity. The army since landing had fought five considerable actions, costing altogether nine to ten thousand men, but had made little or no progress. The country was singularly difficult; the sand-hills afforded neither fuel nor cover; the plain of North Holland, always low and marshy, was so soaked by continuous rain that troops could not be encamped, even if there had been means of transporting tents; and all movements were confined to dykes and roads, of which the latter had been much damaged by the enemy.

So far the army's supplies had been carried on the canals; but even so it had been impossible ever to keep more than two days' victuals in hand, and seldom even so much. The canals had now come to an end, and, owing to the want of wheeled carriage, every step in advance increased the difficulties of transport and supply. Moreover, it was well known that, owing to the state of the roads and the lowness of the land, military operations generally became impossible in Holland in November.

The Russians were disheartened, and there was no friendly feeling between them and the British. A renewal of the attack would be hazardous in the extreme, for the French had been reinforced; and even if they were beaten it would be impossible to follow them owing to the state of the roads, the lack of waggons, and the presence of the Dutch on the eastern flank. Defeat, on the other hand, would mean utter disaster. Abercromby wrote privately:

Were we to sustain a severe check I much doubt if the discipline of the troops would be sufficient to prevent a total dissolution of the army. This is melancholy, and is the natural consequence of young soldiers and inexperienced officers—all-powerful if attacked, but without resource if beaten.—The lieutenant-generals to Dundas, 6th October; Abercromby to same, 8th October; York to same, 7th and 8th October 1799.

Accordingly the duke retreated on the following day, Oct. 7th, leaving his wounded behind him for want of means of conveyance, and on the morrow re-entered the lines of the Zype. So terrible was the state of the roads after weeks of rain that his few waggons took two days to cover nine miles; but, though the French followed him closely, the army suffered little loss. An attack was indeed made by Daendels upon Prince William's brigade on its retreat from Hoorn, but this was repulsed with little trouble. Even within the lines, however, the difficulties of supplies recurred, there being but nine days' provisions in store.

The commissary had sent ships to Hamburg and Bremen for flour more than a month before, but, owing to foul winds or other causes, not one had yet returned. Abercromby thereupon wrote to Henry Dundas that the sooner the army re-embarked the better, though even with the best management it could not hope to evacuate Holland without loss of horses and artillery. The Helder by itself was untenable, and could not by any means be made secure for the winter. The Zype position, though strong, was so extensive as to throw much labour on the troops, who were already sickening fast; and it was out of the question for the army to winter there, if only for the reason that the navigation to it was generally closed by the middle of November.

The re-embarkation itself promised to be a most difficult matter, for the Zype was the only position that really covered the port, and as the troops were gradually withdrawn from it, the enemy would have the better chance of attacking it with success. Moreover, the Helder could not be strengthened so as to hold out above three or four days against siege-artillery; and, if it were captured, every ship in the Mars Diep would be captured with it. In fact, the situation was as awkward and as dangerous as could well be conceived; and, to distress the Commanders still further, there came at this time the news of Massena's victory at Zurich on the 11th of September, and of the defeat of the Allies in Switzerland. (Abercromby to Dundas, 12th October; York to Dundas, 12th, 14th, and 18th October 1799).

Fortunately Brune's officers threw out a hint of an armistice and a convention, which was eagerly caught up by the duke's staff. Negotiations were accordingly opened on the 14th, Major-General Knox acting very ably on behalf of the British, and by the 18th a capitulation was agreed upon. The conditions were that hostilities should cease and that the British should evacuate the country by the 30th of November, yielding up eight thousand French and Dutch prisoners from England, though without prejudice to the cartel already fixed for exchange of prisoners during the past campaign. The Dutch fleet was to remain in the hands of its captors. Though Brune did not know it, the British had but three days' bread left on the 20th; and indeed Abercromby looked upon the loss of half of the army as so certain that he could not conceive why the French agreed to such easy terms.

However, fortunately for Pitt and Dundas, they did, thanks not a little to the astuteness of Knox. Further supplies of flour arrived shortly after the signing of the capitulation; and with some difficulty, owing to continual storms, the whole of the troops were embarked by the appointed day. By that time sickness had reduced the British to twenty four thousand and the Russians to nine thousand effective men.

Bad luck continued to dog the expedition to the last, for three ships of war were wrecked on the Dutch coast, two of them with all hands, and a transport with over two hundred and fifty of the Twenty-Third on board was also cast away, and only twenty of the soldiers saved. However, the remainder of the troops seem to have reached England in safety, including the Russians, who, after astounding the good people of Yarmouth by drinking the oil from the street-lamps, were finally quartered in the Channel Islands. So ended the expedition to the Helder. (York to Dundas, 20th and 21st October; Abercromby to Dundas, 19th October 1799. Dunfermline's *Life of Abercromby*; Colburn's *Military Magazine*, February 1836).

The enterprise is of interest in many respects as being, in spite of its failure, the first undertaken by the renovated, or rather of the new, British Army. The force was of course raw, unformed, hastily assembled, and therefore utterly unfit to be plunged, as it was, immediately into active service; but, none the less, considered as material, it was the best that England had put into the field since Cromwell's regiments were disbanded. There was singularly little crime among the soldiers, in spite of the demoralising company of the poor underpaid Russians; and Abercromby declared the Militiamen to be, in his judgment, a superior class of men and a great acquisition to the army.

Mingled with them were a certain number of Irish, hot from the late insurrection; and an officer recorded many years later that the best soldiers during the campaign in his own very strong company were six rebels captured at Vinegar Hill, (Colburn's *Military Magazine, ut supra*). Unfortunately the officers were not only deficient in numbers, but many were very young and inexperienced men who had been lifted, by the sudden augmentation of the regiments, prematurely to superior rank. In fact, the hurrying of this crude force into the field at a moment's notice was a shameful injustice alike to generals, regimental officers, sergeants, and men; and it was creditable to them to have got through the campaign, with all their faults, as well as they did. It was, however, a great point that this new material had been found. Abercromby wrote to Dundas:

> In the spring you will have a fine army, if the brigades are put under major-generals who are capable of instructing young officers and training young soldiers. They must remain stationary, and not be allowed to dance all over Great Britain.

Here, therefore, was a promise of a future camp at Shorncliffe, though not yet of a Light Division. (Abercromby to Dundas, 11th September 1797. *Military Magazine, ut supra; Life of Abercromby*). Nevertheless, as has been seen, there were a few riflemen, actual members of the British Army, who took a share in this campaign; and this marked a step in advance, which was soon to be carried still further in the form of the famous 60th and 95th.

Another innovation was the appointment for the first time in our history of an officer in supreme command of the artillery, at whose recommendation Abercromby withdrew the battalion guns from the infantry and massed them into four brigades or, as we should now call them, batteries, each of four six-pounders, (Lieut.-Col. Whitworth to Abercromby, 5th July 1799). But the campaign was altogether an important one in the history of the artillery, for it not only brought that arm into the field for the first time with its own drivers, but launched the Horse Artillery likewise into active service, and gave its baptism of fire to the famous Chestnut Battery, (Duncan, *History of the Royal Artillery*, ii.).

Still more interesting was the appearance of a new corps called the Royal Waggon Train, which, though only formed for the first time on the 12th of August, was at once carried across the North Sea. It consisted of five troops, which on the 21st of September were increased to eight, each of four officers and seventy-one men, of whom sixty were drivers; and a waggon-master-general was placed in command of the whole. The pay of the Waggon-Train was the same as of the cavalry, the men being in fact such troopers of the cavalry as were nearly worn out or "did not match their regiments." (*S.C.L.B.*, 12th August, 21st September; *C.C.L.B.*, 8th August 1799).

Considering that Abercromby sailed on the day after the order for the formation of this corps was issued, it may readily be conceived that no part of it was ready to accompany him. But it appears that fragments of it soon reached the Duke of York, and that, by the time when he had decided to re-embark, he had for the first time a sufficient, or nearly sufficient, number of officers and men to deal with the transport of his army. It seems, in fact, that the Government in this expedition to the Helder despatched the troops first, then the supplies, and lastly the transport; and, since the difficulties of transport and supply were among the chief reasons urged for the retreat and re-embarkation of the army, it is necessary to enter rather more minutely into this dry and difficult question.

★★★★★★

A return of 14th October 1799 shows the strength of the Waggon-Train at that date in Holland to have been 25 officers, 275 officers and men, and 514 horses. The Duke of York wrote to Dundas on 24th October that "the Waggon-Train has been till now inadequate to the service of the Army." I may add that at the present time the number of four-horse vehicles assigned to an Army Corps of 36,000 men, excluding all pair-horse carriages, six-horse carriages, and pack-animals, is 514, the precise figure of the horses at the Duke of York's command.

★★★★★★

An inquiry was held as to the causes why the main depot of supplies at the Helder had so often been on the verge of exhaustion; when both the Treasury and the commissary-general were able to produce vouchers showing that between the 13th of August and the 20th of October there had arrived in Holland from England ninety-seven days' supplies for forty thousand men. The largest shipment was that which left England with Abercromby, amounting to thirty-five days' subsistence for forty thousand men; and yet, though Abercromby had no more than at first twelve thousand and, after the 28th of August, seventeen thousand men, his supplies had already run dangerously short by the 9th of September; that is to say, after twenty-eight days only.

This the commissary-general professed himself unable to explain at the time; though he was able to account for it triumphantly some months later, when it was discovered that many of the transports on their return to England contained provisions enough to victual the men on board for several weeks. It seems extraordinary that the commissaries themselves should have been unaware of this fact; and indeed their ignorance reveals extreme incapacity and want of organisation in this department of the Treasury.

But, apart from this, the commissariat appears never to have calculated for the necessity of retaining at least a month's supplies for the troops upon all the transports, for it was not safe to allow less even for so short a voyage as the passage of the German Ocean. Abercromby's division had been fourteen days on board ship before it could land at the Helder; and, with the dangerous and intricate navigation of the Mars Diep to be encountered in the face of prevailing westerly winds, it might well have been delayed even longer in its return to England. The only retreat of the British, in case of defeat, lay across the sea, and a general who failed to keep his ships victualled against such an event, to say nothing of possible movements of troops by water in the course of the operations, would have been a madman.

But, even if Abercromby's division were adequately provided for, the same is not true of the Duke of York's army. Its strength was reckoned at forty thousand men: it numbered actually from forty-eight to fifty-four thousand; and the Russians required a ration of bread half as large again as the British, (1½ lb. against 1 lb), so that the number of bread-rations required must be taken as at least fifty thousand.

★★★★★★

I give the figures of Commissary-General Motz, being uncertain whether he does or does not make allowance for the extra half-ration required by the Russians. I am very nearly certain that he does not; and if I am right the case against the Treasury is very much stronger than is here expressed.

★★★★★★

At the time when the Duke of York's army disembarked there had reached Holland, Sept. 14, forty-seven days' bread for forty thousand men, or say forty days' allowance for fifty thousand. Of this Abercromby's division had already consumed the equivalent of at least twelve days' supply, leaving twenty-eight days' supply only, or about the quantity that should have been kept on board the ships in case of re-embarkation. During the remaining sixteen days of September there arrived, or were purchased with great difficulty from the fleet and in the country, small quantities amounting to a further supply for twenty-eight days, leaving twelve days' allowance on the 1st of October.

Between the 1st and 19th of October arrived twelve days' further supply, in two consignments; but meanwhile, owing to the accumulation of three thousand Dutch deserters and other adherents of the Prince of Orange, the number of mouths had increased. Hence on the 13th of October there was, both on the transports and ashore, bread for only twenty-three days for the forty thousand men that remained of the force. This amount being less than ought to have been reserved upon the transports against the event of a disembarkation, it was not untrue that, when the capitulation was signed, the army was practically at the end of its supplies.

Sheer misfortune was in great measure responsible for this, for four months' bread-stuffs for forty thousand men had been purchased in the Elbe just before Abercromby sailed; but the ships that carried them were wind-bound for five weeks and did not reach the Helder until the 20th of October. But even if they had been delayed for one week only, which should fairly have been taken into calculation, they would not have reached their destination until a week after the army had disembarked; and the season was so far advanced that time was valuable beyond all price. This, therefore, cannot excuse the failure to furnish the duke with a very large reserve of supplies in the first instance; for want of which he was unable to fill his advanced magazines and to provide adequately for movements upon a large scale. The truth is that the Cabinet came to its decision in a hurry, and left this and many other matters to chance. (See *W. O. Orig. Corres.*).

When even the comparatively simple business of filling the principal magazine was mismanaged, it is not surprising that the far more difficult task of distributing provisions from that magazine was found insuperable. Abercromby, as has been seen, asked again and again for horses and waggons, but without result. The figures as to the waggons and so forth have already been given and need not be repeated; but it is beyond all question that the ministers deliberately burked the whole subject of land-carriage, and determined to trust to water-carriage and to luck. They trusted in vain; for the French, as has been told, on learning of Abercromby's approach, removed every boat and waggon that they could; but this was a contingency that should have been reckoned with. Henry Dundas blamed the weather for everything that went amiss in the matter of transport and supply; but, even if his expectations as to water-carriage had been realised, canals no more dispense with the need for wheeled-transport than railways.

In fact it is difficult to decide whether the recklessness of the government was more conspicuous in the preparation or in the design of this expedition. The dissatisfaction of the public in England over its miscarriage was very great; and the ministers were therefore driven to find new excuses for it. Their first line of defence was the weather, which beyond question was cold, rainy and stormy beyond all human experience, considering the season, and greatly impeded the progress of the campaign. But rain and tempest furnished no explanation for putting a raw force into the field without any transport; wherefore it was roundly asserted that all the maritime resources of England would not then have sufficed to disembark an army at once complete with the necessary train of carriages and waggons. This was probably true; but the obvious reply was that, in that case, North Holland, which was known to possess few horses and waggons, was a very unfortunate field of action to select.

As to the imperfect training and organisation of the troops, Ministers pleaded that, until the initial successes of the Allies in Italy and the sailing of the Brest fleet, they did not feel justified in diminishing the number of the Militia. But considering that the successes of the Allies were well advanced in April, that the French fleet left Brest on the 25th of that month, and that the Act for reducing the Militia was not passed until July, this plea was merely childish. Moreover, the Militia could, with a little care, have been made more effective for home defence when converted into regular regiments than before.

The next step, therefore, was to prove that the expedition was valuable as a diversion in favour of the Allies, and that it played a part in weakening the French numbers at Novi and in Switzerland. Upon this it is sufficient to remark that the Battle of Novi was fought two days after Abercromby sailed, and that Massena's great victory over Suvorof in Switzerland was won a week after the Duke of York had begun to move forward in force.

These pretexts being miserably thin, it was necessary to back them by some military opinion, which was the more difficult since Abercromby had condemned the whole enterprise from the first. So far, Dundas in his correspondence with the generals in this campaign had behaved with a candour that did him honour. He had acknowledged to Abercromby after his embarkation that he had required of him an unduly hazardous service; and he had acquitted the Duke of York in generous terms of responsibility for the misfortunes that compelled him to retreat.

But in the House of Commons his courage failed him; and he or one of his colleagues, prompted by him, quoted a single sentence apart from its context from one of Abercromby's letters, to show that the veteran general had looked forward to a successful campaign. Abercromby strongly remonstrated against such unfair treatment, but in vain. The ministers wrote him many compliments and offered him a peerage; but they would not imperil themselves by telling the truth, and allowed the public to believe that they had acted in accordance with the general's advice instead of directly contrary to it. A century has wrought little change in this respect among British Ministers of War.

✶✶✶✶✶✶

Dundas to York (private), October 1799. *Life of Abercromby*; and see four draft memoranda, evidently prepared to defend the action of Government in *W.O. Orig. Corres.* Whole passages from these occur in the speeches of Ministers in Parliament.

✶✶✶✶✶✶

The ministers, therefore, escaped payment of the penalty for this as for so many previous military failures; but meanwhile it is still difficult to discover what was their real design in sending this large force to Holland. It is, I think, absolutely certain that they had no idea of entering upon a regular Continental war and of making Holland the sphere of operations; otherwise the fleet could have been used to transport the army to the coast of Friesland, thence to strike on Arnheim and to invade the province by line of the Waal. Ministers hoped, no doubt, that at the first appearance of British troops the Dutch would rise, expel the French and restore the *stadtholder*; but this was a matter that could very well have waited until France was brought to her knees by the Allied Armies and the British fleet, when it would have followed as a matter of course.

What, then, was the need to hasten British troops over the North Sea with orders (for such was the purport of Abercromby's instructions) to land somewhere and do something? The explanation appears to lie in the intense distrust which the British Cabinet not unjustly entertained towards the Court of Vienna; and in its desire to hold a pledge which should bind that Court to some approach to honest dealing.

✶✶✶✶✶✶

The only right suggestion is that which the king made to me

on Wednesday—that we should make our force sufficient to be quite certain (at least as much as the thing will admit) of occupying the whole country ourselves before the winter. It is only in that way that we can put ourselves in a situation to talk to Vienna in the only style which ever succeeds in making them hear reason. . . . If we decide to return the provinces to Austria, it should, I think, be only in consideration of her co-operation in the attack on France. If we return them to Austria during the war we lose our only tie on them. Grenville to Dundas, 27th July 1799. *Dropmore MSS.*

★★★★★★

It should seem as though Pitt dreaded lest France should be crushed and Europe parcelled out by Austria and Russia without reference to England. Holland therefore being the country with which British interests were chiefly concerned, he determined to intervene there in concert with Russia by military operations, so as to secure a decisive voice in the ultimate fate of the United Provinces, and to bring Austria to reason by threatening to hand them to Prussia. But, be this as it may, the fact remains that he did send a powerful force to the Helder for no sound military object, and that it was forced to withdraw with disgrace.

That there were grave military blunders committed by the commanders-in-chief both of the British and of the Russians is unquestionable; but, in the opinion of the best judges, the difficulties of the country were so enormous that a successful invasion of Holland from the Helder was practically impossible. The brunt of the blame for the mishap, therefore, must lie with the ministers who persisted in pursuing their own designs despite the emphatic and repeated protests of their best military adviser.

Nevertheless, the powers of Europe including Britain had allowed a fateful opportunity to slip from their grasp. The government and armies of Revolutionary France had originally thrown themselves into conflict at a time when the country was disorganised and all but bankrupt. The French Army was in disarray, devoid of an effective command structure and manned by inexperienced citizen soldiers. By all accounts the tenure of the Revolution should have been shortlived. Instead, the future would bring forth from its ranks one of the finest military figures the world had known. Napoleon and the French would soak Europe in blood before all the hard lessons had been learnt at last by everyone.

www.ingramcontent.com/pod-product-compliance
Lightning Source LLC
Chambersburg PA
CBHW032044080426
42733CB00006B/185